D0380831

SANCTUARY

THE NEW UNDERGROUND RAILROAD

Renny Golden
and
Michael McConnell

ORBIS BOOKS

Maryknoll, New York 10545

Second Printing, April 1986

The Catholic Foreign Mission Society of America (Maryknoll) recruits and trains people for overseas missionary service. Through Orbis Books Maryknoll aims to foster the international dialogue that is essential to mission. The books published, however, reflect the opinions of their authors and are not meant to represent the official position of the society.

© 1986 by Renny Golden and Michael McConnell
Published by Orbis Books, Maryknoll, NY 10545
All rights reserved
Manufactured in the United States of America

Manuscript editor: William E. Jerman

"Revolutionary Hope" was originally published as "Response" by Renny Golden in *Sanctuary* edited by Gary MacEoin, © 1985 by the Tuscon Ecumenical Council; used by permission of the author and Harper & Row, San Francisco

Library of Congress Cataloging in Publication Data

Golden, Renny.
   Sanctuary: the new underground railroad.

   Bibliography: p.
   1. Sanctuary movement.   2. Refugees—Central
America.   3. Church work with refugees—United
States.   I. McConnell, Michael.   II. Title.
HV645.G57   1986   362.8'7   85-25906
ISBN 0-88344-440-2 (pbk.)

The patience of God is so great that it prolongs the time of our judgment, but our slowness to obey God produces much suffering. This delay means hunger, torture, and the crucifixion of millions of human beings in the Third World.

The powerful of the earth represented by the multinational corporations like Coca Cola, Del Monte, or Esso have subverted the law of love by the law of the strongest. For those in this country where the supreme God has become power, only those filled with the love of the crucified One of Nazareth could dare to obey the law of God before the unjust human law.

God suffers. God suffers in the malnourished flesh of the poor. God cries in the tears of Mary, the tortured mother in Uspantan, Guatemala. Sobs in the pain of Juan, tortured by the Kaibiles in Huehuetenango, looks at us with interrogating eyes in the 119,000 orphans who have survived the massacres in the Guatemalan altiplano.

Thousands die every month in Central America so that we might wake up and learn to love. To love is to give of ourselves, to encounter the truth. To love is to give your life for your friends. To love is to abandon our easy life so that the oppressed might have a human life. To love is the unique human form of life. While you are reading this book, ask yourself if you live, if you know the profound joy of friendship, of fraternity, of justice, and of trust.

Sanctuary is the fruit of love. Yahweh invented the law of sanctuary so that people might learn to love the stranger, the poor, the widow and those that flee to save their lives even though they might have committed a crime. For this they instituted the cities of refuge.

We, the people of the New Covenant, have been called to make of our own lives the refuge for the weak and abandoned. Those who do not love by giving their lives for their friends do not know God. In our relation with the poor we prove if we are legitimate heirs of Jesus or only unsurping the name of Christian. This is the question that emerges from each page of this book.

The writers of this book have been wounded by love. By that wound God was made human, servant of all and was allowed to be cursed with the death of a criminal. By this wound Fr. Miguel D'Escoto has wanted to fast and condense in this voluntary surrender the suffering of millions of poor, hungering and thirsting for justice. It is a wound that kills our egoism and gives us new life. This life and this love resonate in every word and in the delicateness and the intensity of the call to convert ourselves from fear to true love. The authors share with us life, sufferings, hopes, and the wealth of faith that they encountered from outside the borders of their country. They suffer with God because inside of this great nation anything can be bought, anything can be obtained except the profound joy of being and loving.

In this book we touch the extremes of suffering inflicted on the poorest of the poor that even pierces the heart of God. We touch the hope that we can one day truly become human beings and call Christians to participate in the incarnation of Christ, so that we might be able one day to participate in his resurrection.

Read this book with the heart of compassion.

JULIA ESQUIVEL

CONTENTS

Rosemary Radford Ruether

FOREWORD

In ways that most U.S. citizens neither know nor understand, the United States, since the Second World War, has developed a permanent war economy. The purpose of this war economy is to maintain U.S. control throughout the world in defense of the Western empire and its ability to use the cheap labor and resources of formerly colonized regions of the planet. This war economy pursues military escalation in the two spheres where it perceives this control to be threatened—the nuclear arms race with the U.S.S.R., leader of the Second World, and counterrevolutionary repression in the Third World. Much of the war against the Third World is carried out through surrogate armies maintained by military elites whose power the United States funds within those Third World states.

This war economy has increasingly depleted the U.S. national economy, diverting innovative technology from the civilian to the military sector of society. Key industries, such as the steel industry, railroad and car manufacture, and electronics, have shifted to other parts of the world, leaving vast areas of unemployment in American cities. Key social infrastructures of American society—hospitals, schools, programs for the aged, the poor, and the mentally ill—have been drained to feed the war economy as the first priority of the American government.

This war economy has an even more devastating effect on those Third World regions where the United States seeks to maintain Western control. To repress radical movements for change, including those that have come into power through democratic electoral procedures, the United States has increasingly supported military governments that have eroded all substance from the political structures of self-determination, though sometimes maintaining a facade of "elections" to keep up the fiction, so dear to Americans, that we are in these countries only to protect "democracy."

These national security states maintain brutal internal armies and secret police, and covertly support bands of right-wing terrorists who kidnap, torture, and kill those who raise the flag of protest or seek changes. This repression is most brutal among the most impoverished of society. Any peasant group that, even in the most timid form, tries to organize for land reform is brutally repressed with extreme violence. The repression also reaches out to critical individuals and groups—journalists, university professors, students, church groups, lay ministers, priests, nuns, even bishops.

This war of repression has left no road open for change in regions such as Latin America except that of armed revolution. Efforts at change through reform governments, democratically elected, such as that of Jacobo Arbenz in Guatemala (1954) and Salvador Allende in Chile (1972), were wiped out by right-wing military coups engineered by the CIA. All efforts to throw off economic dependency, repressive military government, and control of the foreign policy of these countries in favor of greater self-determination and a more equal sharing of national resources by the people are immediately labeled "communism" by the American government. Thus the Third World struggle for liberation is falsely conflated with the American competition with the Soviet superpower portrayed as trying to take over these Third World nations as part of a rival empire counter to that of the United States.

A paranoid or Manichean view of global reality as divided between the Kingdom of Light, ourselves, and the Kingdom of Darkness, the Soviets, gives Americans the pervasive impression that their values, their prosperity, and their freedom are under attack by an "evil presence" slowly loosening their hold on the world. This interpretation of global reality creates compliance and even enthusiastic support for continual expansion of the war economy and its interventions, its dealings throughout the world.

The prime area of such repressive control, backed up by local militia and, at times, direct military intervention by the United States, is Central America, seven tiny states, with a combined population of less than 25 million, that form the "bridge" between North and South America. These countries are, for the most part, desperately poor; Honduras and Guatemala are poorer than the others. Their economy has been structured for centuries into monoculture export crops, particularly coffee, cotton, bananas, and sugar. In a pattern that goes back to Spanish colonial times, but which has been exacerbated in the last century due to foreign-controlled agribusiness, most of the arable land is owned by a small elite, leaving only tiny, stony plots of land, insufficient to support a family, for Indian and *mestizo* peasants. More and more of this peasantry have no land at all and thus must work as serf labor on agribusiness plantations. This helps increase the enormous gap between rich and poor, with vast wealth for the top 5 percent of the population, and grinding poverty for the bottom 50 to 70 percent. Over half of the populations of Guatemala, Honduras, and El Salvador subsist at the starvation level, "living" on half the caloric intake necessary for normal human functioning.

Only in Nicaragua has a revolutionary government come into power that is trying to turn around this situation. A brutal family dictatorship that owned most of the land and wealth of the nation, and maintained itself with a personal army that massacred all dissenters, which the United States had funded ever since it helped repress an earlier effort at reform led by Cesar Sandino in 1934, was overthrown in 1979. Calling itself Sandinista after this earlier national revolutionary hero, the Nicaraguan popular revolutionary government has attempted a variety of basic reforms of land use and social services in a mixed and privately-owned economy. The efforts of this government to carry forward needed changes have been severely hampered by the counterrevolutionary war that the U.S. government has mounted against Nicaragua, using for the most part rearmed national guards of the former Somoza dictator.

These counterrevolutionaries—contras—are based in Honduras and carry out strikes against Nicaraguan villages along the border, massacring civilians, destroying crops, and blowing up industrial plants, as well as attempting to block harbors. The United States hopes to topple the revolutionary government, either by a direct military victory of the contras, or by so impoverishing the economy through diverting all its resources into war that it will lose popular support. The repression being maintained in Guatemala and El Salvador, as well as the militarization of Honduras, the base for counterrevolutionary activity, are aimed at preventing similar revolutionary governments from coming into power in other Central American countries.

Counterrevolutionary repression has led to vast refugee populations. Salvadorans flee to refugee camps in Honduras, Guatemalans flee north to Mexico. Some number of these refugees, from El Salvador and Guatemala particularly, find their way to *el norte*, the United States and Canada. Unwilling to admit that these refugees have fled by reason of real danger to their lives, the Reagan administration insists that they are merely seeking better economic opportunities and thus refuses to grant them the status of political refugees that U.S. laws mandate. To grant Salvadorans or Guatemalans political asylum would be to admit that repressive systems are in effect in their homelands—systems funded by U.S. tax dollars.

Responding to the plight of these refugees, who live with immediate expectations of death if they are deported back to their countries, as the American Immigration and Naturalization Service demands, North American churches and synagogues have created a sanctuary movement. Although it transports and harbors only a small number of refugees, this protest movement puts the religious community in direct confrontation with the U.S. government.

Not surprisingly, this sanctuary movement, ignored at first, has come under attack by the American government. Seeking to drain its funds, divert its energies into self-defense against criminal charges, and discredit it to the American public, the government has indicted sanctuary workers on a number of counts. The sanctuary movement, far from fading away, has continued to grow. More churches have declared themselves sanctuaries. Hundreds of thousands of North Americans have vowed to engage in civil disobedience if the United States should intervene militarily in Nicaragua. For the first time since the end of the Vietnam war, the United States government is faced with a major challenge to its policies of global control, a challenge spearheaded by the American religious community.

In this book, Renny Golden and Michael McConnell tell the story of the sanctuary movement. It is the story not only of the North Americans who risk fines or prison terms for sheltering refugees. It is, most of all, the story of the refugees themselves, the repressive violence in their countries that has torn them unwillingly from their native soil, their difficult treks through the war zones of Central America and through Mexico into the United States, suffering continual privation and violence, and their fear-ridden lives in that "home of the free and land of the brave," which so contradictorily offers them safety with one hand and seeks to take it away with the other.

This is a book that all North Americans need to read and ponder. For, in its light, the hypocrisy and duplicity of U.S. foreign policy is contained in microcosm. The refugees and their protectors are the "chickens come home to roost." Their very existence throws into question U.S. foreign policies of more than three-quarters of a century that, in the name of democracy and anticommunism, have sought to maintain American control through repression of revolutionary movements of self-determination. If Americans are able to see through this facade and recognize its fallacy, recognize the enormous toll it has taken upon our own welfare and, even more, upon the welfare of the peoples of the Third World, then the credibility of the government may be called into question. Americans will then have to ask, not only about the legitimacy of Third World revolutions that seek to throw off our control, but also about how to curb the policies that are spawning poverty and repression within our own country as well.

ACKNOWLEDGMENTS

It is a small and perhaps insignificant gesture to acknowledge those who have made this book possible at the risk of their own lives. We do acknowledge, however, the Salvadorans and Guatemalans, living and dead, especially the refugees, who have journeyed into our midst to bring us the truth. We acknowledge the Nicaraguan people fighting for its life even now, and the church of the people, which has lived revolutionary hope in the midst of devastation.

We wish to thank our sisters and brothers in the sanctuary movement for the light their committed presence strikes in these ominous times, especially those summoned to carry the flame further.

We thank our *"compa"* Mary Ann Corley, who encouraged us most, gently editing our first efforts, walking every step of the way by our side.

For wise advice and invaluable editing we wish to thank Rosemary Ruether, Beth Maschinot, and Sheila Collins. To Ewa Pytowska and Jim Harney, who advised, supported, and challenged early on, a special thanks.

To Julia Esquivel for calling back from the path up ahead. And to the editors and staff at Orbis Books for their special help.

To Brinton Lykes and Emily Hewlitt for giving us a peaceful place to write when we began this adventure. To Jean Butterfield for giving us space. And to women friends in Boston who were supportive of this work.

To the members of the Chicago Religious Task Force on Central America, who supported our efforts even when they had to take up the slack our writing time created, we offer a strong embrace of thanks.

When we started, someone asked us how two persons write a book together. We wonder how anyone does it alone.

INTRODUCTION

*If history is to be creative, to anticipate a possible future without denying
the past, it should . . . emphasize new possibilities by disclosing hidden
episodes of the past when, even if in brief flashes, people showed their
ability to resist, join together, occasionally to win.*

Howard Zinn

The hot desert wind furled and unfurled the banners painted with signs of
hope. A small group of women from the Los Angeles religious community
gathered outside El Centro detention center near the Mexican border in
southern California. Hundreds of Central American refugees are imprisoned
there in the desert behind 10-foot-high Cyclone fences topped with spirals of
barbed wire and guarded by the U.S. Immigration and Naturalization Service.
As the women vigiled outside, the imprisoned men, awaiting deportation,
threw a bed sheet over the barbed wire. The sheet pointed north and bore the
words, *En el nombre de Dios ayúdanos* ("In the name of God, help us"), the
bright red letters painted with a mixture of punch and their own blood.

Even such a small act of resistance is risky. Since 1980 the U.S. government
has been deporting from five hundred to a thousand Guatemalans and Salvadorans each month back to the violence of their homelands. They know that
their chances of survival, once they disembark at the airport outside San
Salvador or Guatemala City, are slim. The road from Ilopango airport to San
Salvador is known as the "road to death," where Santana Chirino Amaya was
found with his throat slit after his second deportation from the United States.

"In the name of God, help us." That sign, stuck to the fence of a desert
prison, symbolizes the cry of a people rising from Central America and
written, not only in the blood of the prisoners at El Centro, but in the blood of
tens of thousands of the poor. The imprisoned, the fugitive, the deported, the
campesinos organized and struggling for freedom—even the dead—cry out.

This is the story of North Americans who heard that cry and chose to stand
with the dispossessed. They persuaded their faith communities to declare their
buildings sanctuaries for refugees from El Salvador and Guatemala. Scores of
religious communities have sheltered undocumented refugees in direct defiance of the U.S. government interpretation of the Refugee Act of 1980. The
U.S. government calls what they are doing criminal, punishable by a $2,000

1

fine and up to five years in prison. By declaring sanctuary, white, middle-class congregations experienced something of the risk that the popular church of Central America and the clandestine church of Mexico have endured for years. The offer of sanctuary was an act of authentic solidarity by the North American religious community—a solidarity of defiant love.

This is also the story of the refugees and the truth they brought with them about daily life in their countries. Many felt a calling, much like the prophets of the Old Testament, to tell the story of their people. As Felipe Excot, Guatemalan catechist in sanctuary at Weston Priory, Vermont, said, "We have come here to expose what has been hidden all of our lives." The hidden ones of history are speaking to those of us who thought *we* were the center of history. History is being told and a theology articulated "from below." Sanctuary, at its best, has not been a place to hide in, but a platform to speak out from, as the poor of Central America bear witness to their reality.

Their stories divulge an almost unbelievable truth. Here is the story told by a Guatemalan pastoral worker:

> All day long we were fleeing. We hid in the mountains, but the women wore clothes of many colors, and from the helicopters they could see us very well. We saw the helicopters begin to fly in circles, surrounding us all. They began to machine-gun the people. The only way of saving ourselves was to run to the ravine and throw ourselves into it. It was quite steep. On arriving at the ravine, a woman behind me fell. She carried a child on her back and one in her arms. The one in her arms fell to the ground. . . . She was all covered with blood and her hand dislocated. She shouted to me, "Help me, help me with my child. Look, I can't carry it, I can't hold it any longer!"
>
> I took the child without looking at it. . . . A moment later I heard the child moan. Then I looked at its head. It was split almost in two.

The majority of North Americans do not know the truth of the present Guatemalan situation. To most U.S. citizens Guatemala is an unknown country "somewhere in Central America." Yet, with support from the United States, the Guatemalan government has massacred a hundred thousand civilians since the mid-1960s. A virtual holocaust is happening a three-hour plane flight from our border and we do not know about it.

Although the media ignore Guatemala, what they report about El Salvador fits a systematic pattern of deletion. News reports, particularly on television, center on diplomatic maneuvers, the injury or death of North Americans, guerrillas stopping a bus, or long lines at the polls. Those are the pictures relayed to the U.S. public. The indigenous truth of the people, their lives, their sorrows and hopes, lies on the cutting room floor.

A sound man for a major network television crew, after spending five weeks in El Salvador "covering" the war, writes:

If you rely on television as your source of information about what's happening in El Salvador, you won't know . . . about the thirty people found tortured and shot in the head at close range on one street on one day in San Salvador. You wouldn't know because TV news directors have decided that you aren't interested in the day-to-day terror of the Salvadoran people. And so this terror carried out by our ostensible allies goes unreported. We are told that the best received piece on Salvador was a story on how people still enjoy the beautiful beaches in the midst of civil war.

Sanctuary is a place where refugees can speak the truth. Even in the refugee camps, the desperation to tell their story is evident to visitors. The refugees hand quickly scrawled notes to North Americans who visit there, pleading with them to share their stories. They write, "We cannot leave these camps. It is up to those who visit to share the truth." Suzanne Doerge, a leader in the sanctuary movement in Cincinnati, relates this story from the Honduran camps:

Five worn figures huddled with us around the wooden table in the priest's tent. One gas lamp created a circle of light that brought us together for a few brief hours, blocking out the constant danger of U.S. helicopters hovering over us. They gave us the gift of their stories animated by their hands, scarred by sudden mountain escapes. A soft voice with no hint of revenge told of her papa cut to pieces and the heads of her brothers stuck on sticks. Her mother had cried out for her children, but the soldiers gunned her down in the street. The daughter crossed the Lempa River wearing only her underwear and traveled that way for fifteen days. Their village was bombed and their houses burned. Why? Because they were catechists.

The United States government calls these persons illegal aliens, who come here "solely for economic reasons." Since 1980 only 341 of them have gained political asylum out of nearly thirty thousand applicants. Those in the sanctuary movement call them refugees with the right to live here. More than seventy thousand U.S. citizens have actively participated in breaking U.S. law, as interpreted by the government, in order to "feed the hungry and shelter the homeless." Most sanctuary churches knew from the beginning that it was insufficient to merely bind up the wounds of the victims without trying to stop the cause of those wounds. Welcoming services for refugee families at sanctuary sites became occasions for decrying U.S. foreign policy and mobilizing the community at large to stop the flow of arms from the U.S.A. to Central America. Telling the truth was coupled with putting an end to the horror of that truth. Inspiration for such action came from the rich and heroic tradition of sanctuary but also from the example of the Central American church itself.

The church of Central America is a church that has incarnated itself among the poor who struggle for liberation. Compared to that church the sanctuary movement is like the Roman Saul struck down from his horse of safety and walking the road to Damascus with poor sojourners. A lightning bolt has begun to obliterate the imperial vision, illuminating the path of the God of history. Like Saul/Paul, the sanctuary movement still gropes in semidarkness, holding the hands of exiles who lead the Anglo community further into the light.

The North American church is not a liberation church as such, although some of its historical tradition is revolutionary. But at critical moments sectors of the Christian community and the Jewish community have reclaimed their prophetic tradition and opted for the liberation cause, challenging the oppressive structures and laws of their own government. In colonial times, U.S. churches protected escaped political prisoners from British agents. Quakers, particularly in Rhode Island, were noted for their harboring of religious dissenters, even from other colonies.

During the abolition period, churches provided refuge and protection to fugitive slaves in direct defiance of the Fugitive Slave Law of 1850. In this century, grass-roots immigrant churches and synagogues have defended the rights of workers against exploitive owners. At times, clerics, immersed in the struggle of the poor working class of this country, were in conflict with their own institutional hierarchies, which upheld the rights of owners.

At Selma, Alabama, the explosive moral force of the black liberation church, as it walked, sang, and died for the sake of freedom, awoke the North American religious community. The United Farm Worker's movement entered the pages of U.S. labor history, led by a Chicano who called upon supporters to fast and pray and boycott as an act of solidarity with farm workers.

The sanctuary movement grows out of this prophetic tradition in America. But its uniqueness is that it has provided the oppressed with a forum to call the First World Anglo church to conversion, a conversion of heart and deed, while linking itself to resistance traditions of the past.

METHOD

The structure of this book reflects our methodology and our theology. We begin each chapter with a story. Like the theologians of Latin America, we begin with the concrete reality facing the people. It is *that* truth that calls us to action. We believe the refugees are the opening through which we can come to understand the peoples of Central America and, in the end, understand ourselves and U.S. complicity in the violence of Central America.

When we tell their stories, we do not follow the feature-story approach of daily news presentations that are content to skim the surface and move on to the next story without searching for the causes of human suffering. We do not tell their stories for the sake of "human interest," but out of political and moral necessity. We tell them because of the urgency of the moment. The refugees' experiences are the festering sores through which, if we are courageous and honest enough, we can get back to the causes of their wounds, and not content ourselves with bandages. We seek to name their persecutors as we trace their footsteps of flight back to where they came from—a people struggling for freedom. In that way they will not be victims only, but creators of a new world, makers of history.

PROBLEMS AND HOPES

We recognize that within the sanctuary movement there have been instances of paternalism and racism and sexism. Refugees, at times, have been overprotected by host congregations. Planning committees have excluded refugees from decisions that affected their personal lives. When refugees did speak up at some gatherings, Anglos listened to them politely, but their suggestions were largely ignored.

It might be that one reason why this movement has attracted so much media attention is because of an inherent racism that judges newsworthy any risky act undertaken by whites, but not the same or even riskier actions undertaken by blacks or native Amerians or Hispanic Americans. When six hundred blacks in Operation Push in Chicago issued a declaration of sanctuary and welcomed a Salvadoran family of five, the media were not there.

In spite of these vulnerabilities, the sobering, hope-inducing fact remains that religious communities *have* reached across race and class barriers to offer sanctuary to Central Americans. This has been of profound importance, especially when it was not primarily an act of charity, but of solidarity.

At root, what the churches are defying is not just the interpretation of an immigration law, but the whole pattern of exploitation based on race and class that the United States initiated in 1827 with the Monroe Doctrine and has upheld through thirty-six invasions of Latin America since the year 1900. That is why this movement appears dangerous to the government and enlivening to the churches. It might even be called a revival, an awakening in the life of the ecumenical community that has given new historical commitment to the faith and new credibility to religion, even to those who had long been skeptical of "the church." Whether this points to a new era of faithfulness, mirroring the grass-roots resurgence of the church in Latin America, will depend on how far we are willing to go along with the fledgling solidarity of sanctuary.

This book is a history of the sanctuary movement from the perspective of participants, and so, in that way, it is a people's history. It is the story of a small but significant portion of the North American religious community that resisted U.S. foreign policy and U.S. immigration policy in order to stand with its Central American brothers and sisters. It is the story of what happens when the concerned say, "Enough!"

The sanctuary movement has arisen in a nation that trains and arms the killers of innocent persons and then deems it criminal to shelter the victims of that slaughter. We have written this book because we believe that authentic compassion cannot thrive without increased resistance. The sanctuary movement is still in progress, still able to decide how great its resistance and its compassion will be. We are at a point in its history where it can dissipate as suddenly as it erupted, or it can grow—broaden and deepen into a movement that will effectively resist, at fundamental levels, unjust U.S. domination in this hemisphere.

Finally, this book is meant to be a call to action. We are not disinterested journalists standing back from the situation, but organizers and participants immersed in the sanctuary movement. We have encouraged countless communities of faith to obey God's law. By this book we are encouraging others to do so. If that implicates us in a conspiracy, then we call it a conspiracy of love, which is another name, we believe, for the church. In view of the one hundred forty thousand civilian deaths in El Salvador and Guatemala, we feel that advocating anything less would be the real crime.

I give my support to any Catholic parish that would want to be a sanctuary for Guatemalan and Salvadoran refugees.

Most Rev. Rembert G. Weakland
Archbishop of the Catholic Diocese of Milwaukee, 1982

1

CHOOSING LIFE

Do you even know what exile is?
I'll tell you,
            exile
is a long avenue
where only sadness walks.

Otto René Castillo

El Señor came to our side, the side of the humble;
the boots and the tanks crush us.

Misa Popular *of El Salvador*

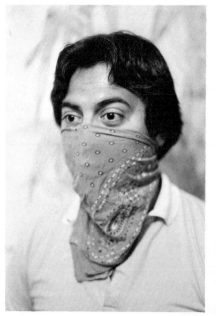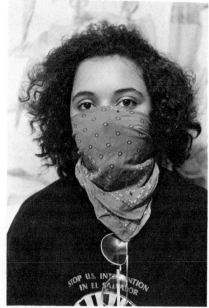

Pedro and Sylvia

WITNESS: PEDRO AND SYLVIA

(Pedro and Sylvia have been in sanctuary in Albany, New York.
Their testimony was taken and translated by Carol Wintle.)

*The first time I went to the office of the Salvadoran Human Rights Com-
mission to report that forty persons had been captured, it was filled with
residents of San Antonio Abad, a neighborhood of San Salvador. I was
instructed to take the testimony of one of the women. She told me the security forces came into her home, beat her son, and raped her daughter.*

*While I was typing this testimony, an explosion went off in front of the
building. My typewriter crashed to the floor, papers flew all over the
room. One side of the office collapsed and several persons were
wounded. I was frightened, confused, and hardly able to speak. There
was rubble everywhere. Three unidentified dead bodies, covered with
acid, had been thrown on top of the rubble. On top of the bodies, a note
signed by the death squad stated, "This is going to happen to you all."
That day I had to decide whether I was going to continue working in that
office or not.*

*Pedro, who was working at the time as a reporter for the national university
newspaper, joined the Human Rights Commission Board as a representative of*

university workers in 1978 and went to work full-time at the commission a year later.

The day after the bombing of the Human Rights Commission offices, the board of directors called a meeting:

> Archbishop Romero came and told us to continue to work—to keep on going forward, and that is what we did. From that day on, I and the other staff members were continually being threatened by phone calls and letters, at home and at work.

Shortly after, uniformed men seized the secretary of the commission, María Magdelena Enriquez, as she left her home one morning. María's boyfriend followed the captors' car, which took her to the office of the National Police. Several Human Rights Commission members went to the National Police and asked to see María. The police denied any knowledge of her. The commission published María's picture in the papers, asking anyone who saw her to report it to a commission member.

A few days later, peasants found the bullet-ridden body of María Magdelena. Commission members went to a local judge to request permission to remove her body. The court required the head of the commission, Ramón, to submit his personal identification papers and retrieve them the next day from the security police headquarters. The next day Ramón went and regained the documents; a few days later, he was killed several blocks from the office. "Security police wanted it to look like robbers killed him," Pedro remarked as his voice choked and a tear formed in the corner of one eye. However, persons in a bar near the spot witnessed the killing and identified the assailants as military personnel.

Later on, death squads killed Ramón's replacement, two succeeding directors, four other commission workers, and board member Archbishop Romero. When the photographer for the commission was killed, Pedro took his place. For the next three years, Pedro combed city streets and country roads looking for bodies and finding some fifteen to twenty each day:

> On my first day as photographer, the driver showed me where to search for bodies. We came upon a woman lying in the road. Villagers had covered her with cardboard. I took a picture of her face and turned to leave. The driver stopped me, saying, "No, that is not how it is done. You have to document the torture."

Pedro removed the cardboard and saw that the woman had been beaten on her breasts:

> This upset me very much. She had been pregnant. Her stomach was split open. Inside her stomach the fetus had been cut out and in its place was the head of the woman's husband. Several yards away lay the body of her

husband. The fetus was placed where the head should have been.

This is what my job was like, day after day. I would have to put bodies together, like pieces of a puzzle. Sometimes I had to pick up bodies of those whom I had worked with.

Commission research revealed that the military arm of the government committed most of the murders. All over the country, Salvadorans were seized by armed men at home, at work, in school, or on the streets—and were never seen again. Sometimes those captured and put in jail were able to inform the commission of their whereabouts. Each time commission members went to the jail looking for them, prison officials denied they had custody of them. Sometimes prisoners were able to supply the commission with the names of those who had captured them. Later, if any of these prisoners or ex-prisoners were found dead, it was obvious that the police had murdered them.

Eyewitness accounts by commission members exposed the collusion between the military and the death squads. In one case, a commission worker happened to be near an auto mechanic shop when two men entered, beat up and captured the mechanics there. He photographed the whole episode:

We gave copies of the pictures to the parents of the mechanics and the parents went to Vides Casanova, the head of the National Guard, and asked him to free their sons. Vides Casanova said there were no prisoners there. The parents showed Casanova the photographs of their sons being seized by the National Guard. Casanova looked at the photographs and asked who took the pictures. One mother said, "You can kill me, but I won't tell you who gave this to me." Casanova said, "OK, come back tomorrow and I am going to see if your sons are at some other police station. Bring the photographs because someone might be able to recognize them."

So the next day they went again. Casanova said they were not able to find the two prisoners. "If you don't tell us where they are, we are going to go to the newspapers and protest this," the parents stated. Casanova responded, "Let us enter into some negotiation here. You give us the photographs and I will give you the bodies of your sons. Unfortunately, your sons are dead. But you want the bodies, don't you? So, you give us the photographs and we will give you the bodies."

So they gave Casanova the photographs and he told them where their sons were buried. This is how the collusion between the heads of the security forces and those of the death squads was uncovered. The death squads and the military are the same. They work during the day in the military and at night with the death squads.

"At other times the police would be very open about their actions," explains Sylvia. "When I was in school, it was common for the security forces to come into the school, beat students, and take them prisoner." She and her fellow *classmates were left with little recourse but to organize demonstrations to protest these actions. Protesting the government actions put Pedro and Sylvia in jeopardy. For an entire year each stayed at a different friend's house each night, for living together would have made it easier for the death squads to find them. The police came looking for them several times, but they never found them.*

In 1983, the military went to Pedro's house. "I wasn't there," recounts Pedro, "but my 16-year-old cousin was. They raped her, tortured her, and threw her in jail, saying she was a communist. She became pregnant from the rapes; when this became evident they beat her until she miscarried." To this day Pedro's cousin is still in jail.

Due to the danger they faced daily, Sylvia and Pedro left the country. Pedro went to Guatemala legally with other journalists and later fled to Mexico. Meanwhile, Sylvia managed to escape and joined Pedro. In Mexico, both worked for the international office of the Human Rights Commission, but immigration officers harassed them several times, requesting bribes to prevent deportation. Eventually they became part of the sanctuary movement for the security it provides and the opportunity to speak to North Americans about the violence in their country.

Church persons helped Pedro and Sylvia cross the border in Arizona. They walked for three hours at night across the desert and were later sheltered in churches in Nebraska, Iowa, Colorado, and Illinois before arriving in New York.

Pedro's testimony about the human cost of U.S. involvement is simple and direct:

Every bullet that travels from the United States ends up in a dead peasant. We don't need that kind of aid. North Americans think they are fighting communists. They are being lied to by their government. I believe there is still time for the people to uncover the truth.

COURAGE TO SAY YES

December 2, 1982. There were flash floods that night. One major bridge was out and the rain was coming in torrents. The radio was warning everyone to stay at home. But still they came. Over seven hundred persons nearly filled the cathedral of St. John in the heart of Milwaukee to welcome into sanctuary *campesinos* from El Salvador and Guatemala. That night, St. Benedict the Moor and Cristo Rey became the first Catholic parishes in the United States to declare themselves public sanctuaries.

In the dark cavernous cathedral, parish members, carrying candles, formed a protective arc around the altar as a living sanctuary. They symbolized the conviction that sanctuary was not primarily a place, but the collective will of a faith community taking a stand for life. Archbishop Rembert Weakland, the first Catholic bishop to endorse sanctuary, articulated that option for life:

[We] truly believe in the sanctity and sacredness of all human life. I had to weigh this act of civil disobedience with the very real threat to these people's lives if they were to return to their homeland.[1]

Bishop Weakland had experienced in his own life part of the compelling history of sanctuary. As a young student in Rome during World War II, he heard stories of how the monasteries in Europe, especially those near the German border, harbored Jews fleeing the Nazi terror. Later, as abbot primate, he dealt with many cases in which Benedictine monasteries offered sanctuary. "I cannot tell the best of these," he said, "without jeopardizing some of my friends, but they are moving tales of heroic sacrifices of life."

That night as parishoners introduced the *campesinos*, their faces hidden by scarves and hats to conceal their identities and protect their friends and relatives in Central America, the congregation broke into thunderous applause that ended with seven hundred pairs of hands clapping in the unison Latin American style. It was a spontaneous gesture of welcome, solidarity, and unity.

During the previous week a front-page confrontation had taken place in the Milwaukee *Journal* between sanctuary organizers and the INS. Ronald Swann, in charge of the Milwaukee INS office, called the church members "nothing more than a smuggling ring." Those comments only seemed to widen and solidify the support for the churches until by the day of the welcoming service, a front-page editorial endorsed the undertaking and called the church members "courageous" for what they were doing. Their stand for life was forcing the wider secular community to choose sides as well.

The act was courageous, particularly for Cristo Rey, a Hispanic parish in Racine, Wisconsin. Identification with the victims brought them to their decision. Many in the congregation were once refugees themselves and even when they voted on sanctuary, many were undocumented. One parishoner said, "We were afraid, but in spite of that, we had to take a stand."

Rachel Parra, a Chicana and secretary of the parish council, read publicly that night the congregational statement of intent to confront the law:

We take this action after much prayer and deliberation. It is our belief that the current policy and practice of the United States government with regard to Central American refugees is illegal and immoral. If this is indeed a country based on the inalienable rights of every person to life, liberty, and the pursuit of happiness, we, as American citizens, have the right to call on our government to respect these rights where violated. We consider our action to be small and insignificant when compared to the courageous action taken by the refugees who are willing to risk deportation and death that their people might live.

Thus, before the television cameras, she openly indicted herself in this "criminal" act. For two weeks prior to the service she had been nervous, had had trouble sleeping, and feared she would not have the strength to speak those words. Every day she prayed to the Virgin of Guadalupe for strength. After the service a woman approached Rachel to comment on what a courageous thing she had done. Rachel responded, "The people in our parish who are undocumented and still voted yes, *they* are the courageous ones."

Ramón and Mercedes Sánchez, two of the refugees taken into sanctuary that night, had not been politically active in El Salvador, but one of their teenage daughters belonged to a student organization, and that involvement was enough to draw the military to their home. It was 1 A.M. on February 5, 1981, when soldiers burst into the house shouting, "Everybody on the floor!" When the family of eight was herded into the main room, the soldiers raped the 13-, 16- and 18-year-old daughters, forcing the parents and younger children to watch. In return raids on the home the soldiers first took away the 16-year-old daughter and days later the 18-year-old.

After the second daughter disappeared, never to be heard from again, Ramón broke. "I went crazy," he says simply. "For seven days and nights I searched for my children's bodies in cemeteries and fields." He saw the dead, old and young, the mutilated bodies of his people. Traveling without food or sleep, the grieving father finally met an old woman in Santa Ana who recognized his daughter's description as that of the one in the cemetery "without an arm." Ramón dragged his whole life and his last traces of humanity to that small cemetery plot. There, amidst the debris of death, was the body of his child, mutilated and swollen, her severed hand being chewed by a starving dog. Later he learned that the other daughter's body had been burned.

A Salvadoran newspaper published photos of the dead daughter's bodies, providing Ramón's family with proof of their persecution and a possible way out of El Salvador through connections with the Mexican embassy. After being smuggled to Mexico City, they were left on their own. An engineer offered them work at a ranch near Jalisco. They were misled and abandoned, without food, funds, or clothing. Though only forty-five minutes from a town, the family was isolated for four months and close to starvation when the pittance they received for work from the engineer, combined with money that friends had sent, allowed them to make their way to Tijuana. There a "coyote" (a border-crossing guide) took them across "on credit" for $1,500.

Ramón still carries photos of his daughters and shows them to strangers. He seems to distrust their imagination even more than he questions his own incredulity. He shows the pictures, whether you want to see them or not—you *must* look at them. The ritual is a hint of the trauma he bears but does not talk about. Ramón's oldest son Jesús says nothing; his depression is severe. The Cristo Rey community treats Jesús very gently, hoping that the young man will find his way into the light.

A few weeks later, a Chicago NBC affiliate interviewed the family. Ramón's brother spoke for him because the pain of remembering was still too overwhelming for the father. After recording their story they returned to Chicago and interviewed the local INS office for its reaction. NBC reported that the INS would deny the family political asylum in the United States: there was no written proof of why their daughters were killed.

EN EL NOMBRE DE DIOS

The sanctuary movement was born from an encounter of North Americans and Central Americans—not around a conference table but on the road, in the desert, along the barbed wire of border crossings. Through that face-to-face encounter, the religious community was confronted with a grave moral problem. Central Americans were fleeing their homelands because of violence and terror, and were being met in the United States by government officials who deported them directly back to that violence. In 1981 and 1982, as the sanctuary movement was beginning, the United States, the only country in the world sending Salvadorans directly back to their homeland, deported an average of one thousand per month.[2] Out of the fifty-five hundred who had applied for political asylum during those years, only two were granted it. The refugees asked for help—*"En el nombre de Dios, ayúdanos."*

At first the religious community near the border responded with food and shelter, and attempts to work through the legal machinery set up by the INS. They posted bonds to get refugees out of detention camps, putting up their own cars and homes as collateral, but the best they could do was buy time. After two years of such work, not one of the fourteen hundred refugees they had helped had gained political asylum. It became clear to them that the hearing process was not designed to grant justice for immigrants but only to carry out the foreign policy of the executive branch of the federal government, which insisted that Central American refugees were motivated exclusively by economic interests. History, meanwhile, has recorded fifty thousand civilian deaths in the war in El Salvador from 1980 to 1984, and one hundred thousand deaths at the hands of the Guatemalan army since 1954.

Authentic help finally came, exactly as the refugees had asked—in the name of God. On March 24, 1982, on the second anniversary of the assassination of Archbishop Oscar Romero of San Salvador, the Southside Presbyterian church in Tucson, Arizona, and five East Bay, California, churches declared a public sanctuary for Guatemalan and Salvadoran refugees. It told the INS quite bluntly to stay out or risk breaking sacred law. The sanctuary movement was born.

The sacred law the Presbyterians referred to came from Moses, thirty-five hundred years ago. Yahweh, the God of the Old Testament, was the initiator of sanctuary, commanding Moses to set aside cities and places of refuge in Canaan, the Promised Land, where the persecuted could seek asylum from "blood avengers." These cities of refuge were for the Israelites, "as well as the stranger and sojourner among you" (Num. 35:15).

The Judeo-Christian faith was born in the travail of escape. God liberated the Hebrew people from the bondage of the pharaoh's dictatorship. God was the force acting in history on the side of those first refugees, leading them from slavery to freedom. In the centuries that followed, the Israelites remembered God as "the one who brought us out of the bondage of Egypt" (Exod. 20:2). God's identity was rooted in action and proclaimed in verbs of struggle—

leading, delivering, freeing. The proclamation of sanctuary draws inspiration from the centrality of the exodus and its aftermath.

The Israelites also saw God as the ultimate refuge: "God is our refuge and strength, a very present help in trouble" (Ps. 46). But sanctuary and refuge were more than passive safety or a secure hiding place: "Defend me, take up my cause against the people who have no pity; from the treacherous and cunning man, rescue me, God. It is you, God, who are my shelter" (Ps. 42). "Defend me," "rescue me," and "take up my cause" are expressions of advocacy and liberation. Sanctuary is not merely a safe place to hide in but a prophetic platform to speak out from. It is a strategy of action, a plan of struggle. It is a stipulation in the covenant relationship between God and the faithful, and between the faithful and their neighbors.

In both the Old and New Testaments the stranger or sojourner is never spoken of in any other terms but welcome. The wayfarer is to be taken in and cared for because "you were once sojourners in the land of Egypt." Jesus immortalized a foreigner, the nameless Samaritan, to illustrate his precept of neighborly love.

When the Southside Presbyterians declared sanctuary, they were not drawing only on scriptural tradition, but reviving a civic tradition with a rich and moving history. The concept of sanctuary was so compelling that it was recognized in Roman law, medieval canon law, and English common law. In the 1600s every church in England could be a sanctuary. During the seventeenth century the whole North American continent was seen as a sanctuary from the political and religious persecutions of Europe. Pennsylvania and Rhode Island were exceptional examples of tolerance and shelters for the outcast. Sanctuary became a part of the accepted understanding everywhere in the world of what it meant to be American. That sentiment was engraved on the Statue of Liberty: "give me your tired, your poor, your huddled masses, yearning to breathe free." When one of the first Salvadoran refugees taken into sanctuary, Daniel Vargas, was asked by reporters why he had come to the United States, he replied, "The only thing I knew about this country was that it was a nation of immigrants, so I thought I would be welcomed."

Two of the most heroic periods of the tradition date from the 1850s in the United States, and the Second World War in Europe. After the passage of the Fugitive Slave Act (1850), which made it illegal to harbor or assist a slave in gaining freedom, northern churches became stations on the underground railroad, in defiance of federal law. More recently, monasteries hid Jews fleeing the holocaust, providing food, shelter, and protective identification. In southern France, a Protestant parish named Le Chambon, under the leadership of its pastor, André Trocme, collectively decided to be a sanctuary, specifically citing the law of Moses. Trocme's son estimated the parish hid over three thousand Jews. Throughout the underground it became known as the safest place for Jews in all of Europe. It continued its clandestine work even near the end of the war when fleeing Nazi troops were massacring entire villages if even one Jew was found hiding there.[3]

Although the declaration at Tucson could draw on a heroic history, it arose as an immediate response to an urgent situation. In the next two and a half years it would grow beyond the imagination of its originators. It would touch the hearts of Catholic sisters in Concordia, Kansas; workers in Ohio; farmers in Iowa; and Catholic bishops in Seattle and Milwaukee. The sanctuary movement attracted and emboldened many supporters, even though it meant defying the "official" interpretation of federal law and risking a $2,000 fine and imprisonment.

El Pueblo

For the first time in this century, war victims—the human beings at the other end of our bombs, artillery fire, and covert actions—were not an anonymous enemy that could be labeled "gooks" or "chinks." Instead, they were Juan, José, Albertina, Angélica, and Ramón. The wreckage of U.S. foreign policy arrived on our shores as living or half-living persons. Daniel Vargas, in sanctuary at the Wellington Avenue United Church of Christ in Chicago, said, "We left El Salvador because we were walking around like dead people, and we didn't know where to go."

They were battered. Some bore the physical scars of torture or burns from napalm or phosphorous bombs. Others were withdrawn, barely able to whisper of the atrocities they had lived through. There were also the less visible scars—the nightmares, the heartache over dead children, unhealed ulcers, arthritis aggravated by lying on damp ground or wading through rivers—and the haunting memories, always the memories.

They were the survivors but they spoke for those who had not survived or whose survival at that very moment hung in the balance. They came as a remnant of a people making an uncertain exodus into anything but a promised land. They always remembered those back home, not only friends and relatives but *el pueblo*. The Spanish word *"pueblo"* connotes the poor majority who are struggling and organizing themselves to forge a new history. The survivors' bond with *el pueblo* is not only by blood and race or culture; it is a moral bond. That bond was the first glimpse many North American religious persons had of the depth that solidarity had taken in Central America. As more and more stories unfolded, overlapping each other to form a thick texture of both terror and resistance, the North American religious community was to learn more about the meaning of solidarity, more than it had expected.

Each victim had a name and a story. Most of the stories have vanished forever. Immigration lawyers, writing on yellow legal pads, are retrieving some of these stories from the oblivion of history. In church basements throughout the country, missionaries speaking to a handful of the faithful are reconstructing an oral history of a people in the midst of struggle. And human rights groups are meticulously researching an almost unbelievable truth. But the stories being heard and passed around the most come from the refugees who take up the call of sanctuary. They have told individual stories rooted in a situation of civil war and village massacres. The refugees are the voice of the voiceless, telling the story of a Central American people, and laying a moral and religious claim on the people of North America.

Salvadorans and Guatemalans came north seeking refuge, a safe haven, and they brought with them a truth about their countries kept from the North American public. The refugees spoke about their lives in Morazan, Guazapo, Chalatenango, Quiché, and Huehuetenango. These places began to take on the features of the haunting spectre of other places and times—Saigon, My Lai, Hanoi, Phnom Penh. . . .

The cry of a suffering people was finally making its way north, carried by a refugee community, persecuted and exiled from its own land. Its very presence in the United States laid a moral claim upon the religious community, placing before it the fundamental faith decision: life or death.

That same choice faced Oscar Romero during the three years he was archbishop of San Salvador. He had opened himself to the stories of the poor, feeling directly their experience of pain. It was out of the people's anguish and poverty that he said:

> The radical truths of the faith
> become really truths
> and radical truths
> when the church involves itself
> in the life and death of its people.
> So the church,
> like every person,
> is faced with the most basic option of its faith,
> . . . life or death.
> It is very clear to us
> that on this point there is no possible neutrality.
> We either serve the life of Salvadorans
> or we are accomplices in their death. . . .
> We either believe in a God of Life
> or we serve the idols of death.[4]

Half a million Salvadorans and hundreds of thousands of Guatemalans entered the United States seeking life. They fled a violence fueled by arms paid for by American citizens. The choice between life and death became for them as concrete and as clear as the choice for or against U.S. military aid to Central America. Churches, synagogues, Quaker meetings had to choose sides: the refugees or secular authority, God or Caesar, life or death. Sanctuary, a unique religious tradition, offered faith communities a channel for action. The refugees themselves finally compelled the faithful to engage in the widest form of resistance since the civil rights era. And behind the refugees were *el pueblo*, the people, linked by a trail of tears and bribes and terror. The long, painful road leads back to its source, the U.S.-supported violence in Central America and the people organizing and struggling for life. That violence and that struggle formed the historical context in which sanctuary took its birth and grew into a nationwide movement.

CENTRAL AMERICA: THE HISTORICAL CONTEXT

El Salvador

The pervasive presence of death in Central America abruptly entered the North American religious community in December 1980 through the martyrdom of five persons in El Salvador—one Salvadoran archbishop and four North American women missioners. Their lives and deaths became the lens through which North Americans came to better understand the martyrdom of a whole people and the widespread persecution of the church.

Martyrs die for their faith; the North American church was to learn from them the meaning and extent of that faith. As Ita Ford, a few months before her death, wrote to Maryknoll Sister Melinda Roper, "If we are to make a fundamental option for the poor we must choose sides. Correction: we have chosen." In two short sentences she summed up the solidarity that was sweeping the grass-roots churches in Central America. In the end, that choice cost them their lives.

But they were not the first. For Salvadorans the blood of martyrs, spilled by dictators and the armies that served them, dates back to 1932. That was the year of the great *matanza*, the massacre of thirty thousand peasants. Government forces killed them because they demanded the basics of life—food, shelter, land. José Anselmo, an old man now living in one of the liberated areas of El Salvador, remembered the 1932 massacre. His father, although not part of a political group, was hunted down and killed by the military because, as José put it, "he was a just man."

Organizing the people started in the 1970s. The Catholic Church, through its *comunidades de base* or popular church communities, expedited the organizing with a theology that brought dignity to the *campesinos*. They began thinking of themselves as children of God, worthy of the right to life. They began asking why they should not occupy and use, or try to rent or buy, land left vacant by wealthy landlords. Why should weeds grow on private property while their children starved?

The year 1977 marked the beginning of the persecution of the church. Security forces murdered two priests and arrested, tortured, and expelled others from the country. The White Warriors Union, a right-wing terrorist group, threatened to assassinate all Jesuits who did not leave the country. During the turmoil, Oscar Romero became archbishop.

Rutilio Grande symbolized the actions and theology of a whole range of priests and pastoral workers during this period. The Salvadoran Jesuit headed a pastoral team in Aguilares. He had gone there to immerse himself in the life of the villagers, to raise their awareness of what life could be, and to share with them the liberating message of the gospel. He spoke to them of the dignity that God the creator had intended for them—a dignity one gained only in history.

He said, "God is not somewhere up in the clouds, lying on a hammock. God is here with us, building a kingdom, here on earth!" What probably sealed his fate was a sermon he preached, less than a month before he was assassinated, on the occasion of the expulsion of a priest whose radio program reached thousands of rural Salvadorans.

In that sermon, emphasizing the fellowship of all Salvadorans, he criticized the wealthy, the "Cains" who cry out "I bought half of El Salvador and that gives me certain rights. My word is law because I paid for the right." Grande called that attitude a "denial of God, who gave us a material world without property boundaries. . . . We do not hate anyone; we love even these Cains. Even they are our brothers. But their contradiction of love creates moral violence that violates us and violates society." He had given new life to the villagers of Aguilares, who thought of him as a saint. He stood clearly against the death perpetrated by the oligarchy, and that stand, as would happen again and again in the future to countless others, meant his own death.

Government informers spied on his work and sermons. At 5:55 P.M. on March 12, 1977, while driving a jeep on a lonely dirt road on his way to say Mass at El Paisnal, he was shot twelve times by 9mm. armor-plated dumdum bullets from Mantzer automatic rifles, the kind issued to police. Any one of the shots would have been fatal, except the one in his foot. Two *campesino* friends, Manuel Solorzano and Nelson Lemus, and three small children, rode with him. The barrage killed the one *campesino*; the other had a bullet in the middle of his forehead fired at point-blank range. The three children escaped to tell of the tragedy.[5]

Over a hundred thousand persons gathered for the funeral mass of the three. Thousands packed the San Salvador cathedral and the National Guard turned away thousands more. This massive response by the poor, on a work day, in violation of state law forbidding such gatherings and faced with machine guns in the streets, marked the beginning of a more courageous alliance between the people and the church, now fully awakened to how deep the violence had seeped into Salvadoran soil.

Grande's death brought a more militant stance to the church. Romero broke state law by refusing to wait for permission to bury Grande. He held public meetings in defiance of the state of siege. He refused to attend official state functions until the murder of Grande was cleared up. At this point he began speaking in the name of the poor and naming the violence against them, not only in the form of death squads but also in the form of landlessness, unemployment, hunger, and poverty.

The archdiocese became a lifeline and a source of information and hope for the people. The archdiocesan radio station began broadcasting scripture readings, religious and protest songs, official church statements, and reflections. Bulletins from the chancery office and Archbishop Romero's sermons became the only source of news: all the public media were censored.[6] These were courageous actions and further placed the church on the side of the poor and against the overt, institutionalized violence of the state.

In 1980 El Salvador was virtually unknown to most North Americans. That agonizing year awoke the North American church and marked a watershed for the opposition forces in El Salvador. The popular organizations that had been organizing nonviolent strikes and demonstrations were at their zenith. On January 22, one hundred fifty thousand persons took to the streets in San Salvador in the most massive demonstration to date.[7] The government retaliated with repression that eliminated nonviolence as a means of change in El Salvador and led to the beginning of civil war in 1981. Repeatedly, security forces shot unarmed demonstrators in the streets. On March 24 Oscar Romero was assassinated while saying Mass. In November government forces abducted, tortured, and murdered the six highest opposition leaders while they were meeting at the National University. The security forces violated the university precincts, traditionally a place of sanctuary where violence was not allowed. On December 2, Ita Ford, Jean Donovan, Dorothy Kazal, and Maura Clark were raped and assassinated by National Guards, with every indication that they were ordered to do so by the powers that be.

By the end of 1980 the death toll had mounted to a staggering 8,398, as documented by the Human Rights Commission of the archdiocese. By December of 1980 there were seventy thousand refugees. Their numbers would grow to half a million by mid-1984.[8] The mass slaughter and mass exodus of a people had begun.

The assassination of an archbishop and murder of women missioners profoundly affected North Americans, especially Catholics. Central America emerged as a moral issue; new peace and justice groups formed as a response. The blood of martyrs watered small pockets of a renewed church in North America committed to justice. That renewal created, in turn, the seedbed for the sanctuary movement. The anniversary of their deaths became new holy days in a growing movement within the churches. By 1982 churches declared sanctuary on those days to symbolize that the work and faith they died for was continuing. Romero, a few weeks before his death had said, "If they kill me, I will rise again in the Salvadoran people." As sanctuaries in Tucson and Washington, D.C., and Weston Priory declared on March 24, it could be said that he was also rising again in the North American people.

At first the North American church did not grasp the roots of the crisis in Central America and the past role of the United States government there. But it would soon understand better the scope of U.S. intervention. Only one month after newspapers all across the nation printed the picture of the four women's bodies being removed from the shallow grave, the United States government restored $5 million in military aid to El Salvador and sent twenty advisors. Two months later it increased the numbers to $25 million and fifty-six advisors.[9]

Members of Congress, workers, university leaders were making comparisons to Vietnam. With the advent of U.S. advisors, the vietnamization of the war became complete. Huey helicopters expedite counterinsurgency tactics and search-and-destroy missions. Counterinsurgency is a military term for a war against a civilian population. The FMLN (Farabundo Martí National Liberation Front), the coalition military opposition group, was too evasive.

Therefore, the plan was to kill the civilians who support the opposition by bombing them or destroying their crops in an attempt to starve them.

Counterinsurgency planes drop antipersonnel bombs that explode two feet off the ground. They are designed to maim and kill—to terrorize the local population. White phosphorus bombing was reported on six separate occasions in early 1983. A 42-year-old refugee reported the effects of these bombs:

> It drops a liquid fire that disintegrates your clothes. Your dress, your clothes disappear. The women fell on the ground, their dresses burned away, they were naked and their hair had burnt off, ashes came out of their ears—it was horrible. The same happened to the children. In our village, we opened up the wound of a girl who had been hit by a mortar. We stuck a needle in her arm where she had been hurt and smoke burst out. And that's what kills, that smoke penetrating under your skin. That smoke, that vapor consumes you for hours.[10]

Jim Harney, a North American who has been in the liberated zones, explains how the U.S.-supplied Huey helicopters operate:

> The people are living on the side of the volcano in Guazapa. They grow rice and corn, build mud houses or simply live under the trees because the bombs would destroy their homes anyway. Under the trees the planes can't see them as easily. The children's faces are covered with scabs because they have no protection from the mosquitos. The people have set up schools and *poder popular local* (local government). One day I was lining up the little kids from one of the schools for a group photograph. Suddenly, a Huey helicopter came strafing the area. All the kids, their teachers, and I dove into a *tatú* for protection. A *tatú* is a small tunnel with extra dirt on top to give added cushioning from the bomb blasts. We all crowded into a 5′ × 6′ space until the helicopter left. I was terrified myself, I don't know the psychological damage this does to the children.[11]

Raids like that can come at any time, or, as one mother said, "breakfast, lunch, and dinner." She usually nursed her baby in the *tatú*. One morning in the *tatú* she commented, "This is the breakfast that Ronald Reagan brings us."[12]

What is significant about the bombings on Guazapo are their regularity and their increase since Napolean Duarte was elected president in March 1984. Duarte maintained throughout the bombings that there were no civilians on Guazapo. U.S. officals said the same thing about areas being bombed during the Vietnam war. One such place was Quangngai, where an estimated five hundred persons were killed by U.S. air strikes. The U.S. government contended that they were all North Vietnamese soldiers. But the *New York Times* reported that "three out of four patients seeking treatment in a Vietnamese hospital afterward for burns from napalm or jellied gasoline were village women."[13]

In 1981 U.S. military aid increased, and the bloodshed increased (during the first four months of that year, there were seventy-seven hundred war casualties). In December President Reagan announced that sixteen hundred Salvadoran soldiers were coming to Fort Bragg, North Carolina, for training. It was a way of circumventing the advisor limit and it signaled an escalation of the war. The next month Congress passed a watershed foreign-aid bill, expanding presidential authority to make emergency transfers, and ratified continued military aid to El Salvador. The U.S. sent $55 million in military aid, including eight A-37 counterinsurgency jet fighters and four O-2A spotter planes that would direct the A-37 barrages. The air war was now in full swing. The A-37s flew thirty missions a day carrying out massive attacks with 300-, 500-, and 750-pound general purpose bombs that "softened up" an area for infantry sweeps.[14] By August 1984, Americas Watch and the Lawyers' Committee for International Human Rights, two private New York-based groups, charged that the Salvadoran armed forces had killed thousands of civilians and displaced hundreds of thousands with "indiscriminate" aerial bombing, shelling, and military sweeps.[15]

Jim Harney tells of his own experience of a bombing raid in July 1984:

My next to last night in Guazapa I stayed in the house of Armando and Esperanza. There were about twenty of us sleeping on the floor. When dawn came the sun shone through the cracks in the house, illuminating the inside in an almost mystical way. I got up and helped prepare some beans for breakfast. There were only enough for a few people and they offered them to me. I refused because the children were so hungry. They insisted, saying, *No tenga pena* ("Don't worry, don't be ashamed"). Again I refused. Finally, one of the community leaders came over to me and said, "We have analyzed this situation carefully. We are all used to going without eating and you are not. You have to leave tomorrow and we don't want you to get sick—*eat the beans.*"

After I ate, Armando took me out to the corn field and rice paddy he was growing. He took some of the rice in his hands and held it up proudly in the sun. Suddenly, from over the mountain, came a plane. We did not hear it until it was almost on us. Ten feet from us was a *tatú* but Armando ran for one farther away. I followed and we both dove into the hole just as the plane dropped a 250-pound bomb that destroyed his entire crop. After the plane left we looked at the damages. If we would have gone into the closer *tatú*, we both would have been killed. When we got back to his house we saw it was totally destroyed. He said nothing. He and his wife gathered up their remaining belongings and an hour later they went to a meeting of the local governing group. Everything he owned was gone and he said nothing. If the plane would have dropped a 500-pound bomb, we would have all been killed.[16]

Public opinion, according to the polls, was running against intervention in Central America. One government concession was to initiate a certification process. Under law, the president had to report to Congress every six months showing a decrease in human rights abuses by the Salvadoran government. This had to be certified before Congress authorized more aid. The first certification, in January 1982, flew in the face of reports from human rights groups claiming that the right to life did not exist in El Salvador. Dr. Margaret Daley Hayes, the chief Latin American consultant to the Senate Foreign Relations Committee, when confronted by religious leaders in Chicago, attributed the violence in El Salvador to the *campesinos* who were always getting drunk and cutting each other up with machetes.

Twice a year the certification charade was staged in order to justify U.S. foreign policy in El Salvador. Churches began using the dates for certification as times to declare new sanctuaries in an effort to bring the truth to the U.S. public through the testimony of refugees. At first, many church persons, especially of mainline denominations, believed that if Congress only knew the truth or listened to the testimony of refugees, it would stop the war. One sanctuary church held an alternative certification hearing with refugees in sanctuary giving their testimony. They videotaped the proceedings and sent it to their senator. He never responded.

By 1984, at a "summit" meeting in Washington, D.C., of fifty religious groups concerned about Central America, even those working at lobbying efforts on Capitol Hill saw limits to how much Congress could do to stop U.S. intervention. Many of them advocated direct action as the only hopeful alternative.

The continued violence in Central America and the administration's hardline response radicalized the religious community. Refugees poured into the United States with stories of persecution. Salvadoran authorities considered peasants subversives if they had a picture of Rutilio Grande or Archbishop Romero in their homes. Death squads targeted catechists and lay ministers (trained to conduct Bible study in the absence of priests). Security forces threatened or killed anyone who gave humanitarian aid to the poor, including nurses, doctors, and refugee aid workers.

Typical of the stories filtering north was that of Pilar, a catechist who was taken into sanctuary at the University Baptist Church in Seattle, Washington. Rev. Donovan Cook, one of the early leaders in the sanctuary movement helping to open sanctuaries in the northwest, told this story of her life:

Pilar was an associate of both Archbishop Oscar Romero and Jean Donovan, the American missionary who was raped and murdered. Because of her involvement with them and with the grass-roots Bible study movement, the Salvadoran authorities wanted her. Pilar and one of her children were arrested and jailed. In jail, she was beaten, tortured and raped in front of the child, who was severely beaten by the Salvadoran authorities.

Ironically, the only care Pilar received while in prison came from the maximum-sentence prisoners she was confined with. The junta had placed her amidst the prisoners in the hope that they would further abuse her.

Critically injured, Pilar and her child were taken from the prison and thrown into the back of a truck, among the corpses of tortured bodies, to be driven to the outskirts of town and dumped. Miraculously, Pilar was able, with her child in her arms, to fall out of the back of the truck and escape into the countryside. After crossing the border out of El Salvador, Pilar fled to Mexico and the United States, leaving her child behind. Her central aim in fleeing was to tell of the atrocities occurring in her country.[17]

Guatemala

If news about El Salvador waned at times, news about Guatemala was nonexistent. But refugees entering sanctuary from Guatemala brought the same stories of horror and repression. U.S. complicity was more hidden, embedded in a 30-year history.

The stories the refugees told had their roots in the 1954 overthrow of Jacobo Arbenz by the CIA with the help of the United Fruit Company. Guatemala was enjoying a decade of democracy after over one hundred years of military dictatorships. Arbenz initiated a land reform that expropriated 413,000 acres of United Fruit Company land. All that land was lying idle and the Guatemalan government reimbursed United Fruit $600,000, based on the company's own valuation that it made for tax purposes.[18]

In May 1954, the U.S. government learned that a shipment of arms had reached Guatemala from Czechoslovakia. The U.S. claimed Soviet intervention and charged that Honduras and Nicaragua (then ruled by the Somoza family) faced invasion from Guatemala. The United States used this argument to justify increased arms shipments to Honduras and Nicaragua. The CIA later armed Castillo Armas, who invaded Guatemala with a few hundred men. A special State Department/CIA Guatemalan group trained a "liberation" force of mercenaries and Guatemalan dissidents at a United Fruit plantation in Honduras. But the key military action of the overthrow was the frequent bombings of Guatemala City by U.S. planes with U.S. pilots hired by the CIA and based in Nicaragua. The CIA coupled this with a massive psychological warfare campaign of misinformation in the newspapers, designed to terrify the population and persuade the army to surrender. The plan was very intricate; it involved huge loudspeakers that broadcast the sounds of airplanes bombing the city, and the use of Guatemalan radio to transmit false reports of massive troop movements and defeats by the Guatemalan army.[19]

Arbenz resigned and Guatemala has since been ruled by military dictatorships. Poverty intensified; repression and terror rose to holocaust proportions. Human rights groups estimate that the government has killed one hundred thousand persons since 1954. The exposé of covert CIA activities revealed to the whole world the real intentions of the United States in the hemisphere.

Violent anti-U.S.A. demonstrations took place throughout Latin America. An Argentine doctor visiting Guatemala was so struck by U.S. imperialism and the lengths the U.S.A. went to in order to maintain control that he became convinced of the necessity of armed struggle. His name was Che Guevara.[20]

From 1967 to 1976 the United States acted as the sole military contractor to the Guatemalan dictators to the tune of $35 million. During the reign of terror in 1971, twenty-five U.S. officers and seven former U.S. policemen worked with the military. Colonel Carlos Arana Osorio, selected by the army to win the 1970 elections, swore to eliminate all guerrillas even "if it is necessary to turn the country into a cemetery." The armed forces raided the National University, assassinated three law professors, arrested sixteen hundred persons, and murdered as many as a thousand others in twelve weeks.[21]

Although the Carter administration cut off aid to Guatemala, U.S. military schools still trained Guatemalan officers in counterinsurgency warfare. In 1981 Reagan squeezed out $2 million for covert activities in Guatemala.[22] One month later he approved $3.2 million worth of military jeeps and trucks to be given to General Lucas Garcia, a name that sends chills down the spines of many Guatemalans because of the number of disappearances and deaths during his regime. At the beginning of 1983, Reagan lifted a five-year embargo on arms sales to Guatemala by approving the sale of over $6.3 million worth of spare helicopter parts and military equipment.[23] A projected 1985 budget earmarks $10 million in direct military aid.

Helicopters and trucks sound innocuous and are sometimes even classified as nonmilitary. But they could not be so understood after seeing pictures drawn in the refugee camps in Chiapas, Mexico, by Guatemalan children who survived village massacres. In the sky are black helicopters with black dotted lines connecting them to the bodies lying on the ground, some with their arms severed from their bodies. All that breaks the dark outlines are the arcs of red crayon spurting from the bodies, and the orange flames consuming the huts.

An Indian woman from the village of Chichicastenango in the El Quiche region, who was able to flee from Guatemala, relates the story of the destruction of her village by Guatemalan soldiers using counterinsurgency techniques:

> The days were passing and we could hear bombs falling on villages in the nearby areas. And we could hear them shooting at the people from helicopters that had machine guns.
>
> Then the first of December came. At dawn we heard shots from far away. We also heard that there were a large number of small trucks all around us. When we heard that the army had entered the village and had killed some people who were guarding the entrance, we couldn't do anything else but leave—all of us in any way possible.
>
> At about 11 A.M., when we thought we were already safe inside the woods, we heard the helicopters coming closer; they surrounded us. The children—like children are—were very restless. That's how they found out where we were.

So they started—in less than five minutes—to bomb us, to shoot us. So we started running deeper into the woods. The children started to scream and run. The women called their children because they were getting lost. They couldn't find them. And it was a race. We were running, running, running, throwing ourselves down on the ground, a cloud of dust, dirt, all wounded in the woods. We were going to be smashed any minute.

Some women ran back when they saw that their little ones weren't with them. The mothers called their children; the children screamed back. The worst off were the ones who were four, five, and six years old and could hardly run themselves. They were the ones who fell behind. That's why many women desperately ran back to get them.

But with horror we saw that all the soldiers were coming behind us throwing grenades and shooting with machine guns. Many of the women who ran back fell, hit by bullets. We couldn't go back to see if they were dead or only wounded, because it was impossible; those hundreds and hundreds of people from the village ran and ran, desperately. We ran for about six hours. We were seeing people with their heads totally smashed open, their hands ripped off, and their legs dangling.[24]

The effect of the helicopters goes beyond the reach of their bullets. Bishop Samuel Ruiz of Mexico recounted a story told by the peasants of a town called Boca Chajul, who were under the threat of death from the Guatemalan military and had to leave their village very quietly to avoid detection:

The mothers of the families pressed their infants against their breasts, in order to prevent them from crying, so they would not be discovered. After . . . tightly pressing their children against their breasts [for some time], and realizing that they were far away from their native town, three women found that they had suffocated their children. These women will remain traumatized for the rest of their lives, having accidentally killed their children, although they know with [their] silence . . . saved the lives of about a thousand others.[25]

In 1983, the same year the United States resumed military aid, Amnesty International called Guatemala the country where human rights are violated more than anywhere else in the world. Previously, in its 1981 report, Amnesty International exposed the Guatemalan government's program of systematic torture. It called the government of Guatemala "murderous."[26]

Others have accused the Guatemalan government of genocide—the systematic killing of a whole people or nation. It is not a word to be used lightly or superficially, because it entails a severe indictment of the actions and motivations of an oppressor group. In 1983, the Permanent People's Tribunal met in Madrid, Spain, to hear testimony from expert witnesses, members of the clergy, and Guatemalan Mayans on the situation in Guatemala. The tribunal, composed of Nobel Prize winners, theologians, and experts in international law, concluded that "the massacres and terror unleashed against the indigenous peoples, with the demonstrated purpose of partially destroying them, constitute genocide."[27]

In 1979, the Third General Conference of Latin American Bishops was held in Puebla, Mexico. A now famous statement from that conference epitomized what was happening in their part of the world:

> From the depths of the countries making up Latin America a cry is rising to heaven, growing louder and more alarming all the time. It is a cry of a suffering people who demand justice, freedom and respect for the basic rights of human beings and people [§ 87].[28]

That cry had already reached North Americans in the sanctuary movement, not as a news release or set of statistics, but in their face-to-face encounters with refugees. They would ask refugees what they could do to help and the refugees would answer simply, "Stop your government from sending guns that kill my people." As the sanctuary movement grew, U.S. military aid increased and the war escalated. The sanctuary movement had to face the U.S. military buildup and formulate a response.

Honduras

By 1982, informed sanctuary churches were saying that a U.S. war in Central America had already begun; what was still only a threat was the full-scale unleashing of U.S. firepower and an invasion by U.S. troops.

The U.S. buildup in Central America, particularly in Honduras, has been followed closely by religious and secular groups concerned about the increased militarism of U.S. foreign policy. By mid-1984 Honduras had become a U.S. armed camp with a series of "temporary" military maneuvers that guaranteed U.S. presence in the region through 1988. These maneuvers, with amphibious landings and parachute drops, were clearly an exercise in invasion tactics. At least one battleship, the USS *Kennedy*, was armed with nuclear-powered missiles. At Cerro La Mole, a mountain in Honduras, the U.S.A. built a radar installation and communication center aimed at surveillance of Nicaragua (also capable of monitoring all telephone conversations in Honduras).[29] Honduras is the key country for U.S. military operations in Central America, as was shown in the 1954 overthrow of Arbenz in Guatemala.

In 1984 military aid worth $190 million was shoveled into the second poorest country in the Western Hemisphere, where forty children die every day of hunger and disease—a situation that ordinary food and common medical supplies could eradicate. Most Hondurans have never turned on an electric light or a water faucet, but instead of being given plumbing, electricity, or hospitals, they get tank traps, oversize airfields (suitable for C-130 troop transports), munitions dumps, and a marked increase in venereal disease. Since 1981, reports of torture, clandestine cemeteries and jails, political murders and disappearances have increased. Documented evidence and eyewitness accounts have made it clear that military intelligence, police, and security forces have been responsible for most of the atrocities committed. U.S. Ambassador John D. Negroponte and Elliott Abrams, assistant secretary of state for human rights and humanitarian affairs, admitted that violations of human rights exist, but "not as a problem or a deliberate policy."[30]

Hondurans know what is happening to their country. On April 5, 1984, twenty thousand of them marched to demand: (1) an immediate investigation of and punishment for all human rights abuses, (2) immediate release of all political prisoners, (3) withdrawal of foreign troops, (4) an end to joint U.S.-Honduras military exercises, and (5) elimination of the Regional Military Training Center in Puerto Castilla.[31]

The sanctuary movement was neither silent about nor oblivious to the military buildup. The Wellington Avenue United Church of Christ, one of the first sanctuary churches, organized a demonstration to protest the Big Pine military maneuvers in Honduras. Big Pine was the name given to the 1983, 1984, and 1985 exercises. In January 1984, on twelfth night, the traditional day to take down Christmas trees, the church asked congregations to bring their trees to the Federal Plaza in downtown Chicago. The purpose was to rededicate the pine tree as a symbol of life rather than a rehearsal for death in Central America. As each person called out the name of a civilian killed in Guatemala or El Salvador, or of a victim of the contra attacks in Nicaragua, the crowd shouted, *"presente."* In traditional Latin American style, the gathering was keeping alive the spirit of the person who had fallen in the struggle for freedom. As one of the speakers that day said:

> We stand here beside the Federal Building, in the shadow of death, in order to witness to life. We invoke the spirit of those who were killed in order to push our commitment forward. As you leave today, remember one name. Pray for it, meditate over it, do whatever you need to do to incorporate the life of that person and the hope of the Central American people into your life. In Central America they have a saying: "For every doctor or teacher or fighter who falls, two will take their place." Let us commit ourselves to take the place of those who have fallen.

As was the case with many events connected with sanctuary, this was an act that demonstrated the essential unity of spiritual renewal and political protest. It showed that the essential dichotomy facing the church was not spirituality vs. politics, but life vs. death. The North American church was still, perhaps, twenty years behind the Latin American church in the levels of choices being made, but it had set out in a similar direction. At least a rudimentary bond of solidarity was being created and a glimpse of what might be demanded in the future was forming as the Reagan administration was setting in place the machinery for all-out invasion.

As massive as the military buildup is, there were indications that the North

American public knew of only the tip of the iceberg. Research pointed to a real war beneath the "publicized covert" war. The Center for Defense Information is an organization founded by ex-generals and admirals who saw the need for outside monitoring of the Pentagon and Defense Department. In May 1984 one of its key researchers told a group of religious organizers that in five years of doing research, he had never come up against so may dead ends. When researching U.S. military buildup, even reliable contacts would not talk and the standard reply was, "That's classified information."[32]

Even so, what was known was vicious enough.

At Fort Huachuca in the Arizona desert, the U.S. military was secretly building a radar and communications system that could carry on the surveillance activities needed for warfare in Central America. A communications satellite receiver is pointed toward El Salvador and computer equipment capable of analyzing night troop movements is operational. The sensing devices tested there can detect a rabbit moving on a volcano.[33]

The technology that stands ready for use by the United States is of immense proportions. Gatling guns of CIA-operated AC-130 surveillance planes are capable of putting a bullet in every square foot of a football field every sixty seconds. Just off the coast of Nicaragua and El Salvador are U.S. battleships that can deliver 802 tons of explosives over twenty miles every thirty seconds. B-52s launched from aircraft carriers, Panama, or even the continental United States could carry out carpet bombing of liberated zones. Behind that stands a potential U.S. invasion force of at least a hundred thousand troops that could be augmented with troops from Honduras or Guatemala.[34]

Allan Nairn, New York-based journalist, writes:

> Because events of the last five years have closed down, one by one, the possibilities for cheap, back-door means of defeating the Central American revolutions, the nature of this country's goals will now have to be discussed explicitly. So will the price it is willing to pay in order to achieve them. Now, if the United States wants to restore its dominance in Central America it will have to pay for it—with young men in rubber bags and gunners who remember how they pulled the trigger that killed those unarmed peasants.
>
> The historical question that was first raised in the hills of El Salvador and Nicaragua has come now for an answer to the living rooms of the United States. As Americans consider their response, the apparatus of intervention stands ready. It is a machine of immense destructive power, but it will not take off on its own. It sits on the runway, engines revved, flight plans drawn for Morazan and Managua—awaiting orders.[35]

Members of the sanctuary movement knew that whether those orders are given or not would depend largely on the response of the churches. Could the moral outrage of North Americans be heightened so they would act decisively to stop the violence against the peoples of Central America? Stopping that violence would demand of the churches that they insert themselves between the atrocities of the present and the horror of the future. Dietrich Bonhoeffer's assessment of the duty of the churches during the Nazi rise to power was coming true again:

> To be sure, the church must bind up the wounds of the victims crushed beneath the wheel. But there comes a time when it must insert its life like a stick in the spokes to grind that wheel to a halt.

Whether the sanctuary movement would say yes and be that stick was still uncertain in the early days of the movement. What was certain was that the roots of the movement stretched back to the desert—the desert where refugees like Anna Toledo de Cruz are daily caught and intimidated by U.S. immigration officials.

We endorse public sanctuary as an ethical and legitimate response to the persecution of refugees and as a means of alerting the American people to the human cost of U.S. military policies in Central America. We believe dramatic witness is called for in the face of our government's disregard for the basic human rights of refugees.

American Friends Service Committee
January 1983

2

THE NORTH AMERICAN SANCTUARY MOVEMENT

fire has gone out of fashion
why then should we carry it
within our hearts.

Roque Dalton

No human being is illegal.

Elie Wiesel

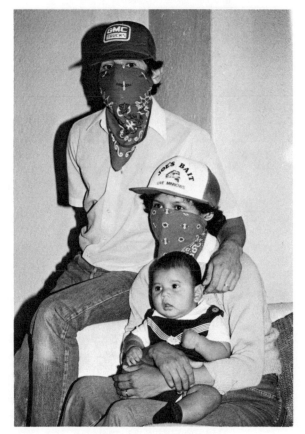

Federico, Anna, and Carlitos

WITNESS: ANNA

(Anna has been in sanctuary in the United States.)

"My name is Anna Toledo de Cruz. My husband's name is Federico and I have a son five months old. I left Guatemala because of the situation in my country and because I was a member of the Catholic Church. The church founded the Credit and Savings Cooperative, where I worked. It was called FENACOP (National Federation of Cooperatives) and its purpose was to serve the people. It taught the poor how to read and write, and how to live and work without rich exploiters. The government does not like it when persons awaken and open their eyes to the reality of the exploitative situation that exists in our country.

"After I worked at FENACOP about two years, the government tried to kidnap me. Many workers there have been kidnaped, so we knew we had to be

careful. In my particular case I had realized that some men were watching me. Ununiformed government agents followed me.

"One day I was getting on the bus to go home when I saw two men on a motorcycle watching me. Then I thought, If I get on the bus, it will be easier for them to kidnap me; they had done that with others. Then I decided to escape. I left, running the other way on a dirt road. Those roads are very desolate, no public transportation or cars, so you have to walk. While I was walking I heard the noise of a motor. So I hid behind some bushes. I threw myself to the ground and I heard them saying, 'She's around here somewhere or she's going to pass by here. Maybe she escaped from the others but she's not going to escape from us.' They were driving a military jeep. I felt lonely and scared. My heart was jumping but I couldn't let myself breathe for fear they would hear me. I felt like a small, hunted animal. Finally the jeep passed on and I started running again. Fortunately, I saw a woman with a baby and I started talking to her. She was able to protect me. The government agents just stood there watching me. They could have killed me but they wanted me alive. That day I decided to leave the country.

"There are many reasons for my persecution. Some neighbors told the army that we were guerrillas because my father was a member of the union where we lived and he was a catechist in the church. Almost every Catholic is accused of being a communist, just because we practice what the Bible says—'to love one another.' In other words, the church practices living in community and we help each other. We have meetings and other community services in order to help others. But the Guatemalan army says those meetings are not related to the church but are for the purpose of discussing communist themes and how to help the guerrillas. In my case, they thought I was the same as my father; besides, I worked in the cooperative.

"Other members of my family had disappeared; my brother and his wife disappeared in September 1982. We haven't heard anything about them.

"I resigned my job and was given severance pay. At that time I was very nervous and I took sick. So I told them I was leaving because of the sickness. In other words, I didn't tell the truth. In my country you don't always know who it is you are talking to. If you are talking to government agents, they will denounce you.

"I used the severance pay to buy what I needed to leave the country—a bag, a pair of shoes—and to pay a driver to take me out of the country. First I was taken to Guatemala City. Then I left for Mexico.

"On my way to Mexico I saw many things. For example, I was hiding with some friends who gave me refuge because I couldn't leave right away for Mexico. There I had the opportunity to meet some guerrillas. I realized that they were not as the government says. The government says they are foreigners—Cubans or Nicaraguans or Russians. But they are our own people. You can see our characteristic features. They are our own people.

"I stayed there for three weeks and then left for Mexico. In Mexico I had a chance to go into sanctuary. I didn't come to the United States to make money or for any other ambition. For me the most important thing is to help my

people because I love Guatemala. I know that I am not a U.S. citizen and that I am taking food from you. I have to thank you. You don't know what it's like to suffer as we have, and yet you still help us. I thank you for that. Through the people of the United States I want to help my people because there is so much suffering in Guatemala.

"I left Guatemala during the Rios Montt regime. During the time I was fleeing, I met my husband. I became pregnant and delivered my child during my flight from Guatemala. Then I came to the United States. I made the decision to come here because sanctuary was going to help us and because we wanted to keep helping our people by talking to the North American people about the reality of our country. Many North Americans are unaware of what is happening in Guatemala. They give money, food, and clothes to my country and so they are surprised when they hear that there is still so much poverty. Help is sent but we don't receive it. It stays in the hands of the government. The economic aid that is sent to Guatemala ends up back in the United States in the bank accounts of military officers.

"On my way to the United States I went from Chiapas to Mexico City to Hermosillo and then to Nogales, Arizona. In Nogales I had many problems. It was late at night when we slipped through a hole in the barbed wire. I carried my baby on my back, Guatemalan style. Suddenly a bright light was shining in my eyes and two INS (Immigration and Naturalization Service) agents grabbed my arms. They wanted to send me back to Mexico at 1 o'clock in the morning. They thought I was Salvadoran and said that the Mexican immigration officials would deport me to El Salvador. I insisted I was Mexican. It was the only way I felt I could save my life. They kept asking me questions about Mexico, to which I responded, No conformes (or I'm not going to answer your questions). They didn't believe me, so they put me in a small room with just a chair, no bed or anything else. I had to sit all night with my child in my arms. The interrogations continued the next day.

" 'Where are you from? What is your address? Who is helping you? Who did you work for?'

"But I didn't respond. I said, 'I'm not going to respond and I'm not going to sign deportation papers, because I want to have a hearing before an immigration judge. I know I have a right to have a lawyer.'

"They were so mad that I knew my rights. So they started to threaten me by taking my child away. I told them not to do that, because I was breast-feeding him and if something happened to him, they would be responsible. I knew I had the right to remain silent and make one phone call. So I told them I was not going to respond and that I wanted to make a phone call. They never allowed me to do so.

"The taller of the two agents leaned over me and said, 'Those rights are not for women. Here in the United States women have no rights.' His eyes were burning as he spoke.

"I shot back, 'That's not true.' Where I had read about it, it didn't specify that those rights were only for men. I wanted them to respect my rights.

"*Getting angrier, they started raising their voices, 'Who told you that you have those rights? Who told you that you can remain silent? Who is helping you; come on, say it.'*

" *'Nobody,' I replied. I just sat there watching them.*

" *'You must not understand,' the tall one said sarcastically.*

" *'No, I understand. It is you who don't understand,' I said.*

"*They passed me to a series of immigration officers who all asked me the same questions. About 1 P.M. they told me they were taking me to Mexican immigration officials.*

" *'I'm not going to go,' I said. 'I'm not going to leave the United States voluntarily. You have to force me to leave and even if you force me, before I leave you have to sign a paper for me saying that you forced me to leave this country.'*

"*Then they took me to Nogales, Mexico. I was detained at the Border Patrol office. They took me to a Mexican immigration judge. He asked me many questions and after I answered he said that I wasn't Mexican.*

"*The judge peered over his glasses at the U.S. agents and said, 'She's neither Mexican nor Salvadoran; she's Guatemalan.' He looked directly at me and said, 'Tell the truth because only Salvadorans and Guatemalans are eligible to stay in the United States.'*

"*The U.S. agents were ready to leave me in Mexico and let the Mexicans deport me to Guatemala.*

"*At that point I was desperate and wasn't sure of the correct thing to do. I resolved inside myself to be strong and I told them, 'I'm going to say the truth, but before that you have to swear, as representatives of the U.S. government, that you are forcing me to leave and that I am not leaving voluntarily.' They even raised their hands and swore to that. 'OK, I am Guatemalan. Besides that, I'm not going to say anything else unless I'm in front of a judge with my attorney.'*

"*They took me back to Arizona to fill out some documents. I asked, 'Am I in detention? I need to be in jail because I can't tolerate that room any longer. I have to stand up all day holding my baby. I need to eat because I am nursing my baby and he is sick from not eating.'*

"*They told me at 4 o'clock in the afternoon they were going to send me to a jail or a church. They didn't say exactly where. I had been detained for thirty-two hours in Nogales with nothing to eat and under stress and psychological torture. When they saw that I was not going to answer their questions, they handed me documents to fill out.*

" *'I'm going to tell you my name and the name of my son, and that's all, even though I have the right to remain silent. Why do you keep asking me these questions when I told you I should have an immigration judge?'*

" *'Yes,' they replied, 'you're right.'*

"*Then they locked me in the same small room. In the next room someone started tapping with a coin. In a while, the door opened and a man wearing a drab, olive green uniform came in. He looked Central American. He didn't have his name on a nameplate, like everyone else. It wasn't the uniform worn by the immigration agents.*

"As he came through the door, he shouted, 'Listen, you fuckin' bitch, you're going to speak up right now. Who do you think you are? You think you're so clever. Who's advising you? Tus padres, verdad? (a derogatory reference). Your parents in the church, right? Are the people from the church helping you?'

"I just watched him because the screams were so loud. They scared me; and my son, just two months old, was jumping and crying. I was very, very scared because the situation reminded me of what was happening in Guatemala. There were moments when I thought he was going to torture me.

"He insulted me by calling me names that were very gross. He asked me where I was from and what my name was. I didn't respond to anything, because I knew any information would endanger my family and others back home.

"He pointed his finger at me in a menacing way and said, 'Look, you're not going to trick me, I'm a Central American.'

"It was worse for me when he said he was Central American because I was sure then that if he got the information he wanted, he would accuse my family of being in league with the guerrillas.

"When I didn't respond, he yelled in my ear, 'What, don't you understand what I'm saying? Are you deaf and dumb?'

"I finally told him what I had told the agents before: 'The one who doesn't understand is you. I have said several times that I want to see an immigration judge. I already have a lawyer, so that's why I don't have to respond to you.'

"He said, 'You think you're clever. From where have you gotten that information?'

"I said, 'Just because I'm not a professional doesn't mean I'm ignorant.'

" 'But from where have you learned about those rights and all that bullshit?'

" 'From reading books.'

" 'And from where have you got the books?'

" 'From buying them at bookstores.'

"He left very angry, slamming the door and making a signal to the others that he hadn't gotten any information from me.

"This happened on June 24, 1984. I was scared they were going to take me somewhere else. The only hope I had was that they would believe I had a lawyer.

"Finally the immigration agents took me out of the room. They became friendlier after they thought I had a lawyer. They said, 'You are going to sign these documents and you're going to have a hearing and a judge.'

"They took pictures of me, fingerprinted me. They took eight pictures and filed four of them, but when they filed them, one was missing. The Central American who threatened me took it. Then in Guatemala it appeared on television; the announcer gave my name and said that I was a university student who had traveled to Cuba. I was accused of being a guerrilla and a reward was offered for turning me in to a security officer. That is why I can't return to my country.

"I was then put in prison in Tucson for three days. They told me I had to pay a fine of $7,000—$4,000 for me and $3,000 for my child. I asked for it to be lowered; a government lawyer tried to have the fine increased.

"On the following Friday I was in an army hospital, in a guarded room. An official arrived and told me I could go free, without any fine. It was strange. Suddenly they let me go. Others have found it hard to believe. They said it was a miracle."

JIM CORBETT: CONSPIRING WITH THE DESERT

The Quaker had never "conducted" anyone before. A frightened young Salvadoran sat stiffly next to him, his fist gripping the door handle. It was spring 1981 and Jim Corbett was maneuvering his van through the backroads of the Sonora Desert, carefully avoiding the Peck Canyon roadblock. The truck rolled past strawberry hedgehog and golden cane cholla—the desert in bloom, ancient witness to other outlaws, other refugees. For these two, it would be a first. If they made it, the refugee, Miguel, would remain in Rev. John Fife's Southside Presbyterian church in Tucson, the first church to offer sanctuary in the United States. And Jim Corbett would conspire with the desert to rescue refugees many more times.

Three years later Corbett had chalked up a "coyote" record: he had brought seven hundred Central American refugees across the border to safety.

Jim's record had not gone unnoticed. As early as 1983 INS officials had posted wanted notices of him on their office walls. The government position is adamant. So is Jim's:

When the government itself sponsors the torture of entire peoples and then makes it a felony to shelter those seeking refuge, law-abiding protest merely trains us to live with atrocity. . . . The presence of undocumented refugees here among us makes the definitive nature of our choice particularly clear and concrete. Where oppression rules, the way of peace is necessarily insurgent.

Corbett's rescue work now takes him as far into Mexico as the border regions of Guatemala. Objective danger increased for him. But it was the first risk that caused anxiety.

Corbett recalled another anxious moment of those early days. He was to pick up a family of eleven, crossing through a hole in the border fence. A young boy guided the family to a "safehouse" on the Mexican side to await Jim. In the middle of the night the woman of the house panicked and called him, hysterically demanding that he pick up the refugees at 2:30 A.M. He knew it would mean driving the van up against the fence in the full moonlight. His low-keyed response deflated the woman's ballooning fear. She quieted and agreed to resume the plan of a daytime pickup.

Corbett could not have imagined back then that his exploits would spark a "domino" response. In the three years since then, church after church has turned to harboring refugees.

In spite of the impressive beginning in Tucson, Corbett is characteristically unpretentious and straightforward in assessing its role:

> Reports that we here in Tucson have built an underground railroad or established a sanctuary movement are false; we are simply in the process of discovering the church. In whatever measure the church is the church, it will try to protect the oppressed from organized oppression—which usually means protecting them from the state. The oppressed are often betrayed by clergy and congregations who give primary allegiance to the law and order of established powers, but throughout Mexico and along the border the church remains the refugees' best prospect for protection.

In late spring of 1983, when the impervious desert was again sprouting cactus, I met Jim in the basement of the University of Arizona Library. He was photocopying reduced topographical maps of the Mexican-Texas border areas, carefully marking river beds and crossing points. He would bring the maps to newly initiated sanctuary churches along the Rio Grande. Refugee crossings had failed on two occasions. Jim was certain that well-marked maps and the use of landmarks and floating devices would teach sanctuary collaborators the terrain. Two weeks later, guiding a Guatemalan refugee family through Mexico, Jim aided the first successful crossing of refugees into Texas.

Since 1983 Jim's "coyote" work kept him on the road most of the time. From Chiapas, Hermosillo, Monterey, Tucson, he wrote letters to friends, the Tucson refugee support group, Quakers, sanctuary communities. As the sanctuary movement spread from coast to coast, and political and theological differences of opinion surfaced, his letters became more tactical, more combative, addressing logistical problems with refugee transport through the sanctuary railroad. But in 1982, on Christmas eve, he was still writing letters to publicize the human cost of the war against the poor in Central America. The following passage was written down not in a divinity school but on the run. It was written by someone who had warned that, "Just as the refugees are outlawed, hunted down, and imprisoned, if we choose to serve them in Spirit and truth, we also will be outlawed."

Corbett's Christmas Letter

In Nogales on the afternoon of Dec. 24, I sat with a baby in my arms, hoping he would continue to sleep until his mother arrived, wondering what I would do if she were captured. Christmas crowds provided ironically appropriate cover for the grim game of cat-and-mouse taking place, a game played daily by refugees trying to evade border patrols.

In this case the fate of the young mother and her child hung on the outcome. As the family of a man known to be opposed to the military rulers of El Salvador, they ran a high risk of being tortured and then murdered if caught and deported to their homeland. For almost a year, the woman had been in hiding, nuturing her firstborn and waiting for a favorable opportunity to slip through Mexican and U.S. border guards.

The sleeping baby projected a trusting innocence that called quietly for love and protection. For a few moments I rediscovered the hope and wonder of Christmas.

But Herod's slaughter of the innocents casts the shadow of the cross on the Christmas story. I couldn't help remembering, from two weeks earlier on the Mexican-Guatemalan border, the grief in Mother Elvira's eyes as she told of just such a baby boy, nine months old, whom Guatemalan soldiers had mutilated and slowly murdered, forcing his mother to watch. Only at the risk of wounding the mind can one learn about the methodical torture of dispossessed persons that the United States is sponsoring in Latin America.

The victim might have been the baby in my arms. And it might yet be. As a Salvadoran refugee, he is considered an illegal fugitive and is hunted by those in league with the military terror that drove his family from its home.

Flushed with excitement and relief, his mother rushed in and hugged him. By nightfall she would once again be with her husband, in a small house in Tucson that a family shares with refugees (a house sometimes so crowded that cars parked in back must be used as sleeping quarters).

A few miles away from the reunited family, Tucsonans were gathering at the Federal Building for the forty-fifth weekly prayer vigil for social justice in El Salvador and Guatemala. I joined them. It was a good place to be on Christmas Eve. The service that Father Ricardo had prepared lifted us from awareness of the "darkness of oppression, torture, and death" up through prophetic to celebrative recognition of the revelatory brilliance of that holy night.

It chanced that I was asked to read the passage that begins, "She gave birth to her firstborn son and wrapped him in swaddling clothes and laid him in a manger, because there was no room for them in the place where travelers lodged. There were shepherds in that region, living in the fields and keeping night watch. . . ."

The Desert as Starting Point

Jim Corbett's first encounter with the plight of the refugee occurred when a friend of his picked up a Salvadoran hitchhiker on the border road leading from Nogales, Mexico, to Tucson. After his friend "lost" the hitchhiker to INS patrol officers, Jim spent a troubled night, unable to dismiss his fear that the refugee and others like him would face possible death in their own country. He already knew that young males in particular were considered "subversive" for fleeing their war-torn country.

The next day Jim took to the road, a desert road as obscure and peripheral to the American public gaze as the hidden struggle of Central American refugees. He went first to the U.S. "holding tanks" in Tucson and then to the detention center in Nogales, Mexico, where Central American refugees were held before deportation. These encounters were entry into the American underside; he was opening doors that others wanted to keep closed.

In the Nogales prison Jim saw 20' × 20' rooms where thirty-five young men slept on the floor. They desperately wanted someone to notify their families that they were being returned. In the women's section mothers surrounded by their children spread a white cloth on a nightstand converted into an altar in preparation for the padre who would offer prayerful consolation before they were loaded onto trucks and sent out. Usually the padre offered more than prayers—he suggested an alternative route past the Mexican checkpoint near Hermosillo if they were able to make another attempt at flight. If only to lift their sinking hearts, they all said they would. In a small courtyard in front of the women's section, pigs rooted in garbage. Refugee children were allowed to go outside their small room to feel the sun, to look past the high walls and armed Mexican guards.

Jim spent days at the prison acting as an intermediary, sending letters to relatives, advising and strategizing with refugees whose return would incur the most repressive measures. Most of the stories were heartbreaking. Hearing the truth about massacres was excruciating. He made contacts with Mexican church workers and offered to take refugees through a hole in the border fence. He worked with a team of clandestine Mexican church workers who explained to refugees how they could get past Mexican checkpoints. Refugees learned Mexican idioms, Salvadoran women straightened their curly hair or wore curlers, the children learned street names of the American border town—Nogales, Arizona.

The refugees gave Jim testimonies of massacres similar to that of Río Sumpul where U.S.-supplied helicopters strafed the river filled with fleeing refugees, turning the water red with the blood of six hundred Salvadorans. These testimonies of Salvadoran government-sponsored murder and U.S. support of that government, coupled with Jim's "crash course" in INS deportation policy, made mere sympathy unbearable. He had to *do* something.

At about this time Jim encountered other Tucson groups aware of the refugee dilemma. Following the deaths of Salvadoran refugees left abandoned in the desert by "coyotes," Rev. Dick Sholin and writer Gary MacEoin persuaded the Tucson Ecumenical Council to become the funding umbrella for legal work in behalf of Central American refugees. Subsequently, the Manzo Area Council developed a legal-aid program that would ultimately bail out fifteen hundred Salvadorans. After Jim began working with the Tucson Ecumenical Council—a coalition representing sixty Tucson churches—the Manzo Council incorporated its legal advocacy project with the coalition in order to jointly provide refugee resettlement services.

Still convinced that the legal route was the best way to halt the deportation of refugees back to persecution or death, the Coalition raised $100,000 for a massive bail-out of refugees at El Centro detention center in California, the main holding facility for the U.S. southwest. Tucson ministers and church members had mortgaged their homes in order to raise bond money. For two weeks thirty volunteers baked in the 110 degree desert heat, enduring the same conditions that the awaiting refugees had to endure. They typed out asylum applications on borrowed typewriters. They were able to free from detention over one hundred refugees.

THE LEGAL ROUTE AND THE INS

Major contradictions in legal guarantees for refugees and de facto INS practices gradually came to light. The group learned that a national network of immigration lawyers had documented violations of due process so consistent as to constitute a policy. According to Susan Gzesch, an immigration lawyer who toured Texas detention camps, refugees were not informed of their legal right to apply for political asylum. She claimed:

> The vast majority of Salvadorans are voluntarily returned to their own country by the INS without ever having had the opportunity to apply for political asylum. Many of them return never knowing such an opportunity exists, or if they did know, they were discouraged from applying by INS authorities, who see their primary work as returning undocumented entrants quickly.

Carlos Holquin, staff attorney at the National Center for Immigrant Rights in Los Angeles, denounced another INS practice that exploits the vulnerability and naivety of even Salvadoran children by encouraging them to sign voluntary departure forms, thereby waiving the right they might have to remain in the United States, and their right to apply for extended voluntary departure. Holquin tells of 5- and 6-year-old refugees, unaccompanied by parents, who have signed voluntary departure forms and been shipped back. According to Holquin:

> The children have been shipped back to El Salvador, back to the middle of a civil war, without even being able to speak with an attorney, without even seeing an adult [other than government agents], without having anyone accompany them, just because the INS, in an incommunicado interrogation convinces them that it is in their best interest to sign the voluntary departure form.

On the other hand, Ambassador H. Eugene Douglas, U.S. coordinator for refugee affairs, considers it unfortunate that sanctuary supporters tend to downplay U.S. generosity toward refugees worldwide: "As our government's senior refugee official, I am particularly disturbed by the sanctuary movement, which endangers the American refugee program." For Douglas, a key error of the sanctuary movement is in calling "undocumented aliens" or "migrants" refugees. "By confusing the distinction between migrants and refugees," said Douglas, "the concept of political asylum that Congress placed in the Refugee Act of 1980 will be progressively eroded. . . . If everyone is a refugee, then no one is a refugee."[36]

The UN High Commission for Refugees (UNHCR) disagrees with Douglas. On May 29, 1981, the UNHCR stated:

In view of the conditions prevailing in the country of origin, all members
of the group should, in absence of clear indications to the contrary, be
regarded as refugees. As regards persons who left El Salvador after the
outbreak of the civil war in 1980, we consider that the above conditions
are indeed fulfilled.[37]

In fact, the UNHCR has charged that the U.S.A. is failing to fulfill its
international obligation to refugees. This advisement became public record in
1980 when it was read into the *Congressional Record.* The INS has chosen to
ignore both the advisory opinion and warning of the UNHCR. Not only did
the United States ignore these binding international obligations, but it chose to
disregard the Geneva Convention of 1949 (ratified by the U.S. Senate July 6,
1955) relative to the treatment of civilians during a time of war. The Geneva
Convention prohibits all signatory nations from returning refugees to a war
zone.

In *No Promised Land,* Gary MacEoin and Nivita Riley document persistent
and numerous violations of legal procedures involving political asylum applicants. They quote a sworn statement by attorney Marc Van der Hout, director
of the Central American refugee program of the Most Holy Redeemer church
of the archdiocese of San Francisco, a member of the American Immigration
Lawyer's Association:

In my opinion there has been a concerted effort on the part of the INS
officials to attempt to expedite the departure of Salvadorans in whatever
manner possible. The consistent pattern that I have observed is the
practice of INS officials trying to coerce the Salvadorans into signing
Form I-274, to "voluntarily" leave the U.S. without asserting their right
to a deportation hearing where they could apply for political asylum.[38]

Even if allowed to apply for political asylum, however, Central Americans
rarely are granted asylum. Of fifty-five hundred requests by Salvadorans for
political asylum in fiscal year 1980–81, only two were granted. In southern
Texas, according to immigration lawyer Patrick Hughes, INS Director Hal
Bolden has never accepted a political asylum application by a Central American. Rather, refugees are immediately classified as deportable aliens and
incarcerated in El Corralón ("the corral") until deportation. Of thirteen
hundred refugees who have applied for political asylum in Tucson, none have
been granted it. More statistics show that nationwide over twenty-two thousand applied during 1982; only seventy-four were granted asylum. For the year
1984, out of thirteen thousand Salvadoran asylum requests, only 325 were
granted.[39]

Denials by immigration judges are hammered out daily, perfunctorily rendered with the same claim of allegiance to law as the persecuted can expect
from Salvadoran officialdom. The denial list grows. Deportation planes fly
them back weekly. In the U.S.A., federal immigration policies require refugees
to show written, certified proof of persecution in order to qualify for asylum.

Ricardo Ernades, a Salvadoran trade unionist, claimed he had grounds for seeking political asylum. The California immigration judge reviewing his case demanded concrete proof substantiating Ernades's claim. In his petition, Ernades stated he had been shot at three times because he was active in the union in his factory. He said further that assassins shot and killed a cousin they mistook for him. The killers left a note on his cousin's chest stating that they had been seeking Ernades. Finally, Ernades identified the men who shot at him as National Guardsmen out of uniform. In spite of these experiences, Ernades was refused political refugee status: he had failed to provide written proof. He told a *Los Angeles Times* reporter that there would be only one way to produce proof: "He can see the concrete proof by my death when I get home."[40]

While applications such as these were being denied, the INS continued to deport thousands to El Salvador and Guatemala. "For FY [fiscal year] 1981 some ten thousand five hundred were returned to El Salvador of sixteen thousand apprehended."[41] Unofficial estimates for the first months of 1982 put the number at more than a thousand a month.

In 1984, responding to mounting charges from the sanctuary movement, as well as congressional pressures, the Reagan administration issued a survey taken by the U.S. embassy in San Salvador on the deportation of 482 refugees from April to July in 1984. The government report concluded that deportees received no ill treatment when returned to El Salvador. The administration rejected a study by the ACLU, which found (within a limited period of time and with only half of the names of *reported* victims of human rights) that over one hundred fifty deported Salvadorans were killed, arrested, or "disappeared." The government stood by its survey. For the government, it furnishes the hard evidence that disputes the claims of sanctuary workers and other human rights activists.

Responding to the government survey, the ACLU claims that it "was carelessly conducted, with no attention to detail, reliability, or personal security, and its findings, or lack of them, can be granted little credence." The ACLU critique of the report repudiates the number of persons surveyed. Although the total number given is 482, only 233 of them were actually contacted. Of that sampling, 120 were directly interviewed, 39 of them by telephone. Those surveyed by mail were urged to contact the U.S. embassy "to speak about a matter of mutual interest," which was not revealed in the letter. In a country torn by civil war, where the slightest digression from anonymity could evoke suspicion of subversion, responding to this type of request would be, to say the least, ill advised.

Embassy officials admitted they were unable to reach many refugees in the "combat zones"—two-thirds of the country.

Of the 81 respondents who reported "no mistreatment," many were contacted by telephone by an unknown interrogator. In the tense atmosphere of El Salvador, it is safe to surmise that they would say exactly what they thought the interrogator would want to hear. Such a survey method is flagrantly unreliable.[42]

INS Refugee Policy

When asked if INS officals would attempt to close Chicago sanctuaries, Chicago INS press representative Bob Eastbrook had this to say:

The so-called refugees in churches are way down on our list of priorities. . . . We have enough illegal aliens without making raids on churches. Speaking personally, I think the churches want a confrontation with a government agency to publicize their opposition to America's handling of the situation down there [El Salvador]. . . . I feel badly when it's implied INS, an arm of the people, is involved in morally objectionable proceedings, almost like Nazi tactics. I don't agree our policy is morally objectionable, because refugee political asylum cases are judged on an individual case-by-case basis.

When questioned about the fact that in 1983 (according to INS statistics) only 2 percent of Salvadoran applicants were granted political asylum, Eastbrook said that the miniscule number only provided that the policy was being consistently applied and that all Central American refugees must be telling "the same type of story and that the merits of their claims are all found wanting by officials."

This admission summarizes the INS policy. If contrasted with the individual "merits of the claims" policy used for refugees from communist countries, the starkly different acceptance pattern of refugees from "friendly" nations such as El Salvador and Guatemala would be exposed. According to immigration lawyer Marc Van der Hout:

The Salvadorans have the best case for political asylum I've ever seen. The denials show the political nature of the government's attitude toward them. If these were Russian ballerinas or Romanian tennis players, they would have no problem.[43]

The INS 1983 record of granting asylum confirms this differential pattern. Political asylum claims made by refugees from Afghanistan were 82 percent successful, from Iran 72 percent successful, and from Poland almost 30 percent successful. From El Salvador, where fifty-five thousand persons were killed in three years, only 2 percent of the claims for political asylum based on fear of persecution were granted. The reason the INS gives for its refusal to grant political asylum is that Central Americans are not political refugees but only economic refugees.[44]

In an interview with *Frontline* (WCBH Jessica Savitch Show), Elliott Abrams, assistant secretary of state for human rights and humanitarian affairs, and director of the State Department branch that determines refugee status applicability, said, "My sense is that from the Caribbean and Central America, the majority of people emigrating to the United States are not refugees. They are people seeking a better life for themselves by finding better employment."[45] In 1982, when Peter Larrabee was director of El Centro, the INS detention center in California, he echoed the state/INS position relative to Central Americans: "They are just peasants who are coming to the U.S. for a welfare card and a Cadillac."[46]

The connection between the foreign policy of the government and INS refugee policy was elucidated by Antonio Rodriguez, director of the Los Angeles Center of Law and Justice:

> The White House knows its [immigration] policy violates U.S. refugee law. It is quite open about this. . . . Reagan understands that to give asylum to a single Salvadoran would mean the recognition of the fascist, genocidal nature of the acts of the junta that force the refugees to flee.[47]

From the government point of view, granting politial asylum to Central Americans en masse would amount to admitting they were being persecuted and thus indict the U.S. government for aiding their persecutors. But granting Central Americans voluntary departure status would not "embarrass" the government and would save lives. Extended voluntary departure (EVD) status, based on the U.S. Refugee Act criterion for applicability, would grant Central American refugees a safe haven in the U.S.A. for the duration of the wars in their countries. When the wars ended, they would return home. Even this humane solution, in spite of two congressional bills to support EVD, has been denied. For refugee applicants from a communist country, EVD is readily granted. Afghans, Iranians, and Poles benefit from EVD status.

Even within the narrow limits the State Department has set for Central American asylum applications, there have been procedural violations.[48] According to investigators from the UN High Commission on Refugees:

> There appears to be a systematic practice designed to secure the return of Salvadorans, irrespective of the merits of their asylum cases. Our impression is that the proceedings were carried out in a *pro forma* and perfunctory manner designed to expedite the cases as quickly as possible, and that the detainees were not given an effective opportunity to adequately present their cases and show good cause.[49]

Although the Tucson bail-out efforts "bought time" for refugees, the group began to realize that the "legal route" was doomed. For the one hundred refugees they had bonded out, a political asylum hearing would follow, which would result in denial in 95 percent of the cases.

The Tucson "bonders" recognized that they had bought about two years of freedom for the refugees, including about a year and a half in court appeals. Before the final appeal, however, the refugee would be required to go underground rather than face definitive denial and deportation. Furthermore, the bail money of Tucson church and support workers would, in each "no-show" final hearing, be forfeited to the state. Jim Corbett referred to the bonding funds as "ransom money," proclaimed the process futile, and escalated the Tucson response to U.S. immigration policy and law. He began evasion services that would help refugees circumvent INS policy entirely.

Before the Tucson group began evasion services, which would lead it deeper into rescuing of refugees, sanctuary, and the construction of an underground railroad, the group summarized the collective wisdom gleaned from the months of legal efforts to aid refugees. It was agreed that there is no justice for Central American refugees under present INS policy and with present State Department and INS personnel. The system and the foreign policy that controls it are misconceived. For any church or agency to encourage refugees to voluntarily enter this system, other than as a last resort, would be at best a mistake, and at worst, complicity in the violation of human rights. Evasion services, sanctuary, and an extensive underground railroad were the answer. John Fife summarized his assessment:

> Initially we were involved with undocumented people, raising bond money, and getting lawyers to assist people who had already been arrested by the INS. We had been doing this for six months or so. Well, I am not mentally retarded and after that much involvement and with legal defense efforts, I realized they were neither effective nor moral. After a while it became apparent that this was an exercise in futility. You recognize very quickly that nobody is going to get asylum except a tiny minority.[50]

Abandoning the Legal Route

In September 1982 the Manzo Council filed a $30 million law suit against the federal government for unlawful deportations. With the Manzo Council taking on the government in the legal arena, Corbett turned to increased evasion services. He and the Tucson Ecumenical Council shared a growing recognition that such efforts were still only binding surface wounds on the body of a people bleeding internally. They could bring only a few across the border safely, but hundreds of Central Americans continued to be apprehended and deported. How could they simultaneously continue clandestine evasion services and raise a public moral outcry that would awaken the North American public to the plight of Central American refugees?

In November 1981 some members of the Tucson Ecumenical Council met to search for the next step in their faith journey. How could they become effective prophets? How could love be made efficacious with regard to the refugees? Included in the group were Jim Corbett and four early leaders in the sanctuary movement, Padre Ricardo Elford, who worked with Papago Indians, writer Gary MacEoin, Rev. Dave Sholin, and the now well-known Presbyterian minister who would be the first pastor to declare his church a sanctuary, Rev. John Fife.

Fife's participation in the Selma march during the civil rights movement may have prepared him experientially and spiritually to declare the Southside Presbyterian church a public sanctuary—a sacralizing of the border, as it were. That is, the sanctuary movement has called forth, in symbol and practice, a new march, a new willingness, as in Selma, to believe in the God of history and trust in the God of the oppressed. Choosing sides always implies both spiritual and physical action. Corbett said:

We decided to go public because we had all become aware that a full-scale holocaust was going on in Central America, and by keeping the operation clandestine we were doing exactly what the government wanted us to do—keeping it hidden, keeping the issue out of the public view.

On March 24, 1982, the anniversary of the death of Archbishop Romero, Fife hung two banners on the small, pink stucco church in the poor section of Tucson. One read, "This is a sanctuary for the oppressed of Central America." The other read, "Immigration: do not profane the sanctuary of God." From that time on, INS cars would intermittently circle the church, alert for a "run" by a pickup truck to gather refugees crossing a border point. Until April 1984, when Phil Conger, director of the Tucson Ecumenical Council, was arrested, the INS never caught anyone, in spite of the fact that many nights there were as many as twenty-five refugees sleeping on the church floor, many of whom had been helped across the border. The number of refugees who have passed through Southside Presbyterian church is in the thousands. When questioned by the press, John Fife publicly acknowledged that he was harboring such numbers. He was doing this under the nose of the border patrol.

Leon Ring, chief of the Tucson division of the border patrol, considered the number exaggerated: "It is not as widespread as they would like to publicize it." Ring refused to "touch" Southside Presbyterian church:

Certain arrests could have taken place if we would have wanted to, but we felt the government would end up looking ridiculous, especially as far as going into church property—anything where ethics involved would be questioned. These church groups wanted publicity. They were baiting us to overreact. We have been deliberately low key.[51]

The "baiting" remark probably referred to a letter the Southside congregation had sent to both the U.S. attorney general and the director of the INS stating the community's intention to offer public sanctuary as the only moral option available to persons of conscience intent upon saving lives. If the federal government wanted evidence for conviction, the sanctuary churches and synagogues were all offering signed confessions. Following is the text of a letter written to Attorney General William French Smith by Rev. John Fife's Southside Presbyterian church:

We are writing to inform you that the Southside Presbyterian church will publicly violate the Immigration and Nationality Act Section 274(a). We have declared our church as a "sanctuary" for undocumented refugees from Central America. . . . We believe that justice and mercy require that people of conscience actively assert our God-given right to aid anyone fleeing from persecution and murder. The current administration of U.S. law prohibits us from sheltering these refugees from Central America. Therefore we believe the administration of the law to be immoral, as well as illegal. . . . Obedience to God requires this of all of us.

Another border state, California, also inundated with Central American refugees, would come to act in concert with the Tucson declaration. Five East Bay area churches—University Lutheran church, Holy Spirit Newman Center, St. Mark's Episcopal church, Trinity Methodist church, and St. John's Presbyterian church—co-declared themselves a sanctuary for refugees. According to Rev. Gus Schultz, the East Bay area religious community had gone through a similar process of clandestinely protecting refugees before arriving at the decision to offer public sanctuary.

LAYING THE RAILROAD TRACKS NORTH

Although an underground railroad had been constructed for border runs and trips as far as Iowa, it had yet to replicate the extensiveness of Harriet Tubman's slave underground railroad. Both Tucson and Los Angeles were straining their capacity to absorb and provide social support services for refugees. The Center for Immigration Rights in Los Angeles has estimated that more than three hundred fifty thousand Salvadoran refugees are in hiding in California alone. Los Angeles has more Salvadorans than any other city in the world except San Salvador.

For Tucson more help was essential. Further, if the sanctuary movement was to alert the nationwide religious community to the desperate plight of the refugees, it would have to become a national movement. When the Chicago Religious Task Force on Central America (CRTFCA), a local coalition of religious and humanitarian groups, contacted Jim Corbett and agreed to his plan to conduct a refugee to a Chicago church sanctuary, the railroad had expanded into the center of *el Norte*, and the sanctuary movement was becoming national in scope.

The railroad would not become operational until Jim conducted a refugee to the Wellington Avenue church sanctuary in Chicago and met with CRTFCA members. On that occasion Jim, in his usual low-keyed style, asked if the CRTFCA would like to do this again and again. That is, would it become the national coordinator for the underground railroad. For a day and a half, task force members debated the proposal. Even forty hours of Jim Corbett border stories and desert theology did not utterly break down their hesitancy. They told him finally that they were reluctant to take on a project for which they had not had experience at a nationwide level. But they promised him they would make inquiries nationwide and try to find an appropriate, more experienced collective. After a month with no results, they realized it was "amateur hour" and they would have to shoulder the responsibility.

Another persuasive factor was the Wellington inaugural service and the transformative nature of the actual encounter of the exiled refugee church with the Anglo church. Not only did the congregation grow yet more in political and theological sensitivity, but the city of Chicago and the national media saw through a new lens, the eyes of a tortured Salvadoran youth, the result of U.S. intervention in Central America.

Sanctuary in Chicago

The late August Sunday service was not typical for the congregation of the Wellington Avenue church. In their midst, blinking back tears, a young Salvadoran refugee, wearing a sombrero and bandana to conceal his identity, and still bearing scars and burns from six months of torture, faced television cameras. For the Wellington congregation, the war in Central America had come home.

When "Juan" was presented to the congregation, its thunderous applause dissolved any previous doubts. Juan whispered his gratitude to a translator and silently lifted his left fist in the traditional Latin American symbol of solidarity and resistance. The congregation answered his salute with hundreds of raised fists.

Rev. David Chevrier, sensing the deep community recognition of the holiness of their harboring action, then invoked the ancient tradition of sanctuary:

> We live in a time of encroachment . . . violation of the holiness of even the most basic of human rights. A demonic domination has been unleashed that is profaning the human through torture and terror. It is time to provide a safe place and cry out *¡Basta!* Enough! The blood stops here!

Upstairs in a makeshift room where the congregation was barely able to coax the plumbing to work, Juan spent his days with 24-hour companionship. We visited him there.

When we knocked, he was asleep, exhausted from his overnight ride on the underground railroad from Tucson to Chicago. Our first impression was that of a child awakened too suddenly. Clearly he was bewildered—the long trip, a tumultuous reception, strange surroundings. But even several hours later, when he had warmed to us and told us his story of eight months of torture and a two-year journey to this precarious freedom, there remained a certain innocence. He was a shy country boy from La Libertad.

It was during his student days at the University of San Salvador that Juan was picked up. One day after class, while he was waiting for a bus, a security policeman came up behind him, yanking his hair and throwing him to the ground. At first, because he was not "political," he was bewildered and hoped that mistaken identity would be established when his papers were checked.

But the police did not ask for his papers. They threw him on the floor of a jeep; a policeman pressed one boot against his head and another on his back. When he tried to move, one of them slammed a rifle butt against the side of his face.

Next they blindfolded him, and he felt terror lock a muscle in his neck. He began to breathe deeper to loosen the cramp. Like a drowning person, his whole life spun before his eyes. Had he somehow been a subversive? But how? Of what was he accused? Juan was never to find out. No charges. No trial.

He felt the thud of two more bodies jar the jeep floor. "They piled us up like potato sacks, only they respect food a little more." When the jeep started, he felt terrible sorrow for his mother, then stabbing anxiety when he remembered the pattern of arrest, followed by rape and murder of the prisoner's family.

During Juan's imprisonment, his father "disappeared." Neighbors saw the security forces come to the house. Three months later his mother died of a heart attack. Juan never has located any of his six brothers.

When Juan began telling about his first day of torture, I felt him distance himself slightly; his voice flattened. I was sad suddenly that all we offered was horrified silence—none of us knew, we could barely imagine, what he had been through. Though safe now, he was still alone. He seemed to know it, so he smiled a lot to reassure us, except when he told about his parents' deaths.

They began his torture in a place that was not a jail. He remembered hallways and torture rooms. He never saw other prisoners, because he was always blindfolded when taken from his room, but he heard screams daily. For eight months he held on; others went mad or committed suicide. Near the end he was delirious, and his hope was waning.

They pounded his hands with heavy metal rods, demanding responses to questions he could not answer. They asked for names. When he would not answer, they hit him on the chest over and over. He still has continual pain in his chest and occasional lack of sensation in his spine. They used electric shock, pulled out his fingernails, hung him by his wrists, burned him with acid, broke his arms.

"But what were they after?" we asked. "Was it your student activities?" His answer:

No, it wasn't that. It's true I was part of a student movement demanding curriculum change, an overhaul of the educational system, and student participation in university decisions. But their interest was in my truck-driving years before the university. I had a route that ran into Guatemala toward the Atlantic coast. In both El Salvador and Guatemala I saw many cadavers lying on the roads. Back then, when they bothered to disguise things, they threw the bodies in the road so that high-speed trucks or cars would run over them, making their death appear to be accidents. But if you stopped, you could see the bodies had been tortured. I think they thought I knew something from my travels.

Juan was unaware that a general amnesty had been granted prisoners when they blindfolded him and drove him to what was clearly a jail. The next day he was released in San Salvador. It was 1979.

He dwelt on that day somewhat, how friends and relatives came to greet the prisoners, but he waited in vain for one of his brothers to step through the crowd. Then he began a ten-block walk to a friend's house. He laboriously pulled his ninety-six pounds through the streets. The lonely walk took him six hours. "I was weak, looked awful. . . . When I got to my friend's home, he did not recognize me."

He stayed there three days before the National Guard came looking for him. He learned later that four of the five prisoners released with him had been apprehended and their decapitated bodies thrown into the streets. When the guard came to his friend's front door, Juan leapt out a back window, scampered over a row of rooftops toward Río Acelhuate, a city drainage river, where he dropped into the water and thus covered his tracks.

He slept on the riverbank when he could walk no longer. Under the sun, and under the stars, he forced himself to walk toward Aguilares, where friends would feed him and he could move on toward the mountains to hide. For months he traveled from town to town in the Chalatenango area, seeking the whereabouts of his brothers. He was taken in by friends. Then he made his way to the mountains where time healed his wounds.

Juan finished his story, telling of his escape to Honduras, then Mexico, and finally his connection with the underground railroad created by religious groups on both sides of the Mexican-American border and extending now to Chicago. He had had to go about it slowly, carefully, because in Honduras and Guatemala Salvadoran refugees are targets for military and right-wing death squads. In Mexico Salvadorans are jailed or extorted. Mexican border guards demand payments from families carrying life savings in hidden pockets.

As a final question to Juan, almost as an afterthought, we asked him why he came here, prepared for possible arrest by the INS.

"It is because of the children," he said, the same innocence in his eyes. "They don't die just from guns. They are hungry. I don't want them just to grow up to a strong adulthood; I want them to have an infancy. That's part of why I'm here, to demonstrate that all of us must be willing, not just one person, to stop this suffering. It's a call."

Running a Railroad . . .

The CRTFCA steering committee was composed of ministers, priests, nuns, labor organizers—Christians and Jews—whose efforts had been largely focused on the task of organizing and conscientizing the religious sector of

Chicago to stop the persecution of the Central American poor. Some had been missionaries in Guatemala, most had traveled in Nicaragua, and one priest member left to work in Nicaragua in 1981 in the Zelaya Mountain region where thirty of his parishioners' throats were slit by contras (counterrevolutionaries). Perhaps it was the presence of missionaries—a Maryknoll sister who had been forced to leave the blood-soaked Guatemalan highlands—that deepened the solidarity the Task Force felt with the church of Central America. It was the moral claim of the martyred church of Central America, even more than the presence of refugees in our midst, that propelled the CRTFCA into the sanctuary movement.

The genocidal war in Central America posed to the Chicago task force the same question faced by the sanctuary founders: How to mobilize the North American religious community? The feeling was that the situation was much like that in 1966, when Americans concerned began the prophetic task of calling for resistance to the Vietnam war. After massive letter-writing campaigns, fruitless meetings with congressional representatives, and sit-ins with up to a hundred seminarians, ministers, and religious women in Senator Charles Percy's office, the CRTFCA despaired of legislative pressure on government that turned a tin ear to the pleas of the fallen Romero to suspend all military aid to El Salvador.

The Chicago group turned, therefore, to an organized effort that would awaken religious persons to commitment in behalf of the peoples and church of Central America. Jim Corbett's request opened the door. The CRTFCA abandoned a local organizing project and joint work with a local Salvadoran committee. Task force members put their hands to telephone receivers, beginning a project that would open more than two hundred sanctuaries in churches, synagogues, and Quaker meetings in the next few years. Like the biblical tiller, they never looked back—there was no time for it. They published over thirty thousand copies of sanctuary manuals and booklets that were sent across the country.

Though isolated from border work, they developed closer connection to it when Sr. Darlene Nicgorski (who had lived in Guatemala and had been working with refugees in Guatemala) became a member of the CRTFCA and went to work with the Tucson border group, assisting with the prescreening/ orientation process for refugees bound for sanctuary. The CRTFCA would coordinate the railroad, placing in congregations across the nation the refugees coming from Texas and Arizona. The railroad tracks were laid *poco a poco* ("little by little"), with human labor drenched in the sweat of day-to-day organizing, compassion, and stubbornness. From coast to coast a railroad would extend as far north as Canada and as far east as Boston.

. . . Building a Movement

The calls came, coded conversations—midnight emergency calls from a Colorado highway driver, from the Rio Grande valley, from a pastor in Ohio, from a Methodist housekeeper in Nebraska, from refugees alone in a room in a dark church, from the clandestine Mexican church, from a Trappist monastery, from an Amerindian tribe in upstate New York, from a Concordia, Kansas, retreat center, from a farm collective in Iowa, from a synagogue in Madison, Wisconsin.

The movement was patched, like Joseph's cloak, in many colors. The weave was loose, open. Initially the task force was overcautious, designing elaborate plans to disguise refugees (wigs, moustaches) and change cars at strategic intervals. This often resulted in keystone-cop slapstick confusion. Corbett said that there was no point in secrecy: the INS and FBI, through their extensive surveillance and phone taps, knew everything we were doing. The decision was made to keep everything in the open, to allow the public to see as clearly as possible what sanctuary was and who was involved in it. But this did not preclude caution and security efforts to protect refugees from arrest, especially when they were en route to a sanctuary. To date, no refugee has been taken from a sanctuary or the railroad and deported.

The best protection was media publicity. Jim summed up this philosophy in four words: "Be simple but audacious." FBI intimidation, surveillance, and the arrest of railroad "conductors" would not occur for two years. By then the organization had learned that it would not be its mistakes, but its successes, that would draw fire from government authorities.

From 30 Sanctuaries in 1982 to 3,000 in 1984

The phenomenal growth of the sanctuary movement in such a short time confounded initiators and coordinators. But if grace, socially expressed as an option for the oppressed, erupts in history, faithfulness to such a gift demands our creativity and skills for such a struggle. Just as Oscar Romero had again and again encouraged organizing the people, the CRTFCA encouraged the founding of each sanctuary.

Initially the CRTFCA sent organizers to meet with a church or synagogue deciding on sanctuary. In 1982 sanctuary was declared in Seattle on March 24 and in Milwaukee on December 2. Then came Minneapolis on March 24 and Washington, D.C., on December 2, 1983. By 1983 travel to a congregation was neither necessary nor possible and the target dates of March 24 and December 2 were insufficient to keep up with the many declarations. As many as one or two declarations per week were coming in by summer 1984. For most congregations the witness of so many other church/synagogue declarations, careful following of the manuals, plus phone-call assurances were sufficient. But for those first churches—from Southside Presbyterian, the University of California chapel supported by the East Bay Sanctuary Committee, midwest churches, the Hispanic churches of Cristo Rey in Racine, Wisconsin, and Pico Rivero in the Los Angeles area, to the first black church, Cross Lutheran of Milwaukee, and finally the first east coast church, Luther Place of Washington, D.C.—everything felt risky.

By 1983 grass-roots denominational pressure had successfully committed formal national adjudicatory/conference endorsement of sanctuary by almost every national Protestant denomination. The National Council of Catholic Bishops has not endorsed sanctuary but individual bishops have. In the fall of 1984 Riverside church in New York City, ministered by Rev. William Sloane Coffin, received a Guatemalan family into sanctuary. Two weeks later Rev. Jesse Jackson received a Salvadoran family of five into Operation Push. In declaring sanctuary Jesse said:

> The national headquarters of People United to Serve Humanity (PUSH) in Chicago joins with more than three thousand churches and communities of faith all over America who support 160 sites offering sanctuary to the innocent victims of war and oppression. . . . We are going to create a network as great as the underground railroad that brought slaves to freedom more than one hundred years ago. . . . If Americans had protested sending troops to Vietnam soon enough, our country could have avoided its longest and most tragic conflict since the Civil War against slavery. If Americans had offered sanctuary to the victims of fascism soon enough, the holocaust might have been avoided. If Americans had remembered their commitment to human rights, our citizens of Japanese descent would never have been carried off to the very concentration camps where Salvadoran and Guatemalan refugees are now imprisoned, awaiting deportation and certain death. We must stand up for what is right and we must do it in time, this time.

Refugees: Welcome to Babylon

If the experience of doing sanctuary was jubilant and life-transforming for North American congregations, it was not always so for the refugees. Culture shock, isolation from other Central Americans, lingering fears, deep psychic wounds that would not heal, letters from other refugees begging for help, the loneliness of returning to a room in a church—all these were problems that refugees and their sanctuary supporters had to face. While sharing the collective wisdom accumulated in the national network, the Chicago task force simply encouraged a congregation to live through the crisis, to work out its own solution because for these problems there was no blueprint. In the words of poet Antonio Machado, *No hay camino*—"there is no way," the way is made by walking.

Occasionally refugees shocked their sanctuary congregations by amorous overtures. Machismo is not a quality discarded at the border. Young male refugees sought companionship with women parishioners, at times inappropriately. Some fell in love, in the way captives cling to their captors. For the first few weeks of sanctuary the congregation sets up a rotation of monitors who stay with the refugees twenty-four hours a day in shifts. Such intensive time creates deep bonds. Occasionally congregations would call the Chicago task force and ask what to do about a love affair or the impact of a rough hewn *campesino* on a congregation that had been expecting a stereotypical Christ figure. Corbett's response to such problems was terse: "We never promised we would send them the Holy Family, only the people."

The major problem, more often than not, was the refugees' reluctance to complain about anything or ask anything of their rescuers. Some 90 percent of the refugees were *campesinos* unfamiliar with the urban ways of even their own nation. The refugees' tendency to suffer in silence, because any difficulty was bearable compared with the suffering they had seen, was a communication and cultural barrier that took months to penetrate. For instance, refugees were not able to articulate to a host community their feeling that the congregation was unwittingly overresponding to refugee needs, thus depriving them of a vital sense of independence and initiative. Without refugee feedback, rendered even more difficult by a lack of parishioners fluent in Spanish, what might have been loving community concern, if tempered, became unintentional paternalism.

At a regional meeting of sanctuary groups in Madison, Wisconsin, four midwest sanctuaries met together for the first time. They aired criticisms, with sanctuary workers and refugees meeting in separate groups. In the plenary session refugees voiced their worries. For many refugees a sense of gratitude or *campesino* reticence had prevented a direct critique of U.S. culture or congregational values. The open Latino-style of the gathering encouraged them to speak out. Some of the congregations glimpsed for the first time their own racist texture and that of their culture, as seen through the eyes of the refugees. In such an open dialogue, problems were aired and some solutions discovered.

But for a few refugees, obsessed with fear for other family members' lives, there were no solutions. A few asked to return to their homeland even knowing their possible fate. Survival guilt, particularly in the case of lone refugees, drove them to the brink of despair in spite of the healing touch of the host community.

In spite of these problems, the overwhelming consensus of refugees and congregations was that of a community of solidarity—one with deeply religious roots that grew and stretched out in an earth that knew no borders.

The same meeting provided congregational sanctuary representatives the opportunity to discuss commonly encountered problems. It was consoling and elucidating. One common problem was that faced when refugees, recovered from depression and loss, begin to adjust to their new life and then receive a long-awaited letter from home, begging them to send money to save their family under threat. The refugees at this point have no income and so must request help (several thousand dollars) from the congregation. The congregation must decide if it will commit itself to this project, which means pouring into resettlement work finances that could go toward further organizing/ conscientization efforts toward stopping the war. Congregations have resolved this type of dilemma in creative ways that have maintained the wholeness of the sanctuary movement.

Social Services vs. Evasion Services

By October of 1982 a debate had arisen within the sanctuary movement. Diocesan and adjudicatory refugee social service agencies (and their supporters within the sanctuary movement) challenged evasion services as weakening the capacity of conventional refugee service organizations to assist refugees. "Illegal" actions would jeopardize their legitimacy and erode their ability to maintain funding, resulting in their inability to serve refugees. Jim Corbett confronted these challenges in a statement at Austin, Texas, which became a watershed speech. Jim began by placing his remarks in the faith paradigm of unequivocally choosing the side of the refugee against "prudent" consideration. Then he offered an uncompromising critique:

> Social services often become cancerous, a few refugees absorbing a constantly increasing expenditure while the vast majority go without. . . . When groups establish a paid staff and rent office space, they often begin competing for funds against all similar groups. Even when this doesn't fragment a movement, fund raising usually drains energy. It can also lead to the development of a self-absorbed organization of paid professionals who don't know what to do with volunteers, who can't afford to engage in insurgent action or offend establishment funding sources, and who identify organizational interests and ego factors with whatever service the organization was originally formed to offer.
>
> In short, evasion services and social services in the United States should be organized to make do with volunteers prepared to suffer considerable hardship in preference to becoming involved in fund raising and grantsmanship.

Jim went on to criticize refugee services as paternalistic help that has simply prepared refugees to fulfill a cheap-labor role in the United States. In contrast, he believed the sanctuary movement offered a "way out of the bog of condescension that is created when well-meaning sympathizers develop programs modeled on establishment charities."

The Austin philosophy, however, was not accepted by all sectors of the religious community. Nor did it anticipate that church agencies would actually contract with the INS to "hold" refugees. Some U.S. Catholic dioceses have contracts with the INS to house captured refugees; they are kept on church property before they are deported. One church worker explained the position of her diocese: "Isn't it better for women refugees to have clean sheets and towels before they are sent back than to be kept in filthy county jails?"

James Ridgeway has reported on how Laredo, Texas, has been handling the problem of accommodating refugees headed for deportation:

> [It] has been paying the Catholic diocese $22 a head per day to house women and children until they can be deported. Not more than $2 a day

can be spent on food. In Webb County, which includes Laredo, the INS contracts with the county, the Catholic diocese, and one private individual to provide six holding facilities for aliens. There are no less than eighteen bidders for a women's and children's facility proposed in Laredo.[52]

Casa Romero workers in Texas risk arrest for interfering with INS deportation policy, but other diocesan workers receive payment for their cooperation with INS deportation procedures.

THE UNDERGROUND RAILROAD YESTERDAY AND TODAY

The early development of the sanctuary movement had a resonance with another era of fortitude on the part of North Americans in response to the great sin of North America—slavery. In 1850 Congress passed the Fugitive Slave Law. *Suspected* runaway slaves could be arrested on request, or on sight, without a warrant, and turned over to a claimant. The only "proof" required was the claimants' word that the slaves were theirs. It was all perfectly legal— just like the deportation of Salvadoran and Guatemalan refugees today.

Resistance developed. Opponents of slavery condemned the law, held public forums, formed antislavery societies, circulated petitions, and made bold, heroic efforts in open defiance of the law. There were slave rescue attempts; some were successful. On February 15, 1851, waiter Fred Wilkins, or Shadrach, as he was known, was seized from his job and rushed to the Boston courthouse. While Shadrach was still in court, a group of fifty blacks from the neighborhood rushed into the courtroom, lifted him into the air, and spirited him to a waiting carriage. Shadrach and his rescuers moved away "like a black squall." The rescue was so fast, nobody even pursued them. The rescuers were all later found not guilty by a sympathetic jury.

Attempts to assist runaway slaves through the underground railroad persisted before and after the passage of the Fugitive Slave Law. As the railroad stretched territorially and added more stations, the daring and creativity of the "conductors" increased. Stations were in cellars, barns, attics, church towers, old mills, caves in the woods, and the back rooms of reputable business establishments. An elaborate system of passwords, special calls, or bird calls was used to elude capture. Harriet Tubman, the most famous of conductors, sang gospel verses when passing the cabins of slaves. One verse meant that a "run" was not possible at that time. Another verse signaled an "all-is-ready-tonight" message. Leonard Grimes, a freed slave hackman in Washington, D.C., decided to use his horse-drawn carriage in the cause of justice. He drove from Virginia to Washington, D.C., carrying out a slave family of three. For this he spent two years in a Virginia prison. George Burroughs of Cairo, Illinois, was a sleeping-car porter who worked a run between Cairo and Chicago. Slaves were hidden in the sleeper car and taken to Chicago. Another enterprising freedman, George Lucas of Salem, Ohio, had a wagon with a false bottom. He successfully carried slaves as far as Cleveland, Sandusky, and Toledo, Ohio.

In both the antislavery period and our times, the United States government made arrrests for "illegally" conducting slaves/refugees to safety. The parallel ends there, however, because the sentences now passed on convicted conductors has not matched those served by conductors during the abolitionist era. For example, Calvin Fairbanks, an Oberlin College graduate, went south to bring slaves north many times. He was arrested and convicted more than once, and spent in all seventeen years in prison. A New England minister, Charles Torrey, left his church in 1838 to aid the escape of slaves. Before his arrest he helped approximately four hundred fugitive slaves escape. Torrey died in prison.[53]

Black abolitionist David Ruggles led a biracial vigilance committee in New York. For his efforts in behalf of runaway slaves, his bookstore was burned down and he was almost captured by a slaver. Vincent Harding has written of him:

> There seemed to be a basic purity of heart, a singleness of mind about his devotion to the hundreds of fugitives who came under his care. His committee was a radical one both in its persistent civil disobedience and in the level of its sacrifice. . . . Over a period of some five years, displaying an evangelistic tenacity which led to his being jailed several times before he was thirty and which finally broke his health and took away most of his sight, David Ruggles helped more than 1,000 fugitives to escape.[54]

By contrast, the first modern railroad conductor arrested, Stacey Merkt, was convicted of three charges of aiding, abetting, and transporting, but she was given a sentence of probation. Another modern conductor, Phil Conger, was arrested near the Tucson border, and charged with three counts of conspiracy. The charges against him were dropped on a technicality, however, indicating that the government was not prepared to initiate a full-scale legal/political attack on the sanctuary movement . . . yet.

There are other similarities between these two historical movements built of survival and moral obligation. Current sanctuary leaders parallel some of the original railroad agents and conductors. Rev. John Rankin was a Presbyterian minister whose railroad "safehouse" stood on Liberty Hill in Ripley, Ohio, beckoning fugitives from Kentucky to cross one more river to a place of safety. Like Presbyterian minister John Fife's Southside Presbyterian church, Rankin's home was under heavy surveillance. His sons carried arms, prepared to defend fugitive slaves and prevent their father's abduction. Slave owners offered rewards of as much as $2,500 for Rankin's abduction and assassination. With the aid of Wilmington, the free black community in Delaware, Quaker Thomas Garrett is said to have aided twenty-seven hundred fugitives. It was Garrett who forwarded Harriett Tubman and her "passengers" to the

Philadelphia safehouse, that of William Still, the great abolitionist and former slave.[55]

Quaker Jim Corbett cannot, yet, match Garrett's record; he has thus far conducted only seven hundred refugees to safety. Historical necessity, however, reinvents moral courage. Corbett has said:

> Choosing to serve the poor and powerless, not just as an intellectual posture or a charitable gesture, but in spirit and truth, we will soon be stripped of our wealth and position. And just as the refugees are outlawed, hunted down, and imprisoned, if we choose to serve them in spirit and truth, we will also be outlawed.

Women to the Back of the Coach

Although there is no one woman in the sanctuary movement who can match the "Moses of her people," Harriet Tubman, such a match could be drawn from revolutionary peoples. There are Guatemalan and Salvadoran women of such stature, whose lives and deaths in the liberation cause of their people have become legendary: in Guatemala, Yolanda de la Luz, Rogoberta Menchu, Yolanda de Aguilar, Mama Aquin; in El Salvador, Lil Milagro and La Guadalupe. Among the women refugees there are similar courageous figures but their voices are rarely heard. The reason, then as now, has to do with sex-role expectations regarding leadership. Among refugee families and refugee traveling groups it is the men, themselves initially reluctant to speak before Anglos, who represent the prophetic refugee community.

So too with Anglo women in the sanctuary movement, even though a woman, Stacey Merkt, gained national distinction by being the first conductor to be arrested. When a *Chicago Tribune* reporter was encouraged to cover Stacey's trial, he wrote a half-page feature on her lawyer rather than on Stacey's case.

When a Catholic renewal center in the southwest planned a large symposium on sanctuary, its staffers chose to invite a well-known senator and a male literary figure "out of the blue," in order, as they explained, to legitimate sanctuary. They were particularly concerned to do this after the indictment of sixteen sanctuary workers who had been involved in border evasion services. They did not invite one of those indicted and facing a thirty-year sentence, Sr. Darlene Nicgorski, who had been assisting refugees in the area for two years.

Similarly, when a Catholic diocesan peace and justice committee held an all-day program in the same area, it invited a priest from the Washington Center of Concern to speak on sanctuary rather than Sr. Darlene. When she suggested that refugees be invited, the idea was rejected because "people don't want to hear horror stories." Women refugees from the Latin America Committee, however, were allowed to sell food, the proceeds of which totaled $77. Another priest, author of books on spirituality, was asked to give a talk on the *practical* aspects of sanctuary. Sr. Darlene, who had screened and oriented refugees, and had been putting them on the underground railroad bound for sanctuaries throughout the North for almost two years, was not asked to give that talk. Media has consistently focused on male clerical "charisma" and authority to the exclusion of women who provide the major daily support work and maintenance of the sanctuary movement.

Racism and the Media

Just as the media ignore women, so too they ignore the plight of victimized Central American peoples. The media focus on North American heroism to the exclusion of the death of nations and U.S. complicity in those deaths. In the words of Jim Corbett, "the media are not interested in the indigenous martyrs of Central America, but they are fascinated with the willingness of U.S. citizens to go to some slight risk in order to help refugees avoid capture."

Although the U.S. press eagerly seeks refugee victim stories, it is reluctant to publish refugee accounts of U.S. complicity in the military slaughter of *campesinos*. Some reporters have said that their editors insist that the more tragic, personal, and "simple" *campesino*'s account, the more popular acceptance the story will receive.

When sanctuary organizers attempted to direct the media to Chiapas, Mexico, where two hundred thousand Guatemalan Indians barely survive in refugee camps, the media declined, preferring stories of individual refugees and of individual churches and synagogues housing them. The result of this undetected racism is that the plight of the Guatemalan Indians has not reached national attention. Individual Salvadoran and Nicaraguan deaths still receive more attention than the attempted extinction of native American nations of the Guatemalan highlands where, according to a poet, the land is so full of the people's blood, "it may never soak into the ground."

Significantly, U.S. native Americans have been very much concerned about the plight of Guatemalan Indians. One branch of the Mohawk nation in upper New York state has declared its sacred land a sanctuary. Near Indiantown, Florida, Seminoles have harbored hundreds of Guatemalan Indians, nine of whom were arrested on the reservation by INS agents. Through the collective efforts of U.S. native American lawyers and publicity advanced by *Akwesasne Notes*, the Guatemalan Kanjobal Indians were released and allowed to file for political asylum.

Native American involvement in the new underground railroad was paralleled in the original railroad when Seminoles harbored escaped slaves making their way to Oklahoma and Mexico. Today their descendants are known as Seminole freedmen or black Seminoles.

Similarly, many a history of the original underground railroad primarily chronicles the heroism of white abolitionists, tokenizing the courage and ingenuity of Harriet Tubman and the black community in general. The truth is that the receiving network—the sea into which the runaway fish would swim—was the black community, a community in double jeopardy for assisting fugitives. Slaves who made their way to Sandusky, Ohio, were aided almost entirely by the one hundred Sandusky blacks led by the barbershop owner, Grant Richie.

No underground railroad could have functioned without the assistance of vigilance committees, which were created by and composed of blacks and functioned to absorb runaway slaves temporarily or permanently into the community. Vigilance committees purchased clothing and medicines, and gave money to help fugitives begin a new life. The committees provided the fugitives with letters of introduction and helped them find jobs. Their historical invisibility is due to the bias of a Western interpretation of history that focuses on individual heroism and overlooks the social courage of a people. Such a perspective succumbs to the attraction of white, male, clerical heroism, losing sight of the anonymous black community that continued the social maintenance work necessary for community sustenance. The inspiration and infrastructure for the railroad—and, in fact, the abolitionist movement itself—was created by blacks:

> Most of these white anti-slavery groups built on the base that the independent black struggle for freedom had prepared, for blacks had provided the first abolitionists, the first martyrs in the long battle. . . . By the 1830s black people had provided much of the base and the heart for the abolitionist movement.[56]

Like the vigilance committees of the antislavery era, the Salvadoran and Guatemalan communities clandestinely present in the United States receive, sustain, and harbor hundreds of thousands of refugees—many more than the sanctuary movement accommodates. Even the work of refugee assistance groups, which service thousands more refugees than does the sanctuary movement, pales before the ability of the refugee community to absorb arriving refugees. In major urban areas of the United States, Central American refugees in hiding take in their brothers and sisters, sharing with them what can be purchased with the income of one employed person. Three-room apartments hold ten to fifteen refugees who rarely assess space discomfort in North American terms.

Responsibility to *el Pueblo*, so acclaimed in liberation theology, is not a romantic notion to the Central American; it is a moral and political obligation. Its depth of commitment eludes North American sensibilities. Terrified refugees, confronted with a culture that encourages individual freedom and privatized responsibility, sometimes abandon this responsibility. Many Anglos, failing to comprehend the profound obligation that Central Americans feel toward one another, applaud such a step as an expression of individual freedom and choice.

A more in-depth understanding of the sanctuary movement must lead us beyond race and class blindness, both within the movement and especially from the perspective of elitist North American interpretations of Central American national movements. The corrective for such a reductionist and classist sense of reality is an understanding of the sanctuary movement in terms of the refugees, the voiceless and hidden ones of history, rather than in terms of Anglo, male heroism.

This chapter has not documented the hidden, courageous work of many religious people, especially women, in Tuscon and California who were part of the first glimmers of sanctuary. It, nevertheless, began with the story of an Anglo male, because the study of the social history of a movement needs to point to its beginning. Reflections on Jim Corbett tend to mythologize him. But the best compliment to him is the proliferation and prolongation of the course of action that he pioneered. The dangers he faced alone at the beginning, others have faced since then. His story, though uniquely his, has grown into a mosaic incorporating the stories of many others who took up the work, living out his challenge not to be mere onlookers of history, learning how to be comfortable with atrocity, but to become makers of history.

The 14th General Synod applauds those congregations granting sanctuary to El Salvadorans and Guatemalans, and encourages all our congregations to consider providing sanctuary until such time as extended voluntary departure status is granted.

United Church of Christ
14th General Synod, June 1983

3

THE U. S. GOVERNMENT
AND THE SANCTUARY MOVEMENT

They will lay their hands on you and persecute you, deliver you up
to the synagogues and prisons, and you will be brought before
kings and governors for my name's sake. This will be a time for you
to bear testimony. By your endurance you will gain your lives.

Luke 21:12, 13, 19

watching the days pass like exhausted swallows pathetic wings
    accused of anything for having loved hope and defended life.
When do I get out of here? It doesn't matter.
What does is that in spite of the hatred, the pain,
    the uncertainty . . .
May we keep on
    hauling up the morning.

Otto René Castillo

Photo by Harvey Finkle

Brenda Sánchez-Galan, her daughter Bessie, and Pedro,
a Salvadoran who works at Projecto Libertad in the Rio Grande Valley

WITNESS: BRENDA SÁNCHEZ-GALAN AND MAURICIO VALLE

(Brenda and Mauricio were the first refugees
to be arrested on the underground railroad.)

In 1980, when Brenda was a high-school student in San Salvador, a demonstration erupted near her school. Salvadoran military tanks pulled into the crowd and soldiers shot down fleeing demonstrators. The sisters in charge of Brenda's school instructed the students to go home immediately. Making her way through the streets, the terrified 15-year-old saw Salvadoran military personnel execute persons in the street. She ran to escape their reach. In her flight she saw an old man motioning her to come into a ground-level parking garage. She ran into the garage. There, huddled in the rear part of the building, a hundred persons were crammed. The old man lowered and bolted the door against an approaching government tank. As the sounds of the steel tracks clattered nearer, Brenda looked into the terrorized eyes of the others and saw what they expected.

Then there was silence. The tank had stopped in front of the garage door. A Salvadoran soldier ordered the door to be opened. The old man, in a final act of defiance, refused. In the suspended silence that followed, the adults in the front, with only moments of life left, moved the children hand over hand, overhead, to the rear of the garage. It was their last act of love. The tank pumped round after round of 50-calibre machine-gun fire into the garage. Bodies crumpled upon one another. Brenda remembered lying among the children and whimpering babies, soaked in blood. In the room was the sound of dying. Then the soldiers broke into the garage and began to cart the bodies, like refuse, into trucks. Those still alive were ordered by an officer to be silent about what they had seen or they would be killed.

Brenda remembers that day of infamy as the day she dedicated her life to God. She was no longer a young girl. Fifteen years old, she had seen innocence murdered, her people penned, like silent lambs, before slaughterers. She had faced the absurd and incomprehensible—and she chose hope. She soon left school to begin training to be a medical assistant in order to work with the Lutheran Church and Green Cross at a refugee center near San Salvador. She worked with the center's physician, Dr. Ibarra.

In spite of long and dedicated service to the refugees, Dr. Ibarra was interrogated by the military because of his refusal to submit lists of patients for military approval. Ibarra contended that his role as a doctor was to heal anyone who came for his help. The military insisted that he was helping "subversives."

He was arrested, brought to national police headquarters, and tortured for six months. They wired his thumbs behind his back, tied ropes on his wrists, then hoisted him on pulleys until his arms were pulled from their sockets. Finally pressure from the Swiss embassy ended his agony. He was released and eventually left the country.

Soldiers returned to the apartment building where Brenda and other medical assistance workers lived. They intended to "interview" church medical workers whom they felt were aiding communists. One night Brenda's co-worker was dragged from her apartment and brought to national guard headquarters where she was gang raped and tortured. In the morning the soldiers led her into the town square and forced her to bend over. Then a soldier inserted a machine gun in her rectum and pulled the trigger. She was three months pregnant. The fetus was torn from her womb and sliced in half.

When Brenda heard of her co-worker's abduction, she sought refuge with the Lutheran church. She took nothing with her but her one-year-old daughter Bessie. At the Lutheran church she was told that she could be taken to an underground railroad. She went to Mexico City and found Rev. Daniel Long whom she had met in El Salvador. After hearing her story, Long told her it could be arranged to send her to the United States if she wished.

Brenda longed for and rejoiced in the possibility of safety that the United States would bring. When she set foot in U.S. soil, she offered a prayer of thanksgiving. She was met by church representatives and taken to Casa Romero in San Benito, Texas.

●

Mauricio Valle, through similar tragic encounters with death in El Salvador, had taken up the healing profession of his father and, like Brenda, decided to work for the Lutheran church in a refugee camp as an assistant ambulance driver. Mauricio's father was a nurse working in a refugee camp. Salvadoran military men ordered him to stop giving medical assistance to "subversives" and then accused him of having nursed a specific "subversive" they were after. Soon after this, armed death-squad members broke into their home and beat his father. Mauricio ran to get help from a local official whose intervention saved his father's life.

After this Mauricio fled with his entire family to another part of El Salvador where his father again began working as a nurse in a refugee camp. An anonymous letter arrived at his house saying that the death squad knew where he lived. Then phone calls came in the middle of the night threatening to kill Mauricio's entire family because his father gave medical care to "communists."

The anxiety and fear Mauricio's father felt for his family became unbearable. Every sound at the door might mean his family would be dragged outside and death-squad execution would follow. One night after a threatening phone call his father decided to end the terror by eliminating the cause of the threats to his family. He took a gun, walked behind the house, put the gun in his mouth, and killed himself. In El Salvador the facts that parents must tell their children are beyond the mind's capacity to grasp. Mauricio's father had instructed him beforehand that this act was one of necessity and inevitability. The boy listened. After, he buried his father.

After a year of death threats hanging like a cleaver over their heads, Mauricio's sister lost her self-control. The tight reign she had held over her terror, as a brave reassurance to her anxious father, was released. She became hysterical when another phone call came, repeating over and over that they were close to death, that without their father there was no protection left. For Mauricio's sister death was certain—all that was left was a choice of how to die. She announced she would get it over with. She killed herself.

Mauricio took his father's place as a worker at the Lutheran refugee camp. There he met Rev. Daniel Long. After hearing Mauricio's story, Long suggested to him, as he had to Brenda, that he leave El Salvador. Mauricio chose to stay and help his people.

Sometime after that encounter, Mauricio was accosted by two unknown men on a bus. They shoved a gun in his ribs, pulled him off the bus, and pushed him into a waiting van. His thumbs were tied behind his back and he was blindfolded before being taken into a large barn where he heard the cries of torture and pleas of mercy as persons were dragged outside and shot.

The old accusation against the father was leveled at the son. He was a communist because he worked with church representatives at the refugee center. When he was dragged outside and propped into a kneeling position, he was offered a choice. Did he want his brains blown out or his head chopped off? Just before he was to be executed, a man intervened, claiming they had the wrong person, that he thought Mauricio was not the one they were seeking. He was released with a warning that they could pick him up again whenever they chose.

Mauricio fled to the Lutheran church. He asked Daniel Long to help him escape from El Salvador. With church worker assistance he traveled to Mexico City, crossed the Rio Grande, and went to Casa Romero in San Benito, Texas.

THE FIRST ARRESTS

On February 17, 1984, Brenda Sánchez-Galan and Mauricio Valle got in a car with Sr. Diane Muhlenkamp, Casa Romero worker Stacey Merkt, and a *Dallas Times Herald* reporter, and headed for freedom. The Salvadorans had been apprehensive, but after their long and uneventful journey, and in the company of "courageous" Americans, they felt confident. Danger was behind them now, lurking snakelike in the dusty back roads of El Salvador.

At 5 A.M. when dawn rolled pink wheels of light over the dark floor of the valley, border patrolmen brought their car to a stop. All six passengers were arrested.

Brenda and Mauricio were held in custody without being arraigned or presented to a federal magistrate for five days. They were repeatedly interrogated by five border patrol officers. They both asked that a lawyer be present during their questioning; their requests were denied. Under guard in the INS-designated motel room, alone in a strange country, separated from her baby sick with impetigo, and vulnerable to thinly-veiled threats that she would never see her child again if she did not cooperate, Brenda, who was pregnant with her second child, became hysterical halfway through her interrogation. At one point during questioning, she passed out. All these facts were admitted into the records of their trials.

While Texas immigration lawyers continuously attempted to gain access to Brenda and Mauricio, Stacey Merkt's lawyers began preparation of a legal defense.

Federal prosecutors charged that Stacey Merkt and Diane Muhlenkamp did "willingly, knowingly, and unlawfully conspire, confederate, and agree" to transport "illegal aliens" within the United States. Darlene Gramigna of the Chicago Religious Task Force spoke for many others when she agreed with this charge except for the unlawful part:

Those church workers did willingly and knowingly transport but not "unlawfully" and not "aliens." According to the U.S. Refugee Act of 1980 and the U.N. Protocol Accords on Refugees, these women and thousands of others are enforcing our own U.S. refugee law—[the] INS is . . . violating that law.

The U.S. Refugee Act of 1980 was passed by Congress to bring the U.S.A. in line with the UN Protocol on Refugees, which the U.S.A. had signed in 1968. The protocol states:

No contracting party shall expel or forceably return a refugee in any manner whatsoever to the frontiers of territories where his (her) life or freedom would be threatened on account of his (her) race, religion, nationality, membership of a particular social group or political opinion.

The argument that Stacey's accompaniment of the refugees was a legal act was the basis of lawyer Dan Sheehan's legal presentation in the preliminary hearing held before magistrate Sue Williams. Sheehan, who was a lead counselor in the Karen Silkwood case, claimed that the religious workers were conducting persons authorized to reside in the U.S.A. according to Title 8, Section 1106, subsection 42, of the U.S. code, and in compliance with the U.N. Protocol Accords on Refugees, because Mauricio Valle and Brenda Sánchez-Galan did indeed have well-founded fear of persecution if returned to their country.

If this argument had been accepted, it would have established a legal precedent to the effect that Salvadorans had a legal right to be in the U.S.A. because they have a right to seek political asylum. But Stacey lost. Assistant U.S. Attorney Jack Wolfe, countering Sheehan's First Amendment affirmative argument that Stacey was fulfilling a Christian moral duty, claimed her Christianity was "irrelevant" and he asked the jury to find her guilty of smuggling.

Stacey, knowing she faced a maximum 15-year sentence if convicted, refused to plead guilty, stating that she had "broken no law." During her release on bail, she wrote a letter to supporters and members of the refugee assistance network. She wrote it from Casa Romero, a diocesan-run refugee assistance house near the Rio Grande where she had been working. The following are excerpts from that statement:

> How many refugees have I said goodbye to? Who knows if they will make it past the valley's immigration checkpoints or where they will end up? If pulled off a bus they face deportation and very possible death. Yet everyone of them says it will be OK. "With God it will go well." How long can we close our eyes to the "disappeareds," to the continued increase in killing, to the torture and to the Salvadoran government's participation in this? Who is the criminal? Who will allow it to continue? . . .
>
> Refugees keep coming with the same story of the government's organized killing and repression. Where are our ears to hear? And to respond? I am standing in the belly of the beast. The reality of destruction, oppression, and injustice is so tightly and subtly woven into the fabric of our lives that we don't see it . . . a monster we've created. And we've been eaten. I will not stay in, I will not allow others to be eaten.

On April 13, three months after Stacey's arrest, Jack Elder, director of Casa Romero, was arrested. A Texas grand jury indicted him on three counts of transporting. That arrest marked an escalation against refugee assistance workers inasmuch as Elder was not caught in the act of transporting. INS officers brought refugees to Casa Romero and asked them to identify Jack as the person who had driven them to the bus station. It is not unlikely that the INS planted refugee-informants at the center. Commenting on his up-coming trial Elder said:

> I'm looking for a confrontation. Not to be self-righteous about it, but there's a moral force behind what we're doing that has the potential to

focus some light on foreign policy. They [the administration] refuse to look at the deeper issues. There's a war going on in El Salvador now, there are bombing raids financed by the U.S. government. This is the issue people are fleeing from. . . . One reason I don't feel that uncomfortable facing a possible fifteen-year sentence is because the stakes are the future lives of kids and women in El Salvador.

He, his wife Diane, and their four children had lived for two years in a trailer house next to Casa Romero. For frightened refugee mothers who walked with their children across at least two borders, those buildings have been a beacon of hope. By February 1984, however, "escaping" from Casa Romero became more difficult than crossing the Rio Grande. Reconnaissance flights began over the Texas border, with a national beef-up of a thousand border guards, over half of whom cover the Texas border. INS officers raid Greyhound buses in the Rio Grande valley, demanding that every Hispanic-looking person show identification. The border patrol has placed electronic sensors in the grass in the areas surrounding San Benito to detect footsteps. Diane Elder refers to the area where she worked as the "war zone."

Patrick Hughes, an immigration lawyer from Proyecto Libertad, estimates that the INS deports seventy refugees a day from El Corralón, the INS detention center for refugees. El Corralón ("the corral") sits isolated in the Rio Grande Valley, rising from the grasslands as desolate as Rommel's bunker. Even talking to refugees behind the barbed-wire fence is forbidden. Buses of refugees headed for deportation exit every day through the gates of El Corralón.

In the case of Salvadorans, the INS loads them on planes bound for Ilopango airport in El Salvador, where they are greeted by Salvadoran military. U.S. immigration officials give them a list of all the deportees. In the case of Santana Chirino Amaya, a second deportation led to his death. Amaya's sister testified in a congressional hearing that her brother begged the INS not to deport him back to El Salvador. A month after his return he was found decapitated at a crossroads on the "road to death."*

*A national study done by the American Civil Liberties Union in 1984, entitled "The Fate of Salvadorans Expelled from the United States," dealt with 111 returned Salvadorans who had either disappeared, or been killed, arrested, or tortured. The study was hampered by the fact that ACLU had so few names of reported victims of human rights violations and, because of incomplete Spanish surnames, it could use only half of the names of returned Salvadorans obtained from INS records.

This identification was a phenomenal accomplishment since members of the Salvadoran Human Rights Commission (the documentation center for human rights violations) have been assassinated or targeted for assassination. By late 1984 even this minimal documentation, coupled with publicity generated by the sanctuary movement, led the Duarte administration to allow refugee camps to be set up for deportees returned to El Salvador. Red Cross workers greet refugees at the airport and offer them the option of entering a refugee camp if they wish "protection." According to Elliott Abrams, the Salvadoran government option proved that refugees were safe when deported. Sanctuary workers asked Abrams what difference there was between such "protected camps" and concentration camps. The difference, according to Abrams, was that the refugees were free to enter or not. The sanctuary workers who met with Abrams suggested that imprisonment or possible death was not much of a choice.

In addition to tightened security at the Texas border, the INS was squeezing the Arizona border. One month after Jack Elder's arrest Phil Willis-Conger of the Tucson Ecumenical Council was arrested near the Arizona border. Conger was charged with three counts of transporting. In August 1984 his case was dropped because of a legal technicality.

The response of the religious community to the arrests might have been the Reagan administration's litmus test of church resistance. Right after the first arrest, at least fifteen church groups called press conferences denouncing it—a risky venture, given the conspiracy charges. In Tacoma, Seattle, Olympia, Albuquerque, San Francisco, and East Lansing there were sit-ins and prayer vigils in front of INS headquarters and at federal buildings to protest the arrests. At a prayer service in Phoenix, one participant carried a sign that read, "We have conducted 600 Central Americans to safety. We have saved 600 lives while the U.S. government has aided in the deaths of thousands. Who are the real criminals?"

Following the arrest of Phil Conger, a caravan of over a hundred cars traveled from Southside Presbyterian church in Tucson to Temple Emanu-El for a Passover deliverance service. The 143 drivers and passengers signed this statement:

> We, the undersigned, are transporting undocumented Salvadoran and Guatemalan refugees to the Freedom Seder at Temple Emanu-El. For the same act of transporting refugees, the U.S. Justice Department is selectively prosecuting Jack Elder, director of Casa Romero. After the Second World War, the U.S. government bound itself by law never again to expel or return refugees to any country in which they would face persecution. At Nuremberg and Geneva, the U.S. government also established that everyone has the right to protect refugees. Consequently, our transporting of the refugees is not an act of civil disobedience. Rather, we are demonstrating that, in its violation of human rights here and abroad, the Reagan administration lacks legitimacy as our government. Injustice has disguised itself as authority and is using the executive authority to violate just laws.

The caravan conducting the Excot family to the Benedictine monastery in Weston, Vermont, in March 1983, was another kind of response to the arrests. This caravan surfaced the underground railroad in defiance of threats of arrest, to publicize nationwide a grass-roots religious community unintimidated and more militantly determined than before the arrests. When the twelve-car caravan left Chicago, the cars were festooned with signs reading "Freedom Train," "Refugee Express," and "INS Stop Deportations." Days later the caravan wound into the Green Mountains of Vermont. Hundreds of supporters in seven states had rallied to the passing "train," announced and chronicled by a UPI reporter. When it passed through Washington, D.C., accompanying reporters asked INS national representative Duke Austin what the INS response would be. Austin said, "We will have to put them on notice that sometime in the future they will be held accountable."

Subsequent caravans followed. Fifty cars rolled across the desert from Tucson headed for Los Angeles where another group of supporters would conduct it to San Francisco and from there to Seattle. When the Tucson caravan finally reached Seattle, Bishop Raymond Hunthausen and Seattle Mayor Royer attended the sanctuary inaugural services. In January 1983 Hunthausen had written a pastoral letter to his diocese on the Christian obligation to support sanctuary for refugees.

Following the Weston and Seattle caravans was another traveling from East Lansing to Detroit carrying a refugee who had been a political prisoner in Mariona prison in El Salvador where he had been tortured for more than a year. Within a month Salvadorans launched a caravan from Cleveland, Ohio, to Chicago. In October 1984 a caravan carrying a Salvadoran family of five traveled openly from Los Angeles to the Chicago Operation PUSH public sanctuary. Before leaving Los Angeles, one hundred cars and two buses traveled to El Centro detention center as an act of solidarity with the incarcerated refugees. There the activists announced their plans to enter nearby Camp Pendleton, the largest Marine base in the country and the training base for war games in Central America. As the group of twelve religious women and two men attempted entry to lay roses on a small coffin, they were surrounded by a battalion of marines. "We were attempting to symbolize the death of the poor and to commemorate the lives and deaths of our sisters Ita, Dorothy, Jean, and Maura who shared the fate of the Salvadoran people," said Sister Jo Ann DeQuattro. All were arrested.

Stacey Merkt and Jack Elder

The INS had made it clear that it would not "break" a sanctuary church or synagogue, but there were no assurances about the underground railroad. Bill Joyce, INS assistant general counsel, said in 1982:

> We're not about to send investigators into a church to start dragging people out in front of the television cameras. We just wait them out. . . . This is a political thing dreamed up by the churches to get publicity. If we thought it was a significant problem, then maybe we'd look at it. But there are plenty of "illegal aliens" out there.

By November 1984 the INS apparently thought that the sanctuary movement was a significant problem.

Alan Nelson, INS commissioner, had responded to congressman George Miller's inquiry about the situation of refugees and the efforts of religious communities, through sanctuary, to protect deportable Central Americans. Nelson stated:

In essence, the position of this administration regarding the so-called sanctuary movement is that religious affiliation or motives cannot insulate anyone from the consequences which flow from a violation of the immigration laws anymore than from violation of other criminal or civil laws. . . . Those involved in this movement seek to have the federal government selectively enforce the immigration laws by basing a decision to prosecute not on the statutory illegality of the smuggling activity, but rather on the conditions or motives of the aliens smuggled. . . . INS officials and U.S. attorneys will continue routine prosecutions of all violators of smuggling, transporting, and harboring statutes where they have been apprehended in the normal course of business. No special exemption from prosecution can be tolerated based on the nationality or the political, economic, or social condition of the participant.[57]

Commissioner Nelson summarized the rationale for this INS legal/policy response. There is no basis in American law for the legal concept of sanctuary. But "the United States has the most humane and generous system for the treatment of those fleeing persecution of any country in the world."

By the following month immigration officers had again arrested Jack Elder (who had not yet been tried for his first arrest) and Stacey Merkt. Bishop John Fitzpatrick of the Catholic diocese of Brownsville, Texas, borrowed $27,000 to post bond for Jack and Stacey on December 10, 1983. Stacey was indicted on two counts of transporting and one count of conspiracy. Jack was indicted on two counts of transporting, one count of conspiring to transport, a new charge of "landing" undocumented aliens, and a final charge of "conspiring to land." Because Stacey's arrest violated her parole, she could have faced a long prison term. Similarly, Jack's eight-count indictment and previous arrest could have meant a lengthy sentence if he was convicted. Facing such possibilities, Stacey and Jack issued the following statements. It seems important to quote the full text of both statements because Stacey and Jack have, by their lives, and clear theological and political articulation of their faith, summarized the efforts, goals, and vision of the sanctuary movement.

Stacey Merkt:

"What is happening here is all so impossible, but happening. The endurance of the poor and their faith through this terrible pain is constantly pulling me to a deeper faith response. . . . One cries out: Lord, how long? And then too what creeps into my mind is the little fear or big, that when it touches me very personally, will I be faithful?"

These are the words of Sister Maura Clarke, one of the four religious women murdered in Salvador four years ago. I read them as part of a prayer service we had here at Casa Romero in remembrance of them and also of the opening of the house. These words stick with me. They stick with me because what is happening in Salvador is still "all so impossible, but happening." Nothing has changed, except our increased support of the war. We train the Salvadoran pilots. We provide the planes and the bombs, the helicopters and the ammunition. We have advisors to plan the war and U.S. observation planes to fly over El Salvador and radio information to the military. This air war has increased the number of civilians killed. We have set a house on fire. And locked the doors.

The lawlessness of our government is evidenced in our continued participation in the war. The lawlessness of our government is evidenced in the creation of refugees and their subsequent deportation. And now it is evidenced in false accusations against myself and Jack.

When the war in Salvador touches me, will I be faithful? The war touches us every day, no matter where we are, if we've eyes and ears. Victor, a 16-year-old Salvadoran, left his mother and four brothers behind. His father? Disappeared. One day I gave him a farm worker shirt that said *Marcha para sueldos* ["march for (better) wages"]. He asked me if he could wear it. "In my country you can't wear a shirt like that on the streets. They'll kill you."

I sit organizing my thoughts and I try to come up with new words to express something that is old. I can't. The old words are that I am a lover of life. What motivates me to help people and to work for justice is my belief in a God of life and love. I have seen. I have heard. I don't need five hundred thousand more refugees to convince me that we act illegally when we deport refugees. I don't need fifty thousand more deaths to convince me that there is a war in El Salvador. I don't need a bolt of lightning to tell me that I am to love the oppressed by defending them, liberating them. And I am to love the oppressors by charging them.

Advent, my favorite time of year, is now. Typically, it is a time of preparation and anticipation of Christ's birth. This year I think of it as a time of promise. A promise that in small things, insignificant things, come earth-shaking changes. Why else would we be standing before you? Why else would the Salvadoran army be bombing villages, killing old men, women, and children? Why else would the death squads [make] university professors, union members, church workers disappear? But for the promise of a small, seemingly insignificant love, I will persist. We United States citizens will have no excuse. We will never be able to say, "I never saw, I never heard, I never knew"—that we set a house on fire and locked the door.[58]

Jack Elder:

Yesterday, December 4, the Federal Grand Jury in Brownsville, Texas, returned an eight-count indictment against me for allegedly transporting illegal aliens last month. Since three counts of transporting illegal aliens are still pending against me in Federal District Court in Corpus Christi, it might be helpful to review the real issues at hand.

First, the evidence gathered from expert witnesses across the country in the case of the United States vs. John Elder in September of this year confirms what many of us already knew—El Salvador is experiencing a civil war; U.S.-directed ground sweeps and air attacks are generating many displaced people and refugees; Salvadorans who continue to enter the United States in great numbers continue to be deprived of their rights as refugees under national and international law.

Second, in the face of these grim developments, there have been signs of hope: (1) Faith covenants around the country are debating our foreign policy in Central America. Many have voted affirmatively on sanctuary. They have provided forums for refugees to speak of the awful cost Salvadorans are paying for our increasing influence in their country. And through the sanctuary movement, many churches are rediscovering their prophetic role. They are asking us, as God does, to stand with the poor, the oppressed, and to stand against the powerful and oppression. (2) The growing sense of community among sanctuary fellowship has enabled us to act boldly in challenging unjust authority because we do so collectively, not as individuals. Thousands of Americans, today, have signed a pledge of resistance, to be activated in the event of increased aggression by the U.S. against El Salvador or Nicaragua.

I think the meaning of all this is clear—our leaders have led us into an intervention in El Salvador that is shameful. The displaced, the disappeared, the detained, and the dead of that country cry out to us, "Where is your sense of shame?" It is to these people, my brothers and sisters, victims of our country's plan of death in El Salvador, that I respond: your cries have been heard. As a member of the sanctuary community, and one of the growing number of Americans who are repulsed by the war we are waging in El Salvador, I am proud to be able to live my life in a way that allows my own alleged criminal actions to illuminate our nation's shameful policies. Let no one claim, as did many Germans under Hitler, "We did not know."[59]

The determination of the state of Texas to win the case was evidenced in a gag rule issued by the state attorney's office; it forbade Stacey, Jack, their lawyer Steve Cooper, or the district attorney to discuss any aspect of the case with anyone. After the first arrest, Dan Hedges, the state attorney in Houston, expressed his hope that Merkt's conviction would "warn those involved in the sanctuary movement not to expect preferential treatment."

On March 27, 1985, Judge Filemon Vela, declaring his intention to preserve "the integrity of the legal system," sentenced Jack Elder to six months in a halfway house in San Antonio, Texas, and Stacey Merkt to six months in prison. The judge allowed Stacey to be free on bond pending an appeal.*

At a press conference following Jack's sentencing, Bishop Fitzpatrick said this:

---

*A panel of three judges of the Fifth District Appellate Court in New Orleans have since "set aside her conviction." The U. S. government could reprosecute or drop the case.

I am glad Jack is not being treated like a common criminal; he is no kind of criminal, rare or common. I think there is one more step that surely has to be done. It seems to me that what we need now from a federal judge is an injunction against the INS, an injunction that would halt deportation of the El Salvadorans.

State Attorney Dan Hedges's warning—made after Stacey's first conviction—that sanctuary workers "should not expect preferential treatment" became a reality in less than a year. And the religious workers indicted at that time were not given any preferential treatment; they were given preferential *attack*. For some of the indicted sanctuary leaders, convictions on each charge could mean thirty years in prison. In that "round-up" the government net reached out to snare church workers in Mexico.

A Time to Bear Testimony

"They will lay their hands on you and persecute you . . . and you will be brought before kings and governors for my name's sake. This will be a time for you to bear testimony [Luke 21:12, 13].

On a small side street in Nogales, Mexico, less than a mile from the United States border, the white stucco church called the Sanctuary of Guadalupe and St. Martin stands as a shelter to the sojourner. For those refugees fleeing El Salvador and Guatemala who make it through the roadblocks, bribes, rapes, and deportations, this church has been a safe haven. Padre Ramón Quiñones, pastor, makes daily visits to the Nogales jail where Mexican immigration officials take captured Central Americans. In his small paneled office Padre Quiñones sifts through messages from refugees asking for help. Underneath the clutter of messages lies an unofficial summary of the 100-page indictment the U.S. government handed down against him and fifteen other sanctuary workers on January 14, 1985.

The U.S. government charged them with seventy-one counts of conspiracy and encouraging and aiding "illegal aliens" to enter the United States by shielding, harboring, and transporting them. Approximately forty-nine refugees were arrested and named as "illegal alien unindicted co-conspirators," many of whom will be used as material witnesses against those indicted. The government named twenty-five other North Americans as "unindicted co-conspirators," whom they will also pressure to testify against the sixteen. The government can use the threat of deportation against the refugees and the threat of indictment against the North Americans to pressure them into testifying.

When Padre Quiñones speaks of the indictments, his voice is soft but filled with conviction:

Right now there are ten Guatemalans starving to death in the Nogales jail. They have to sit in cubicles without a roof while the temperatures here are going down to the thirties at night. What as a person of faith am I supposed to do? Ironically, the name of this church is "the Sanctuary." We are being indicted because the church is living up to its name.

The government gathered most of the evidence in the indictment through informants wearing bugging devices who had infiltrated church meetings. Sanctuary workers called the surveillance a threat to civil liberties—inasmuch as the sanctuary movement has always been open. The government, not content with having its own evidence, also filed a motion that sought to severely limit the kind of evidence that could be presented in court. The government seeks to keep the defendants from expressing any of their motivations for their actions. If the judge rules in favor of the government motions, there can be no mention of international law, the Refugee Act of 1980, religious conviction, events in El Salvador or Guatemala, U.S. foreign policy, or stories of the refugees fleeing persecution. Further, if the government has its way, the defendants will not even be able to use the word "refugee" in court or be able to refer to U.S. immigration policy or the small number of persons who have gained political asylum in the United States.

According to one attorney familiar with such trials:

> The serious charges against so many sanctuary workers, including church leaders; the wholesale arrest and holding of refugees as potential witnesses; the methods of infiltration and bugging of church and religious meetings used to obtain this evidence; and the current effort to gag the defendants and their attorneys at trial show that the government has seriously escalated its attack against the sanctuary movement and against all those, including sanctuary refugees and workers, who would oppose its policies. This must be seen as part of the plan to escalate U.S. intervention in Central America and to prevent the building of resistance inside the United States on religious, humanitarian, and political grounds.

Peggy Hutchison, one of those indicted on some of the heaviest charges, reflected on the meaning of the government move: "The sanctuary movement has developed some power and is a threat to the government. It is clear we need to continue the work and expand the movement. The indictments have strengthened me to work harder for peace and justice in Central America." (For a commentary on the indictments, see Appendix 3, below.)

REAFFIRMATION OF SANCTUARY

Peggy Hutchison's resolve to continue and even increase her commitment was reflected throughout the country, beginning with two of her co-defendants. Sr. Anna Priester of Phoenix symbolized the attitude of those indicted. Sr. Anna has Hodgkins disease. Right after the indictment was handed down, she went into the hospital to have her spleen removed. The judge on the case moved to drop the charges against her because of her physical condition. The operation was successful and Sr. Anna refused to have the charges against her dismissed. She said that if it happened, as soon as she was well she would be out helping refugees in the same way as before.*

Nena MacDonald, another of the sixteen, is a nurse from Lubbock, Texas, who volunteered to work with the Tucson Ecumenical Council. Inasmuch as she has two young children, she was asked by the press why she did it. Her reply:

> If I walked down a street in Lubbock and saw a person lying in the street hurt, people would think there is something wrong with me if I didn't help. What I have done with refugees is no different. If people come here to drink from the well of kindness and we turn them away, we will have poisoned the well. Someday when we ourselves may need to drink from that same well, we will find it poisoned with floating bodies.

Eight of those indicted vowed publicly to continue the work. Five days after the indictment, that commitment was dramatically demonstrated when volunteers from Tucson helped seven Guatemalan refugees cross the border. They traveled on foot through the rugged Sonora Desert where vehicles picked them up and transported them to one of the eleven Tucson sanctuary churches. Church workers spent two days and two nights backpacking through the countryside with the family, which included two young children. The family had lost to Guatemalan death squads seven family members including two daughters aged nine and ten. "We knew we were under surveillance. We knew that leaving was the only alternative for persons who are in danger of being murdered in our country. If we are sent back, there is no doubt we would be killed," said the father of the family.

The likelihood of their deportation was confirmed when new 1984 immigration statistics were released. That year the U.S. government granted only 0.4 percent of political asylum applications from Guatemalans. It was the same year that Amnesty International called the Guatemalan government one of the worst violators of human rights in the world. The United States refused 97.5 percent of all Salvadoran applications for political asylum during that same year.[60]

All around the country church responses to the indictments and arrests were quick and strong. Local congregations and national church bodies reaffirmed their commitment to sanctuary as a valid ministry of the church and vowed they would not be intimidated by the government. Top religious leaders from the National Council of Churches, the Leadership Conference of Religious Women, the United Church of Christ, the Catholic Mission Society, the American Baptist Church, and others issued a statement saying, "We proclaim our belief in the moral rightness 'sanctuary.' It will flourish as long as hope,

---

*Nevertheless, the charges against Sr. Anna were dropped.

love, and a belief in the ultimate authority of God live in the hearts of the people." Cardinal Timothy Manning told a capacity crowd at the St. Vibiana cathedral in Los Angeles that, "There is no such thing as an undocumented person. There is no illegal alien in the church."

A symposium on sanctuary planned for Tucson, expected to have three hundred participants before the indictments, drew over fifteen hundred in the wake of the government action. On the day of the arraignment in Phoenix, a city known for its conservatism, eight hundred fifty persons gathered at St. Mary's church to hear the two Catholic bishops from Tucson and Phoenix read a letter they sent to President Reagan. In it they called on him to grant voluntary departure status for Guatemalan and Salvadoran refugees. They voiced their support for the work of those indicted. Sr. Darlene Nicgorski, one of those indicted told the crowd, "It is a sad day when the government tells the church whom it can feed, whom it can clothe, and whom it can welcome. I know I have not done anything illegal. If I have done anything, I am guilty of following the gospel." The eight hundred fifty participants walked five blocks to the courthouse in what one Phoenix resident called the largest demonstration there since the civil rights days.

Throughout the country local church reaction was highly visible and clear in its commitment to continue providing sanctuary. Sanctuary groups called press conferences denouncing the arrests and indictments. Demonstrations at INS facilities and interfaith services of solidarity were held in San Francisco, Los Angeles, Chicago, Milwaukee, Cincinnati, and New York City. In Chicago five persons were arrested when trying to enter a Navy recruitment center in an attempt to publicize the connection between the indictments at home and U.S. military intervention in Central America.

In Piscataway, New Jersey, Rutgers University personnel feared the refugees there would also be arrested. Twenty-five members of the sanctuary support group camped out in the church for a week as added protection for the refugees. The Flores family of six, in sanctuary there, had three children under the age of seven. The father, Ramón, was a medical student in El Salvador. He and his brother and wife, all students, fled their homeland after government security forces arrested, tortured, and imprisoned them for working at a refugee camp in San Salvador. Rev. Henry Atkins, pastor of the church, said, "The policy of the present administration is to move toward a military solution in Central America. One of the forces opposed to that is a large part of the church."*

A new spirit of militancy and increased participation occurred spontaneously from coast to coast. A monthly sanctuary meeting in Seattle, normally attended by fifteen supporters, drew more than fifty. The following day one hundred fifty persons demonstrated their support for sanctuary in front of the federal building there. Calls from local sanctuary congregations to the Chicago Religious Task Force reaffirmed their desire to receive refugees. Christ Presby-

---

*On August 6, 1985 Ramon Flores was apprehended by INS agents as he picked up his seven-year-old daughter from a day camp. Among the arresting agents was John Nixon, an infiltrator posing as a sanctuary conductor who drove the Flores family on the railroad.

terian church in Burlington, Vermont, issued the first postindictment declaration of sanctuary; three churches in Houston were ready to follow. New Hampshire Sisters of Mercy declared sanctuary at the end of December in spite of an unsympathetic bishop and the berating of a right-wing newspaper. They will not retreat after this new government crackdown. Sr. Mary Ellen Foley said, "We feel it is a moral imperative."

The Cincinnati Coalition for Public Sanctuary had just sent a worker to San Benito, Texas, to continue the work of Casa Romero. Speaking for the coalition, Sr. Julie Sheatzley said:

> It is not these people of faith . . . who should be indicted. It is the U.S. government that should be indicted on charges of inducing refugees to flee El Salvador and Guatemala by sending millions of dollars of military aid to those oppressive governments. The U.S. government should be indicted on charges of transporting through their deportation of tens of thousands of refugees back to harassment, torture, and possible death.

THE PRESENT CONTEXT AND THE FUTURE OF THE MOVEMENT

Events surrounding the mid-January indictments became a microcosm demonstrating the reason why sanctuary arose in the first place.

At the end of January 1985, during the weekend of the first National Sanctuary Consultation in Tucson, the Air Force announced a three-day wargames exercise involving eleven air bases, one thousand servicemen, and nine hundred sorties. Two weeks after the indictments the United States sent eight new helicopter gunships to the Salvadoran military, sharply escalating government firepower and further endangering the lives of civilians living near combat zones. In August 1984, Americas Watch, a New York–based human rights group, condemned the Duarte government for indiscriminate bombings in civilian areas that have caused thousands of deaths and tens of thousands of refugees.

During the sanctuary conference itself a telegram was received from El Salvador telling of the disappearance of Emiteria Acosta Detereza, a church worker in the refugee camps of San Roque. Just days before, the Salvadoran military had been looking for her. It was a solemn reminder that the war continues in Central America.

It was in that context that refugees in sanctuary reiterated to the conference participants the need to go to the source of the problem—U.S. foreign policy. Yadira, a student from El Salvador who received a death threat and fled, said:

> We are asking people here to stop the madness of sending military aid to the repressive governments of Central America. This crackdown is a tool, an act of intimidation. They don't want us to tell the truth of what is happening in our countries. They want us to be afraid. *But we won't be afraid.* Only you North Americans can stop the situation there by stopping the military aid. You are the only hope for us. Don't let us down!

Preparation: Eliminate Witnesses

Sr. Darlene Nicgorski has analyzed the government objectives in indicting twelve sanctuary workers and arresting forty-nine refugees:

> The indictments are an attempt to silence the truth by silencing refugee witnesses to atrocities, by silencing church workers assisting refugees, and by silencing truth's entrance into the courtroom. As long as the war in Central America can remain technological, clean, and distant, the reality of the people's suffering does not become real to our U.S. people.

Nicgorski believes the U.S. government is cracking down on the sanctuary movement—with its seventy-thousand members—because refugee testimony about aerial bombardment and massive dislocation in their homelands belies the "improved" human rights situation reported by the State Department.

But why did the U.S. government decide to crack down on the 3-year-old sanctuary movement? To fully understand the timing and force of its attack on sanctuary leaders and refugees, it is necessary to examine the arrests in the light of advanced U.S. military objectives in Central America.

One of the first objectives, as Sr. Darlene has noted, is to keep the war "technological, clean, and distant" because the Pentagon has learned from its Vietnam experience that the true nature of the U.S. involvement in Central America must be kept secret. To that end the invasion of Central America was accomplished through low-intensity warfare directed from militarized Honduras, which was the "best kept secret" of 1984.

A primary U.S. military objective, which can keep the U.S. role in the war "distant," is to strengthen national armies in order to avoid U.S. troop involvement. There are four other phases of counterinsurgency that are meant to keep the war clean and distant but have not succeeded, because pacification involves civilians who keep fleeing persecution, coming to the U.S.A., and telling (particularly in sanctuary) just how dirty the war is. These four phases of pacification, which really reveal the new face of the war, are: (1) control of the civilian population in the liberated zones through government-controlled relocation centers, (2) use of the U.S. government human rights agencies to obfuscate or deny U.S. involvement with internal Central American military policy, (3) repatriation of refugees to relocation centers, and (4) control of independent humanitarian assistance programs for refugees.

Rural Pacification: Refugee Militarization

U.S./Salvadoran military strategy is no longer directed specifically against the rebel forces. Instead the war is focused on the destruction of the *masas* (a term used to describe noncombatants living in guerrilla-controlled areas). The military objective is to cut off the popular base of the opposition by forcing the civilian population out of liberated zones and into government-controlled refugee camps. The *CARECEN* (Central American Refugee Center) *News Bulletin* quotes U.S. Defense Attaché Duryea as stating: "We are making life worse in the guerrilla-controlled zones by keeping constant pressure on them [civilians]. . . . This can't help but make the government areas more appealing."[61]

"Constant pressure" is accomplished through bombardment. These bombings are multiplying internal refugees in El Salvador, as well as driving the civilian population of the countryside into the cities and across the border into an exodus journey that ends in Mexico or the U.S.A. Once displaced civilians are driven into government-controlled relocation camps, they are caught in a web of military objectives, the first of which is pacification of the populace. The objective was accomplished in Guatemala, beginning in 1981, through massive strafe-bombing of civilians and by military massacre raids on Indian villages in Guatemala.

Similarly in El Salvador, there is a government relocation plan, Project 1000, which planned the relocation of half a million internal refugees. According to the *CARECEN News Bulletin,* "The relocation program, popularly known as *Techo, Trabajo, y Tortillas* ["roof, work, and bread"], carries the same name as that given to the Guatemalan government relocation program of 1982–83, which itself largely duplicated the 'strategic hamlets' plans used in Vietnam to control and pacify the rural population in order to drain away support from the guerrillas."[62]

Human Rights Reports: **Ficta** *and* **Facta**

According to the State Department, Salvadoran relocation camps and Guatemalan "model villages" are not linked to bombardments and human rights abuses. In February of 1985 the State Department released its own annual global report on human rights. The report lauded improved conditions in El Salvador and Guatemala, and condemned conditions in Cuba and Nicaragua. At a press conference, Elliot Abrams, undersecretary of human rights and humanitarian affairs, went so far as to cite Guatemala and El Salvador, along with Brazil, Uruguay, and Guinea (West Africa), as countries that have advanced the furthest toward democracy. But a 1984 study published by Americas Watch and the Lawyers Committee for International Human Rights, entitled: "Free Fire: A Report on Human Rights in El Salvador," stated that human rights violations have not decreased, as the Reagan administration claims, but that the occurrence of civilian killings by the Salvadoran army has increased. The report states that the "armed forces of El Salvador, ground and air, are engaged in indiscriminate attacks upon the civilian population in conflict zones, particularly in guerrilla-controlled conflict zones."[63]

In 1985 a study by the congressional Arms Control and Foreign Policy Caucas said the U.S.A. was becoming more involved in a war in El Salvador that is "reminiscent of Vietnam." Even the release of this study, refuting the Central American policy of the administration, did not brake Reagan's roll on the war drums. The 130-member bipartisan congressional caucus accused the administration, on February 11, 1985, of having supplied "insufficient, misleading, and, in some cases, false information on aid to El Salvador." As examples, the report showed that the $1.7 billion in aid to El Salvador since 1980 has not, as the administration has claimed, been used primarily for economic aid and social development; 85 percent of it was military aid. This is an almost direct reversal of the administration claims that 75 percent of the aid was used for economic and social purposes. Additionally the report says that "the administration has provided false information to Congress concerning the number of military personnel operating in El Salvador and about the roles they are performing."[64]

Repatriation of Refugees

When refugees are displaced from border areas, in some cases to prepare potential combat zones, such as the Salvadoran-Honduran front, they become part of U.S./Salvadoran military objectives. In mid-1984 thousands of Salvadoran refugees were asked a second time to move even farther from the border into the interior of Honduras. The Honduran government, in fact, knew the refugees could not agree to a second move, because they would be sent into an economically desperate area of Honduras where the populace had refused to accept refugees. The refugees refused to move. Honduran President Suazo Cordoba then met with Salvadoran refugee representatives and gave the ultimatum of moving there or returning to El Salvador, knowing the majority of refugees would risk repatriation to their own war-torn country rather than move their elderly (many would die from such an arduous move) and families into a hostile environment far removed from their own country, and with little hope of land for planting and sustenance. Although Suazo Cordoba has rescinded the relocation order, by 1985 hundreds of Salvadorans had already returned to El Salvador. When they are shoved back across the border, they are forced into army-controlled "strategic hamlets" because of their desperate need for food and shelter.

The treatment of internal refugees by the Salvadoran military is supposedly the responsibility of President Duarte, but according to Heather Foote of the Washington Office on Latin America (WOLA), the Salvadoran Air Force consults with U.S. General Paul Gorman, former head of the U.S. Southern Command, without consultation with President Duarte. Related to military pacification policy are decisions about the use of AC130 Spectre gunships used against noncombatants in liberated zones.[65]

The pacification of refugees in rural areas is a plan that requires large shipments of food and construction materials for refugee shelters. As pressure from Central American solidarity groups and the religious sector mounted against continued economic and military aid to contras, and to the Salvadoran and Guatemalan regimes, U.S. military groups and their conservative financial backers rerouted money for military pacification plans and contra aid through "humanitarian assistance" programs. In 1984 the Pentagon, along with the conservative National Defense Council, lobbied for a more prominent role in management of humanitarian assistance in Central America. An amendment to the fiscal defense spending bill in 1985 gives the Pentagon authority to transport goods and supplies (on a space-available basis) that have been provided by humanitarian aid groups.[66] The problem with this concession is that the Pentagon has awarded this function to right-wing humanitarian aid groups, thus offering U.S. and Central American militarists a source of economic assistance for pacification efforts with or without official U.S. aid.

Additionally the U.S. pacification effort has other assistance in the field—the Peace Corps. Peter Stevens, newly appointed Peace Corps mission director for Honduras, told a visiting delegation of Wisconsin and Texas legislators and religious leaders that by 1985 there were 550 Peace Corps volunteers in Honduras. That means that Honduras has more Peace Corps members than any other country in the world except Ethiopia.

A fundamental role that Peace Corps workers perform is assisting in U.S. military-directed humanitarian projects involving both the Honduran peasant population and Salvadoran refugees in camps. Peace Corps workers thus unwittingly serve the objectives of the overall pacification plan. As an example of the U. S. "humanitarian" attitude Rev. M. Ted Steege, director of the (Wisconsin) Lutheran Office for Public Policy talked with Colonel Hutton, the chief medical officer at Palmerola Air Base. Rev. Steege reported the following conversation:

> "Basically people are rather healthy here. We don't find any significant malnutrition here, for example," said Colonel Hutton.
>
> "What about the World Health Organization's estimate that 50% of all children in Honduras are malnourished?," I asked.
>
> "Well, I can't give you statistics or argue with yours; all I can tell you is what I've seen. Of course, maybe they just don't bother to bring the worst ones to us, and maybe we don't see many, because by the age of two, 40% of them are dead. In a way, that's all to the good, because when the weak die off, it strengthens the gene pool."[67]

Freeing up Military Assistance

According to Peter Stone, writing in the *Boston Globe*, two retired U.S. generals, who were former CIA operatives and commanders of Green Beret special forces in Vietnam, took advantage of the air shipment opportunity. General Singlaub and General Aderholt are coordinators of a "humanitarian assistance" program called Refugee Relief, which has shipped medical supplies and is scheduled to send food, clothing, and shovels to Salvadorans, Guatemalans, and Nicaraguan contras. The generals, who consult with the Pentagon and CIA on military policy, have criticized both for failing to supply the Salvadoran government and the contras with sufficient aid. A Refugee Relief brochure states: "This type of aid will defray costs that the U.S. government would ordinarily incur, thereby freeing a portion of its financial allocations for additional military and other assistance." Additionally, Singlaub and Aderholt sit on the following right-wing paramilitary boards: the 1,500-member Air Command Association, the National Defense Council, the World Anti-Communist League, the Christian Broadcasting Network, World Medical Relief, the Knights of Malta, and *Soldier of Fortune* magazine.

Federal Aid vs. Church Aid

The traditional agency for official U.S. aid channels is Aid to International Development (AID), which was the assistance program for Latin American development in the 1960s. Initially used to support U.S. corporate investments, AID turned to training Latin American police and paramilitary in torture and assassination tactics.

By the end of 1984 the U.S. strategy was to channel $23 million in refugee assistance money from AID through private voluntary organizations including Catholic Relief Services (CRS). Previously, right-wing humanitarian aid funding sources, such as the Heritage Foundation, were fiscal channels. Conservative humanitarian aid groups like World Vision and SEDEN are already used as ideological and fiscal funnels for pacification of refugees.

The new effort to pull liberal humanitarian assistance groups into this military plan is being met with some resistance by CRS workers:

"The U.S. government is not a neutral party here," said one troubled international relief worker. "This is a military strategy, including bombing, to displace people from areas that government cannot control and a linked strategy to then feed, care for, and pacify those refugees."[68]

In spite of strong CRS regional opposition to accepting AID money, CRS Deputy Regional Director George Ann Potter has not discounted continued dialogue with AID. AID funds $330 million a year to the Salvadoran government for a food program that the government administers; it has been accused of corruption. The other major Salvadoran refugee assistance agency is run by the Catholic archdiocese. The director of all Catholic refugee camps in El Salvador is Father Octavio Cruz. In 1983 AID was so anxious for the San Salvador diocese to accept money for the hundreds of thousands of dislocated that it was ready "to hand Cruz the bills in a brown paper bag," according to one source who spoke to a *National Catholic Reporter* journalist but remains anonymous for security reasons. In objecting to AID help, the diocese based itself on the pleas of Archbishop Oscar Romero to Jimmy Carter that the U.S.A. not send military or economic aid or apply diplomatic pressure on El Salvador. Quoted in the *NCR,* Father Cruz said, "Its [the U.S. government] humanitarian aid comes within a counterinsurgency package." Cruz's cryptic response ties U.S. policy to rural pacification, which is a tactical part of U.S./ Salvadoran military counterinsurgency strategy.[69]

By 1985 the latitude previously afforded nongovernment refugee camps was shrinking, squeezed by the Salvadoran government refugee assistance agency CONADES. All offical U.S. aid goes through CONADES, which frequently uses the military to organize food distribution in refugee camps. Church agencies that transport food into the countryside are being stopped at checkpoints, particularly near militarily sensitive areas, and refused access to desperate refugees. The objective is to force starving refugees into government relocation centers.[70]

When Mary Ann Corley, a sanctuary worker and peace secretary for the American Friends Service Committee, visited the camps with an AFSC delegation in March of 1985, she spoke with a church worker who told her that access to refugees outside San Salvador was becoming more difficult. The worker speculated that eventually there would be no access to the camps. Many are driven to shantytowns on the edge of San Salvador such as "No End Neighborhood." There eight thousand persons are living in an encampment with a National Guardsman every two hundred feet. Said Corley:

> It became clear that anyone who assisted refugees, whether in El Salvador or the U.S.A., would increasingly become the target of their government's attack. Obviously, the form and degree of repression is more stark and brutal in El Salvador. But I believe the sanctuary movement can expect more arrests because the struggle for the hearts and minds of the refugees as part of a U.S./Salvadoran pacification plan is an aspect of the war that is still in formative stages but will continue. My conversations with the Salvadoran poor, who know the government's intent but who struggle for a place to lay their bone-weary children, also convinces me that the plan will never work.

The Government and the Churches

The arrest of sanctuary workers needs to be considered within the framework of the goals and purposes of the Reagan administration with regard to the progressive church. These goals were put forth by Reagan's team in the Santa Fe document (1980):

> U.S. foreign policy must begin to counter liberation theology as it is utilized in Latin America by the "liberation theology" clergy. The role of the church in Latin America is vital to the concept of political freedom. Unfortunately, Marxist-Leninist forces have utilized the church as a political weapon against private property and productive capitalism by infiltrating the religious community with ideas that are less Christian than Communist.[71]

According to David MacMichaels, former CIA foreign policy analyst:

> This argument [of the ideological directions of Central American policy] is laid out in the so-called Santa Fe group paper, which argues that

Central America is an East-West testing ground, that there is a direct conduit from Moscow to Havana to Managua through which revolution is exported. This theory recognizes as incidental the misery and exploitation that exist within the region. It denies completely that the insurgency in El Salvador has any indigenous character. This argument has been the basis on which the government has based its policy.[72]

The Santa Fe document states that the U.S.A. must use a "security system" to meet internal and external threats posed from Central America in order to "further our national interests. . . . Combining our arsenal of weaponry with the manpower of the Americas, we can create a free hemisphere of the Americas." The document outlines a program of military training, and technological and psychological assistance, to Central American countries, which was the blueprint for U.S. intervention in the area. As early as 1980, Reagan's Central American strategy team referred to the Sandinista triumph as "terroristic" and predicted a similar triumph in El Salvador, with "Guatemala . . . the strategic prize of Central America, adjoining as it does the vast Mexican oil fields." To prevent all this, a military security system had to be developed, as well as a propaganda campaign that could sell it and quash dissent. Thus, the second proposal of the Santa Fe document (and the one relevant for groups such as the sanctuary movement, which were capturing national press attention) stated that:

U.S. policy formulation must insulate itself from propaganda appearing in the general and specialized media which is inspired by forces explicitly hostile to the U.S. . . . Coverage of Latin American political reality by the U.S. media is both inadequate and displays a substantial bias favoring proponents of radical socio-economic transformation of the less developed countries along collectivist lines.[73]

The document goes on to identify "radicial activists" as those who lack an adequate understanding of the real political and economic situation of Central American countries, and who contrive to feed a "constant stream of disinformation which abuses our friends and glorifies our enemies."

On the contrary, the danger of the sanctuary movement is its clarity of information, brought into the midst of ordinary, comfortable lives, by the actual victims of atrocities. So powerful and transformative is the testimony of refugee witnesses that the U.S. government had to stop it. The first government strategy was to close down the Texas border by arresting and intimidating the small band of refugee workers in the Rio Grande valley. Months later the government tripled the number indicted, increased charges and the number of refugees arrested, intending to seal the Arizona border and send a message to North Americans and refugees that their actions were criminal and severely punishable. Instead, the sanctuary movement interpreted these government actions as a plan to further eliminate Salvadoran witnesses to the continued bombings of civilians in the countryside under the "moderate" leadership of U.S.-supported President Napoleón Duarte. Sr. Judy Vaughan of Los Angeles saw this "crack-down" related to overall U.S. foreign policy decisions in Central America. "I only hope," she said, "this is not a precursor to intense escalation of the war our government is already directing in the region."

On February 3, 1985, just a week after the arraignments, the government continued its attack on sanctuary. INS officers arrested René Hurtado, a former member of the treasury police in El Salvador, who had been at St. Luke Presbyterian church in Wayzata, Minnesota, since December 12, 1982. The INS arrested and handcuffed him outside the grade school where he was attending English classes.

René has been of particular concern to the U.S. government because he told the media he had been trained in torture techniques by Green Berets. Subsequently, the chairman of the Joint Chiefs of Staff signed an order for the U.S. Army to investigate his allegations.

A member of the U.S. Army Criminal Investigation Division, Ismar Rubio, called René and later tried to visit him. René did not want to see him, because he feared that if his identity was discovered, his family in El Salvador would be in danger. Rev. Richard Lundy sought advice from lawyers and members of Congress, who suggested that René not talk to the army. When Lundy told Rubio that René would not talk to him, Rubio replied, "Tell the congressman that he has given very costly advice to René. When I went to El Salvador, I did not have to talk to the Salvadoran high command but only with U.S. officials, but if I have to go again, I may have to talk with the Salvadoran high command, and then we don't know who will be hurt, do we?"

The government refused bond on René, so he was kept in prison. Demonstrations were held outside the post office building that houses the INS in Minneapolis. Letters of support for René came from several members of the U.S. Senate and Congress.[74]

More Collisions Ahead

The sanctuary movement is a social phenomenon the government seeks to control through intimidation, co-option, or infiltration, in order to discredit it. One reason for the indirect approach is a failure of the administration to develop the kind of right-wing interpretation of moral issues that would win ground. The sanctuary movement has the high moral ground. Elliott Abrams has said, "The battle for Central America is a battle for the high moral ground. And it is much harder for us to win that battle when a lot of church groups are opposing us and saying we don't have it."[75]

U.S. government strategy in relation to the sanctuary movement bears some resemblance to the Banzer Plan named after Colonel Hugo Banzer, who took power in 1971 and became the president of Bolivia. The Banzer Plan is effectively used against the church by ruling groups in El Salvador and Guatemala today. The following are excerpts from the Banzer Plan:

Never attack the church as an institution and even less the bishops as a group. Rather attack the part of the church that is the most progressive.

Control certain religious orders.

The CIA has decided to intervene directly in this affair. It has promised to give us information about certain priests (personal documents, studies, friends, addresses, publications, foreign contacts).

Arrests should be made in the countryside, on deserted streets, or late at night. Once a priest has been arrested, the minister should plant subversive material in his briefcase and, if possible, in his room or home, and a weapon, preferably a high calibre pistol. Have a story prepared disgracing him before his bishop and the public.

By any means of public communication, publish loose, daring, compromising material in order to discredit priests and religious persons who represent the progressive element in the church.

Maintain a friendly relationship with some bishops, with certain members of the church. . . . In such a way we will assure that public opinion does not believe that there is a *systematic persecution of the church but only of a few dissident members* [italics added].[76]

Even though U.S. religious culture is pluralistic and shaped by a highly developed First World society, many of the Banzer Plan strategies can be used by any government wishing to suppress a liberation process while not appearing to persecute the church.

Former CIA analyst David MacMichael, commenting on the administration response to the efforts of the religious community to arouse public outcry, said:

The anger that people like you, especially religious people and alternative journalists, arouse in officialdom, you have to see to believe. They totally reject, not only what you have to say if it conflicts with the official view of reality, but they question your motives, even your right to exist.[77]

Another indirect attack is that of trying to create splits in the movement. This is accomplished by discrediting one side of a different tendency (or the leaders of one side) so that witch-hunts will appear to be deserved. Individuals or groups are labeled "bad" ("communist," "subversive," "radical," "irreligious,") as opposed to the "good" ("mainstream," "institutionally grounded," "negotiable," "naive but sincere," "well-intentioned").

An attempt to create splits was made by Elliott Abrams on a national public radio broadcast. Abrams explained why so many religious persons are involved in the sanctuary movement:

I think that many of the militants, let me put it that way, the militant activists, are really just opposing American policy in El Salvador. I think they mislead many churchgoers around the country and others in human rights groups around the country, thinking that there is some horrendous

1930s-type situation and that if they don't act thousands will die by the end of the week. I've seen some of the material that is handed out by organizers to people in churches. It's horrendously misleading stuff. It's the kind of stuff that would lead any sensible person who reads it to jump into the sanctuary movement. But what I would like to say to people involved in the movement is, Have you gone to see your congressman and senator, have you made it an issue in the reelection campaign, have you exhausted every possible way of addressing this issue in a democratic country before you take the law into your own hands? Because I think the answer is that they sure haven't. This is just a matter of casual law-breaking.[78]

In a similar vein Alan Nelson of the INS pointed out the "political" nature of the goals of sanctuary leaders:

Most of the leaders are candid in acknowledging that the thrust of their movement is to oppose U.S. foreign policy in Central America. It is important that the American public know that this political motive is one of the basic thrusts behind the sanctuary movement.[79]

Abrams and Nelson are correct in stating that the sanctuary movement has understood its faith stance in behalf of refugees as an inevitably political act. In spite of the attempts to intimidate religious persons by labeling their motivations political, not religious, the ploy has not been successful. And in a country that has reelected a president who defines religion in rightist, sentimental terms, popular grass-roots resistance to the point of arrest is significant.

Federal Grand Juries

If the government calculates that sentences are not stiff enough to deter resistance, one obvious tactic is to levy heavier sentences, a tactic in use against peace activists involved in direct actions aimed at stopping the production or use of nuclear weaponry—for example, Ploughshares I and II. But the last and most ominous government weapon that could be aimed at the sanctuary movement would be to call for a federal grand jury. FBI operatives would thus be offered a legal excuse for investigations based on their need to serve subpoenas to potential grand jury defendants. This tactic was used against domestic resistance groups during the Vietnam era. The name of the FBI program at that time was COINTELPRO. Debi Elzinga, a member of CASC (Central American Solidarity Coalition) in Milwaukee, some of whose members were the subject of FBI overtures, has said:

I believe that as U.S. intervention abroad deepens and as the growing emphasis on military spending increases, FBI and government agency surveillance of American citizens will become more and more widespread. This is the lesson to draw from the Vietnam war and the systematic and illegal use of the FBI against peace activists. The tactics of slander, infiltration, and intimidation which the FBI used during this period are amply documented and a matter of public record.

Historically, grand juries were used by our ancestors to protect the accused from government intimidation. But now they are used as a form of inquisitional intimidation against the accused and in support of government power. According to Rev. Dick Gillete:

> Between 1970 and 1973 under the Nixon administration, more than 100 Grand Juries convened in 84 cities subpoenaed over 1,000 activists. Such was the sweep of this inquisitional power that Senator Kennedy charged in 1972, "We have witnessed the birth of a new political animal—the kangaroo Grand Jury—spawned in a dark corner of the Department of Justice."[80]

When a special grand jury is called, the government has a net at its disposal. Grand Jury probes become fishing expeditions to gather in anyone tangentially connected with a movement. The government has used special grand juries to destroy a movement of resistance by intimidating members into testifying against each other. It does not matter that the activities of the sanctuary movement have always been public. The objective of the grand jury is intimidation and disruption. An aura of betrayal is created when anyone agrees to testify before a grand jury. It is an insidious attempt, under the guise of legal investigations, to recruit informants.

Aware of government intent, Milwaukee sanctuary organizers sent a letter to the sanctuary network instructing members on their legal right to refuse to say anything to the FBI and their right to refuse to testify in a special jury investigation. However, in terms of raw, unethical power, the government has the higher ground. Since COINTELPRO, the government has changed the punishment for refusing to testify. Noncollaboration is no longer a civil but can also be a *criminal* contempt charge. A person refusing to testify could go to jail on a civil contempt charge for the duration of the grand jury and then be indicted for criminal contempt, a charge that carries an indefinite sentence. The alarming truth about the use of grand juries as a repressive measure is that anyone who has the moral integrity to refuse to testify can be jailed for years without having been convicted of a crime in a court of law!

In the case of Maria Cueto and Steve Guerra, the sentence for refusing to testify before a federal grand jury investigation of Puerto Rican nationalists was three years. At the time Cueto was the executive director of the (Episcopal) National Commission on Hispanic Affairs; Steve Guerra was a board member of the Episcopal Church Publishing Company. Cueto was jailed for a year when she refused an FBI request to search church files in order to locate information on Puerto Rican fugitives who might have been members of the

Hispanic commission. Cueto refused to cooperate on the grounds that such collaboration would threaten her relationship with Hispanic grass-roots groups and that such a request jeopardized the independence of the church.[81]

Bishop John Allen's failure to support Cueto's refusal to testify, as well as his refusal to prohibit the FBI office search on First Amendment grounds, led to a split in the Episcopal church. In response to this incident the governing board of the National Council of Churches (NCC) adopted a resolution on grand jury abuse. It reads in part:

> It is the governing board's conviction that the use of the grand jury's powers as an instrument of investigation in support of law enforcement, rather than as an evaluator of evidence already gathered, is a distortion of its already quasi-judicial function. The use of the grand jury's powers to harass and pursue political dissidents is a departure from its proper constitutional function and is a great threat to public order, lawful government, and true domestic security.[82]

Congress has never given the FBI subpoena powers, yet agents today routinely threaten uncooperative persons with subpoenas from a grand jury, and often indeed serve such subpoenas on them.

In spite of the NCC denunciation of the use of grand juries for purpose of political repression, there is no guarantee that they will not be used against the sanctuary movement. If members of the sanctuary movement refuse to cooperate in such a probe, they will exemplify moral leadership, prophetic hope, and unbowed faithfulness to the God not of the law but of the people, especially the disenfranchised. The cost of this discipleship, however, would be high, personally and collectively. The cost for the state would be disastrous.

THE STATE VS. THE PEOPLE OF FAITH

Beyond the sanctuary movement, other religious groups in solidarity with the peoples of Central America have similarly "crossed the line." Witness for Peace and the Coalition of U.S. Women Against Intervention have understood prayer, when it is liberative, as efficacious action. Sr. Marjorie Tuite of the Coalition of U.S. Women Against Intervention has said, "Our prayer must, as the Central Americans say, have 'hands and feet' if our prayers truly are an act of solidarity."

These religious groups, as well as other interreligious task forces and Central American solidarity groups, are involved in a National Pledge of Resistance Campaign. The pledge, which has some seventy thousand signers, calls on Americans to act now to stop U.S. intervention, and commits its signers to civil disobedience and legal protests if significant U.S. escalation occurs in the future. The pledge emphasizes that U.S. invasion has already begun; what is feared is invasion on a wider scale.

In addition to these activist religious groups, the institutional churches have been outspoken critics of U.S. Central American policy. The Episcopal Church, the United States Catholic Conference, the Union of American Hebrew Congregations, the United Methodist Church, the American Lutheran Church, the United Church of Christ, the Presbyterian Church of the U.S.A., the American Baptist Church, the Church of the Brethren, and the Disciples of Christ have all issued statements objecting to Reagan's policies in Central America. Indications are that the administration wants to intimidate or muffle that criticism. The Arizona arrests were a blatant attempt to silence the church.

In November 1983 the Senate Subcommittee on Security and Terrorism held hearings on "Marxism and Christianity in Revolutionary Central America." The hearings marked the first time the government launched an investigation into theology. Specifically, the focus was liberation theology. Witnesses were sworn in, a highly unusual practice reminiscent of the McCarthy era. Witnesses were asked for names of church persons connected with liberation theology in the United States.[83]

In October 1982 the Reagan administration appointed Robert Reilly to the long-vacant post of liaison with U.S. Catholics. Reilly brings to the post a strong anticommunist philosophy and years of experience with the U.S. Information Agency (USIA). In late 1984 a group of one hundred fifty religious leaders—the majority from the Catholic community—was given a foreign policy briefing through Reilly's office. The speakers included Otto Reich, "public diplomacy" expert on Central America, and disarmament director Kenneth Adelman. In addition, the group was shown a twelve-minute film, condensed by the State Department from a long Venezuelan documentary, on Pope John Paul's Mass in Managua last March. The film was buttressed by a former Maryknoll sister who has repudiated the work of the Maryknoll missionaries, an ex-Sandinista intelligence officer, and John Lenczowski of the National Security Council who believes liberation theology is the major source of subversion in Latin America. According to a published interview, Reilly sees his role as playing down the conflict between the Reagan administration and the Catholic Church.

Cardinal Bernardin of Chicago was unwilling to acquiesce to pressure from one of Reagan's other liaisons. After an official government visit intended to convince the prelate that the Reagan administration was doing an adequate job in Central America and to dissuade any criticism, Bernardin balked. A short time later, he wrote his most outspoken criticism of Central America foreign policy.

By spring of 1985, after the arrests of religious workers and following the protests of the U.S. trade embargo on Nicaragua, the Reagan administration was involved less with "disagreement" with the churches and more with open wrankling. In April the State Department and the ultraconservative Institute for Religion and Democracy (IRD) cosponsored a conference on religious liberties during which the National Council of Churches was attacked for its stance on religious liberty, considered by Peter Berger "a major scandal of our time, an outrageous and disgusting phenomenon." The IRD produced a "Special Report of Religion and Democracy" (March 1985), which accused the sanctuary movement of having a political agenda, of having no real biblical/historical basis for sanctuary practice, and of misleading the American public about danger to Central American lives. Following the State Department/IRD conference was a state-level conference for law enforcement officers in Idaho cosponsored by the right-wing American Security Council, which focused on the antinuclear movement, the "criminal" sanctuary movement, and the Aryan Nation Groups.

The potential church/state combustion continues at these ominous but contained levels. The stepped-up harassment of the grass-roots sanctuary movement may be a government warning shot intended to disrupt national network efforts by scrambling coordinators to "cover" individuals under attack. This tactic is designed to ignite small fires of infiltration and costly legal cases that force national organizing efforts into legal defense skirmishes and away from building a church movement capable of the concentrated moral and political force that can stop Reagan's military intervention in Central America.

As a final indication of Reagan's intentions, there is the scenario described by lawyer Dan Sheehan of the Christic Institute before the National Sanctuary Convocation of 1985. Sheehan outlined a government plan code-named "Rex 84." In the event of a U.S. invasion of Central America, Rex 84 provides for apprehending four hundred thousand "illegal aliens" and incarcerating them in detention camps at key army defense commands throughout the nation. Further, under the secret provisions of Rex 84, there is a potential arrest list of twenty-six thousand North Americans considered national security risks. According to *The Spotlight,* a right-wing newspaper, Rex 84 "has a carefully orchestrated objective: to apply so-called C and C [capture and custody] measures against political opponents, resisters, or even outspoken critics whom the administration considers dangerous."[84]

In April 1983 the White House issued a highly classified National Security Decision Directive that lists the provisions for activating those prison camps. Money for this project, $8.2 million, comes, ironically, out of the Federal Emergency Management Agency, an agency created in 1978 under President Carter for responses to floods and hurricanes. According to Sheehan both refugees (considered terrorists) and their North American helpers are national security threats who could be primary candidates for such internment. From Sheehan's perspective, the sanctuary movement enters into national security strategy and is, therefore, a part of future U.S. military plans.

To this last harrowing possibility the two hundred sanctuary representatives responded soberly but not fearfully. What sustains sanctuary workers' ability to stand firm is their discovery of themselves as a community. Under the menacing sweep of Reagan's deadly eagle, a people's church is being born. Community is understood by this new liberation movement as the result of faith actions. It is a discovery made in the process of becoming church, when religious persons choose sides and embrace the God of history among the poor and oppressed. This spiritual conviction is the combustive moral force Reagan cannot jail, infiltrate, or kill. It smolders now but it could burst into flames.

The spirit of sanctuary resistance is summed up in the statement of Kate Skelton-Caban, a sanctuary worker from Albany, New York:

> The sanctuary movement is not a movement of a few church leaders. Nor do we seek to be a nation of great leaders. We seek to be a nation of great justice. The courage to do justice belongs to the humble, the common folk, to those who have no title, wealth, or armor to protect themselves from the cry of the people. That is why the indictments of the sixteen North Americans is really an indictment of the seventy thousand North Americans who actively participate in the sanctuary movement. We engage ourselves in this cause for no other reason than that we believe the greatness of a people must rest on the moral courage of its citizens. The administration's efforts to shackle our courage, to silence our beliefs, to imprison our principles, defames all the people of this nation.[85]

[We affirm] the action of the 194th General Assembly endorsing the provision of sanctuary to refugees as an appropriate moral response to our government's policies toward Central American refugees in the United States, even though the current administration may consider this to be illegal.

Presbyterian Church (U.S.A.)
195th General Assembly, 1983

[We express our] firm support and encouragement for those individuals and churches who, from the base of their Christian convictions or for humanitarian reasons, have risked imprisonment in order to save the lives of refugees from Central America by helping them to avoid being sent back to the countries they have fled.

196th General Assembly, 1984

4

THE CLANDESTINE SANCTUARY CHURCH IN MEXICO

Only in ourselves
The light, the dawn,
or nowhere

Otto René Castillo

The highest virtue is always against the law.

Ralph Waldo Emerson

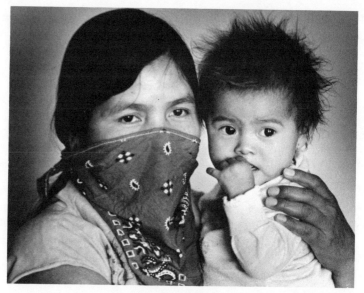

Photo by Tom Dorsey/*The Salina* (Kansas) *Journal*
A Kanjobal Guatemalan Indian Mother and Child

WITNESS: A KANJOBAL GUATEMALAN INDIAN FAMILY

(This Guatemalan family has been in sanctuary at the Manna Retreat House
of the Sisters of St. Joseph in Concordia, Kansas.)

*When Sr. Mary Malherek, a Maryknoller who had done mission work in
Guatemala, found the Kanjobal family of six, they were all living in a shack in
the Arizona desert. The baby Veronica, daughter of Guadalupe and Miguel,
had malaria. Miguel's brother Poncho had intestinal parasites. Guadalupe's
father and mother, Armando and Rosario, were reluctant to leave the border
area where they waited for the opportunity to work, picking oranges in the lush
groves outside Phoenix. It is an area where the only Anglos who appear are* las
monjas *("the sisters") and overseer owners riding pickup trucks. Their reluctance to leave was offset by two realities, equally profound. They could not
forget their responsibility to* el Pueblo *despite their fear of traveling inland.
Secondly, in spite of the fact that Mary did not speak the Kanjobal dialect, she
had lived as they lived in Huehuetenango and she had witnessed the unimagina-
ble suffering of their people. Her invitation was compelling.*

*When sundown turned the orchard leaves gold and draped the desert floor in
purple shadows, the Guatemalan Indian family prepared for a dawn departure
that would begin their journey to sanctuary at the St. Joseph Sisters' Retreat
House in Concordia, Kansas. Sr. Mary crowded shoulder to shoulder with the
family in a circle in the small room that was their home, to pray an exodus*

prayer. Armando read a scriptural passage that asked God to be faithful to el Pueblo *always. As the deep shadows rose, engulfing their open shack, a ring of candle flames held in the hands of the Guatemalan exiles illuminated the desert night. Armando and Rosario began a song that echoes in the* altiplano *("highlands"). The song, "Gracias Señor Aleluya" ("thanks to God, Alleluia") is that of a people whose past is a tapestry of suffering and death, and whose future in an alien culture is unknown.*

The family exodus had begun after a series of attacks on their village in the highlands. While Armando and Miguel were in Mexico seeking wages to feed the family, soldiers in blue and white helicopters hovered over their village back home. Suddenly the sky seemed to explode. Soldiers opened fire on the village and dropped hand grenades. Rosario and her two children, one her pregnant daughter Guadalupe, ran into the jungle for protection from the helicopters. The women made their way to Rosario's parents' small village. When they thought it was safe, the women returned to their half-destroyed village. Within three weeks the whirr of the helicopter struck terror in screaming children who ran into the open fields only to be cut down by the automatic rifle fire that rained death on the remaining women, men and children. As the survivors fled through jungle cover to the mountains, they saw the smoke rise from the burning bodies of the villagers. The soldiers had poured gasoline on a pyre of bodies in the village square and set it ablaze.

Rosario, her children, and other survivors walked for days, terrified, without food, water, or the simplest coverlet for protection at night. They ate weeds and roots to keep from starving. When helicopters continued pursuit, they gathered for prayer and for strength from each other. En route Guadalupe delivered her baby Veronica, prematurely.

When they arrived at the Mexican border, they had to cross the river at a treacherous point where a narrow footbridge spanned the river. Helicopters patrolled the river, exciting the children to near hysteria. Five fell into the muddy waters and were swept away. Guadalupe, weak from delivery, could not cross the bridge. Her mother, therefore, hid her baby granddaughter in bushes and hoisted her daughter on her back in order to cross the river. When Rosario returned for Veronica, she heard another infant crying. Rosario saved both children, having to cross the rickety bridge five times in all. Once in Mexico the helicopters continued pursuit. The military explained that they were chasing guerrillas.

Meanwhile Armando and Miguel had received no answers to their letters. Alarmed, they attempted to cross the border to Guatemala, but couldn't. In addition to concern about his wife Guadalupe and her family, Miguel wanted to reach his 15-year-old brother to persuade him to flee Guatemala. But when Miguel arrived at the border he learned that his brother had been killed by a civil patrol. The villagers who knew the story about his brother's village explained that fifteen or twenty men were blindfolded and taken from the village to be shot.

The frantic inquiries of the two men were finally answered when they met some village survivors who assured them that their wives and children had escaped and were in Mexico. They traced the known refugee routes in Mexico and were reunited with their family. Miguel, carrying the wound of his broth-er's death, rejoiced to embrace a new life with his own daughter Veronica. The six of them then began the trek to el Norte, *working at whatever jobs they could find, crossing finally into Arizona where they had heard that they might find work canning or picking.*

On April 26, at 10:30 P.M. a van carrying the entire family and Sr. Mary Malherek pulled into the Manna Retreat House driveway. Despite the late hour and the social conventions a small Kansas town expects, someone rang the chapel bells. With the St. Joseph sisters applauding, the refugees and Mary Malherek disembarked from the van singing a song: "Gracias Señor Aleluya."

CONDUCTING REFUGEES THROUGH MEXICO: A CASE HISTORY

(Renny Golden and Robin Semer are members of the Chicago Religious Task Force on Central America. In late May and early June of 1983 they collaborated with Jim Corbett in trying to help two Central American refugees make their way through Mexican checkpoints to the U.S. border. Their story, narrated by Renny Golden, follows. The names of refugees and Mexican church workers are falsified, to protect their identities.)

For the first time in four days, we sat in the town *zócalo* (square), drinking dark Mexican beer. A tropical moon flooded the colonial church belfry to a white bone of adobe. The restaurant lights dimly laced the village garden of pink bougainvillea, yellow blossoms, and milky lilies. The night was silver, peaceful as a dark lagoon of stars. It was deceptive, we knew.

The night before we'd walked behind the church, along the cobbled streets of the market. Guatemalan and Salvadoran refugee families were sleeping on the steps of the closed *mercado* ("merchant") stands. Their few possessions served as pillows on their brick beds. Sour, pungent smells of spoiled produce curled along the narrow vendors' lane. Where the refugees sprawled, exposed and raw, a hungry dog, hopping on three legs, stumped through the market, wagging its tail at each sleeping group, looking for scraps of food.

The beers were a relief. We had just completed four harrowing days of interviewing refugees and filming river-crossings along the Guatemalan/ Mexican border. The Kansas television crew we'd brought down were licking their wounds, drinking to their fortitude and, in their individual heart of hearts, writing their memoirs. It *had* been an adventure. But for Robin and me, close calls with Mexican *migra* ("immigration officers"), refugee *orejas* ("ears"—i.e., spies), and *policía* were just beginning.

We finally turned our backs on the cathedral, and crossed the square to our hotel room, to begin preparations for a 6 A.M. flight to Mexico City. Robin and I had made plans to meet privately with Jim Corbett in our room. We had accompanied the television crew to facilitate connections between Jim's rescue work, the U.S. sanctuary movement, and the clandestine sanctuary church of Mexico. We wanted the media to tell the people's story, and to show the conditions of refugee camps. We hoped such exposure would crack the baleful silence veiling the massacres of Guatemalan Indian farmers by allowing survivors to testify to President Rios Montt's genocidal intent. It was a chance for the voiceless ones to speak.

Back at the hotel, Robin switched on the ceiling fan to muffle our voices. But security reasons apart, moving air in southern Mexico is a perpetual necessity. It's hot in Chiapas; steamy and tropical. That night, I remember staring sleeplessly at the fan blades' shadowy rotation for hours, thinking about Jim's asking us to become "coyotes"—help conduct refugees past border patrols.

The plan was simple enough. We'd conduct twelve Central American refugees out of Mexico into the U.S.A. Jim and Robin and I would transport them to Mexico City. From there, we'd split into two groups; Robin and I would head for the Texas border, and Jim for Nogales. Robin and I memorized a border map and its marked crossing points. In a Mexican border town, we were to purchase a rubber raft, to cross the Rio Grande. Once across, we'd bring the refugees to a church that would house them until drivers for the underground railroad picked up the refugees bound for sanctuary churches somewhere in the U.S.A.

As I said, the plan was simple. Jim had done it many times. What we hadn't counted on was the shifting role of Mexico in relation to refugees. Robin and I would never make the Rio Grande. Neither would the young refugees we were escorting.

Even now, it's not clear what "tipped off" the Mexican immigration officers, *la migra*. Our contact and friend, Padre Rodolfo, had come up with a "perfect" plan. Instead of using a van with U.S. license plates ("very dangerous"), Rodolfo suggested that we take the pilgrimage train to the Shrine of Our Lady of Guadalupe, in Mexico City. *"No hay problema"* ("there's no problem"), Rodolfo assured us. *"La migra* never, never checks pilgrims."

Even guileless Jim was skeptical, but he said little. Polite indirectness is a cultural fixture in Mexico. Additionally, when one dialogues with a priest, the ancient bulk of a paternalistic church absorbs investigative questions like the ocean absorbs stones. I was undaunted. Rodolfo thought I was funny and he accepted my directness as part of the familiarity demanded by team membership. Also, he was beginning to acknowledge the political force of feminism.

"Rodolfo, don't be casual about this. We're sitting ducks if *la migra* begins a passenger check," I said, and I laughed a little.

Robin was having trouble translating "sitting ducks" when Rodolfo caught on. He laughed and repeated: *"No hay problema, absolutamente."*

So far, so good. The problem with clandestine Mexican church workers, however, is not what they tell you, but what they fail to tell you. Rodolfo would passionately insist upon one plan, and then, after two phone calls, change it abruptly.

Jim had taken ten of the refugees to a town two hundred kilometers ahead, skirting some of the most difficult checkpoints. It had been part of his plan before we agreed to help. He wasn't sure even then how he'd get so many out; probably by bus. With the padre's new plan, he'd meet us on the train at 1 A.M., thus joining his group with the two young men Robin and I were accompanying.

The twelve potential sanctuary candidates were all priority cases: of the thirty-five refugees in Rodolfo's church courtyard, these were the ones who most urgently needed to avoid deportation. A Salvadoran family of five had seen half its village massacred near Santa Ana. A Guatemalan mother, her children, and her brother were all that was left of another family. Three of its members had been killed by soldiers because of an uncle's involvement in a *campesino* revolt against *padrones,* which took the form of burning off the plantation owner's cotton fields twice.

A teenage Guatemalan added the most risk to the trip; it was why I feared Jim's "coyote" days were numbered. The teenager was the sole eyewitness to the murder of his North American "father," a lay missionary who worked with orphans in Guatemala City. The young man's first story was that Guatemalan soldiers had killed Frank Holdenreid, an outspoken critic of Rios Montt, in May 1983. Brought into the U.S. embassy, he suddenly changed his story. He claimed, perhaps to save his life, that robbers had attacked them, in spite of the fact that Holdenreid's money was not taken. Jim had arranged to get the boy out of hiding in Guatemala City, knowing that the military or police would pick him up if he had been a witness to the death of a North American murdered by the military.

With such a crew, Jim had begun the journey. They traveled in two cars driven by two of Padre Rodolfo's refugee team workers. The journey was vintage Mexican style, jolting Jim's Anglo sensibilities. Teresita was in charge of the operation, for which she "prepared" by deciding, spontaneously, that it was time to go. After an hour of driving, Teresita informed Jim that she had not "firmed up" a church contact in their rendezvous town. Jim Corbett is flexible and calm, but still a "gringo," not accustomed to the Latin flair for sudden changes or sudden disclosures of withheld information. Now he was worried, thinking about driving up to a church, *any* church, in the middle of the night and asking for protection for ten "illegals." Try as he might, he could not be comfortable with a snap-judgment approach to *migra*-dodging. Teresita guided the drivers around a checkpoint and back onto the highway. He remembered that she had been followed by Guatemalan agents who were suspicious that her aid to refugees included more than food and blankets. Her reputation was legendary among the exiled refugee community. Teresita worked from the coastal area, high in the farthest reaches of the Sierra Madres, where thousands of refugees worked on coffee plantations, which exploited their desperation. More even than Rodolfo, she was the trusted *"compa,"* the one who listened to the tales of torture, rocked the diseased and malnourished babies, comforted the humiliated women who had been raped by officials or coyotes or soldiers.

Teresita was continuing her work in spite of Rodolfo's insistence that she leave Mexico until Guatemalan intelligence got off her trail. Rodolfo hoped Teresita would go with Jim and take sanctuary in a church. Teresita would have none of that now; perhaps later, when there was greater danger. What was her definition of danger? The newspapers were reporting increased repression of refugees and their supporters. The Guatemalan military invaded Mexican refugee camps and murdered refugees. Her courage and skill in eluding capture somewhat reassured Jim, but her spontaneous decision-making tightened the muscles in his neck.

With darkness now engulfing the caravan, and within a half-hour of their destination, she pulled the two cars off the road, in full view of passing highway patrols, and announced that it was time for everyone to eat supper. Jim was flabbergasted, and tried politely to insist that they continue. It was no use. She paraded to what looked like a restaurant, to check it out. Jim could see from his front-seat window that there was a problem. Teresita and the two drivers fell into a stalled discussion. It was a Keystone Cops' replay: in the car, out of the car. Jim got out four times, not knowing if he should stay there or proceed to the restaurant. Finally, he walked over to the place. The proprietress was standing inside, waiting for a decision. When Jim looked into the "restaurant," he saw a drunk pawing a woman, and realized why Teresita and the drivers were stalled in their discussion. It was a whorehouse!

Meanwhile, the refugees were using the toilet facilities, leading the Madame to announce grandly that she wanted them to stay over, because "we want this to be a family place." Teresita was considering the offer. Jim, uncharacteristically direct, said he thought such a move would be dangerous. Finally, everyone ate supper and left.

They found a village priest who was willing to hide the refugees for a few days until Jim returned. The padre treated the midnight intrusion with the same ease that Teresita kept for encounters with Guatemalan agents and Mexican officials. For Jim, the evening bordered on the surreal.

The Virgin of Guadalupe Pilgrimage Train

"Walk around the train station to avoid *la migra,*" Jim advised us. "You'll find about seven passenger cars. The last four will be second class."

On the tracks the pilgrimage coaches bound for Mexico City stood placid as burros under a butter sun which was melting toward evening. In the train yard, vendors spread bowls of mangoes, papayas, and limes on dark railroad planks. *Mujeres* ("women") wove through the crowd, graceful as acrobats, juggling great baskets of fruit, tortillas, and beans. With each purchase, the woman would reach into the great tin bushel on her head and pull down food as if it were a magic rabbit. Young boys with plastic bags of cold Fresca, sprouting lemon-, strawberry-, and cola-colored straws, worked themselves into the knot of passengers, hawking. Children squirreled on and off the train, sampling their grandmothers' sacks of tortillas and beans carefully prepared for the two-day journey to the Guadalupe shrine. Most of the pilgrims were old women, who wore plaits of grey braids pulled back from leathery faces.

Once seated, I fingered the wooden cross hanging from around my neck, hoping it conveyed an impression of innocence to the staring passengers around me. Jim had insisted that my fair and freckled skin would be an asset in bringing refugees out. I felt like a hooker in a convent parlor, trying to pass for a novice. If the religious masquerade wasn't effective, I was to say I was a journalist for a religious magazine. Robin, a Jew, was busily reading a pamphlet about Our Lady of Guadalupe. She asked me why I insisted on blue ribbons for the Guadalupe medals we'd bought for our charges, Oswaldo and Ricardo.

"It's Our Lady's color," I explained, feeling knowledgeable offering such irrelevancies. It came from desperation of my sense of uselessness as a *gringa* with poor command of Spanish. Robin looks *latina,* has a half-Mexican son, and is culturally and linguistically integrated into the Mexican scene. Her usefulness was continually demonstrated; all negotiations fell to her. I could feel her exhaustion.

"Do you think we're overdoing it?" she wondered aloud, pointing to the brown scapulars I'd bought for Oswaldo, a 17-year-old Guatemalan (who looked 15) and for Ricardo, an 18-year-old Salvadoran. I felt like I was directing a 50s home movie of St. Ailbe's eighth-grade picnic: scapulars and medals everywhere.

On the train, however, where the *madres* ("mothers") wore flowered aprons over their dark dresses and fingered wooden rosary beads, religious paraphernalia did not border on fanaticism. In fact, it might have worked, our story of taking two young men to visit the seminary in Mexico City after the pilgrimage. But it didn't. When I saw those immigration officials enter the train, moments before the last whistle blew, I knew we were in trouble. (Thanks a lot, Rodolfo!—"*La migra* never checks pilgrims.") I felt my stomach knot. I stood up, hoping that my *gringa* presence could distract interest away from the refugees. I sensed our fate, but wanted to shave our losses.

If they caught us with *"el maestro,"* our religious pretensions would become a joke. *"El maestro"* (the "teacher") was Rodolfo's name for the Guatemalan law student from the University of San Carlos. *"El maestro"* was sitting with two refugee companions and us. He was also part of Rodolfo's "foolproof" plan for refugee transport to Mexico City. Rodolfo, overwhelmed with refugee arrivals in great numbers at his church, and increasingly alarmed at the tightened Mexican security and at the Guatemalan military reprisals against refugees, had taken the opportunity to load the pilgrimage train with twenty additional refugees. Their chances of survival would increase if they could plunge into the human sea in Mexico City. "The little fish can swim in the deep," Rodolfo said.

Rodolfo knew that our charges were sanctuary priorities, and insisted that we need not deal with any of the others. We felt clear about our responsibilities.

That was why I had twice mentioned to *"el maestro"* that his friends in another car were holding a seat for him. It didn't work. He liked talking to Robin, trying to impress her. The effort was wasted. I knew it when Robin translated his story. She became more guarded than she had been with the *campesinos*. It was some hint of class arrogance that put her off. He seemed determined to make her notice him.

I knew the day before, when he walked through the church gate, that he was not a *campesino*. Even covered as he was with dirt from having walked twenty-five hours crosscountry, his dark beard fringed with gray dust, he carried himself proudly, with confidence. He looked like the young Che. His intense black eyes never left you when he spoke, and he gestured with a clenched fist that betrayed his otherwise dispassionate and lolling speech.

"When did you leave Guatemala?," Robin asked him, as if he'd just walked in from a graduation dance. Whether he had calculated that he could trust us, or whether he was just being reckless, I'll never know, but he got right to the point.

"I left at 6 A.M. yesterday, because I shot and killed two Guatemalan soldiers. I am a political activist at the university, supportive of the Poor People's Army who fight for our suffering people. The soldiers had come to kill me; they fired through the door, killing my roommate instantly. I drew a pistol from under my pillow, shot at them, and fled out the window."

His voice was steady, but he sank back a little after the first rush of words. The voice was like wheat, willowy and grainy—not at all the precise expression of a law student. The only emotion he allowed was a small catch in his voice when he spoke of his slain friend. His roommate was a Nicaraguan, ex-Somocista, who'd experienced a conversion to the side of the poor during his year-long relationship with *"el maestro."* They had met when *"el maestro"* arrived, after falling out with his parents, who supported President Montt. *"El maestro's"* parents were from the bourgeoisie; his uncle had run for president of Guatemala two years earlier. He halted in his monologue and stared at his open palms. Then: "I just wish that he had died in his own country, fighting for his own land."

Of all the refugees with whom to be caught, *"el maestro"* had to be sitting with us! It may have been that we brought each other bad luck. If he had not sat with us, he'd probably be with his brother in Cuernavaca by now. It was our group, not *"el maestro,"* they were after. But they considered him part of our group. I watched as the officers walked directly past twenty seats and came to us. The younger officer motioned, held his hand toward Oswaldo. "Papers," he demanded.

Robin's hand tightened on her purse, where she held their counterfeit Guatemalan *cédulas* ("papers"), which were useless without Mexican papers as well.

The captain: "No papers, you come with us."

Robin: "But sir, we're taking these boys to the shrine, and then to the seminary. Can't you allow pilgrims to proceed, please?"

Back and forth. Train whistle. The officer held Oswaldo by the arms. We still wouldn't budge.

The captain: "You can either come now or at the next checkpoint, fifty kilometers away. You'll be arrested immediately."

Our Antideportation Tactics

We began to follow them off. I was simultaneously alarmed and relieved. Alarmed, to think Corbett would try to take ten refugees onto a train that would be checked, and relieved in my assumption that they were simply removing us from the train and would probably release us soon. Wrong. When we got to the police cruiser, they motioned the three men to get inside and told us we could go.

We knew our instructions well, and chorused: "We can't leave them!" Then Robin took over, explaining that they were religious persons, trying to save lives. "You know," she politely pointed out, "that Salvadorans and Guatemalans are endangered if they are deported. If you take them, you'll have to take us too. We can't abandon them as the world has done."

The younger officer seemed puzzled at such a direct, moral appeal, and didn't respond. The captain relented and allowed one of us to accompany them, but not the other. "The other," he ordered, "has to take a cab. It's too crowded, and this isn't a taxi service."

Robin and I were confused when they refused to allow us all in the car because we'd hoped to offer ransom money and the car was the only secure place to negotiate. But apparently they weren't open to bribes. Robin caught a cab and followed.

I sat in the back with Oswaldo and Ricardo, straining to understand what *"el maestro"* was telling the officers. Though I missed nuances, the gist of his confession was clear. He demanded political asylum, explaining that he'd killed two Guatemalan soldiers. With a flourish of "legalese," he rested his case and gestured to the back seat, including us as his *amigos*. Dear God, I thought, we're doomed. Claiming spiritual motives for our actions now will appear cynical. Worse yet, they may suspect that Oswaldo and Ricardo are guerrillas.

At the police station, we were left in a side room, off the holding tank for apprehended Salvadorans and Guatemalans. After a briefing, Robin managed to take *"el maestro"* to one side, away from center stage. She cautioned him to disassociate himself from us. He was tense and distracted, but he agreed.

I paged through a notebook until I reached the page I wanted. It had a list of important persons' names. I angled the list of names before the captain. Then speaking loudly to Robin, I began the facade. "Robin should we call the bishop first, or Padre Ramón? Or Padre Joaquín?" My purpose was to intimidate them with a list of notables, of whom only one person (usually the least influential) would actually respond. Our affiliations seemed not to impress them at all.

The stars lit the small scratch of open space where the deportees were held. It had been hours; we'd have to call the notables. We had met the bishop the day before, and though he was sympathetic, he was not Bishop Samuel Ruiz of San Cristóbal de las Casas. Ruiz had denounced Guatemalan military killers, and had courageously confronted Mexican authorities on the treatment of refugees, challenging the unofficial refugee policy of his own government. He supported his priests' clandestine protection of refugees. But the risks were clear. He had not been able to save Padre Cervantes Hippolito, a public advocate for the refugees, who was found bound, tortured, and beaten to death. It was a year since the priest had been murdered. The warning still held. Given the danger, it was no surprise when a call to the bishop brought no response. In fact, each of the priests contacted begged off. The real surprise was Rodolfo. We called, reluctant to implicate him, but confused and worried about Oswaldo and Ricardo. He said he'd contact another priest. He himself could not come.

The priest never came.

At 8:30, the captain told us we were to leave. Robin fervently repeated that we would not leave them. The captain then, through clenched teeth and in a slow voice, said: "You may not remain here. We are not going to deport these Guatemalans. So you can go now, without concern."

We didn't believe him. It showed.

He repeated himself, and, exasperated, called the younger officer over. "You talk to them. I'm losing patience, and if they don't leave, I'll have them locked up."

It was a "good cop, bad cop" routine. The younger man reassured us that the two refugees would not be deported, but that he could no longer guarantee our immunity, given the captain's mood.

We stayed. The captain and the young officer went off duty. Robin passed the *cédullas* to Ricardo and Oswaldo, under the distracted gaze of another officer. The second time we were threatened with arrest if we stayed, Ricardo tried to reassure us that they'd be all right. If deported, he and Oswaldo could make their way across the Río Suchiate again. He was worried about our safety. We appreciated his caring.

Ricardo had endeared himself not only to us, but also to the refugee team because of his quiet charm. He had also endeared himself to the Salvadoran consulate, where he'd worked for two months previously. The position had allowed him the opportunity for sneaking out false papers for Rodolfo's refugees. An already known complication about Ricardo is that his entire family was in Guatemala and that he had Guatemalan papers, but he was a Salvadoran. His village near La Libertad had been attacked, his brother and uncle were killed. He recounted the horror of young women friends whom he saw raped and beaten. The soldiers later slit their throats. In spite of his bodily grace and easy smile, Ricardo's sadness hung like an impending rain at the edge of each conversation. Rodolfo wanted him to go into sanctuary because he feared his Salvadoran identity would be exposed by newly arriving Salvadoran refugees as they passed through the consulate. Jim Corbett felt that Ricardo would be an articulate spokesman for Central Americans to the North American public, but he also felt that if Ricardo was to be deported back to Guatemala, it would not be too dangerous, because he did have good Guatemalan papers. However, we learned later that Ricardo was also in trouble with the Guatemalan authorities. When we asked why, Rodolfo refused to explain. On the one hand, he reassured us, but on the other hand, he escalated our fears for Ricardo's safety in either country.

Oswaldo gave us less worry. He was a Guatemalan who was competent in evasive travel. Twice he'd returned to Guatemala, hoping to convince his grandmother of the danger in his country and to talk her into leaving for the U.S.A.

At 10 o'clock, long after the deportation trucks made their last run, and urged by Rodolfo to leave, Robin and I left the office, committed to returning by 7:30 A.M., to begin renegotiating a release. Once outside, we called Jim to warn him not to take the train. We spoke briefly and promised to call him in the morning. We then went immediately to the church to meet with Padre Rodolfo. Why hadn't he come? Where was the other priest? What would he do to save Ricardo and Oswaldo? We kept it up.

He began a circuitous discussion about the role of the church in relation to the Mexican government. Everyone knew the official church had to dance to the official government "line" about refugees. The government often stepped on the church's toes. The church was afraid to complain and thus lose its partner, or the dance, or both. The result of this delicate official relationship was the creation, by grass-roots churches, of an intricate pattern of codes and multilevel conversations, which only they understood (sometimes I wondered if even *they* did).

Officially, Mexico was more humane in its acceptance of refugees than was the United States. Unlike the INS, it was not openly violating the U.N. Refugee Accords of 1967, which stated that persons "with a well-founded fear of persecution" should not be returned to their country. Compared with the sinister INS policy, Mexico is liberal, officially speaking. But the truth is that Mexico is unofficially cooperating with U.S. immigration officials at the U.S. border, and looks the other way when Guatemala violates refugee rights or international agreements.

Uno Mas Uno had reported that Guatemalan helicopters had firebombed a Mexican border area that had a high concentration of refugees. Padre Rodolfo had spoken openly about this when he was in the States, but after the Mexican government cover-up, he changed his story. He said they'd made a mistake, and that Guatemala had firebombed only its own side. Rodolfo would say nothing derogatory or criticize Mexico, in order to protect his refugee operation. Also, he explained that the Mexican military could be as brutal as the Guatemalan. The real fear of the base church of Mexico was about to be realized. It was perhaps why Rodolfo was acting so strangely. The bearer of these ill tidings was our last hope for Ricardo and Oswaldo: Padre Joaquín, a Michoacán Indian.

He arrived after Rodolfo's phone call, while we were rationalizing that *la migra* would respond to clerical intervention, but not to us, because we now appeared to be affiliated with the left (thanks to *"el maestro"*).

Rodolfo introduced us and Joaquín nodded. In the next forty minutes, during which time Robin poured out the story and implored him for help, he lit Player cigarettes, one after the other, drank half a beer, stared stoically at Robin's moving lips, and never indicated what, if anything, he would do. Rodolfo intervened and suggested that Joaquín sleep on it. Joaquín turned to him, but didn't nod. Then Joaquín spoke for the first time that evening, addressing Rodolfo. He said he had just learned that a decree by the Mexican government would be issued within the week. The official decree, to be worked out with Rios Montt, would expel *all* refugees back to Guatemala. There would be a bloodbath. Rodolfo dropped his head into his hands. "Three years of work," he mumbled. "For what?"

Rodolfo's task force had successfully integrated refugees with Mexican families, to keep them from the camps where they would be nothing but "cannon fodder," as he put it, because of the raids. The poorest of Mexicans had been protecting refugee families.

But because of this decree, the Mexicans were going to be in jeopardy. Of course, it meant massacres for the Guatemalans. Rodolfo said the borders were to be sealed off, by order of Rios Montt, because Montt's military pacification plan, *á la* strategic hamlets (similar to the Vietnamese-U.S. strategy), could not work with a porous border. Montt referred to the Guatemalan refugee settlements in Chiapas as guerrilla retreat bases. (One hundred fifty thousand refugees, mostly children, and Montt insisted they were *all* subversives!)

After Joaquín had left, Rodolfo walked with us out into the courtyard, which was empty at this late hour. He needed to explain himself, and to explain Joaquín. He asked no one in particular, perhaps the stars, if he should play his hand with *la migra* for only two persons, when soon he'd need to speak for hundreds. He executed a sweeping gesture to encompass the refugee huts in back of the courtyard and mumbled: "Niños, mujeres, todos, todos" ("Children, women, all of them, all of them").

Then he began to cry.

The next morning, we began what would become a two-day vigil at the immigration office. We hoped the captain's prediction that Oswaldo and Ricardo would be released would come true. But it soon became apparent, from the officers and from the secretary, that nothing would happen without approval from *el jefe* ("the boss"). We were prepared for trouble. Rodolfo had used the word brutal when describing that man.

We waited for three hours, watching the first "catch" of the day being unloaded. Still using the journalistic angle, as Jim had suggested, I was writing in my notebook descriptions of the newly-arrived deportees. Five young Salvadorans, their blue jeans wet to the thigh from wading in the Río Suchiate, led the line. After them came a Guatemalan *campesino* family. The young daughters were holding each others' hands; the last child clutched, forlornly, a small, cloth Indian doll. The officers corralled them as perfunctorily as farmers prodding cows. Some of them wore street clothes; others, like our captors, were uniformed. But all bore the same badge of power: from holster or belt, a pistol protruded like a growth, unnatural and grotesque. Each revolver was more ornate than the other. Pearl handles, gold barrels, etched with curly, black embroidery. Even civilian teenage males would mock this machismo. But the officers' aberrance paled before the pretensions of *el jefe*.

El jefe entered the room quickly—a sleek, poised animal. He strutted. Not a street strut, but a military click-click. He was light-complexioned, in contrast with most Mexicans I had seen, and coldly handsome. Behind him, background voices and movements snapped into a still frame. All was intently focused on his presence, the persons in the room hypnotized, stunned, rather than afraid of him. His voice was quiet, restrained, like velvet. Instead of raising it for the listener, he spoke more slowly, half-snarling through thick lips. The room fell into a deeper silence as we strained to hear him. For *el jefe* the issue was not his audibility, but the listener's intelligence. At the end of each paragraph, his sausage mouth would crack into a gallows smile. He would raise his eyebrows and ask *"Entiendes?"* ("Do you understand?"). He did not repeat himself.

El jefe motioned us into his office, sat, folded his hands, indicating with a finger gesture that Robin was to begin speaking. Above his head hung a diploma from the Heroic Military College for the Honor of Mexico; to its left hung a license spelling out that he was a military immigration attorney. What could be worse, I thought, as Robin repeated our plea. An immigration lawyer! My hand brushed an empty mortar shell that served as a decoration on his desk. The shell teetered, but remained upright. He stared at me as if trying to remember my past offenses, then abruptly interrupted Robin. "Tell your friend," he said, enunciating every syllable, "that she may not take notes of any kind." There followed a slice of a smile. "I don't care that she takes notes. It's not important to me that she is a writer. It makes no difference, you see. But . . . it is not correct. *Entiendes?"*

I closed my notebook, confident that we now had one trump card. I shouldn't have used it again, but I did. Hours later, when he had left and reappeared again, I continued to take notes, although I'd been forewarned of his entrance by the office workers' frenzied preparations to hold themselves still, like suspended hummingbirds. I was frustrated by his endless stonewalling, so I thought the reminder of the possible presence of the press might work.

He wheeled around, fifty feet away. He stared at me through his sunglasses. It took me five minutes to realize that the arrogant stare was intended to freeze my disobedient hands. My continued obdurance (which was really more a matter of naivety than stubborness) must have caused the Clint Eastwood posturing—legs spread, arms folded across his chest. He stood like that a full ten minutes, until I'd put away my notebook, like a naughty child. *El jefe* signaled us into his office once more. This time, the warning was clear. No mean smile. He spoke to Robin in a quietly menacing tone, but glared at me.

"If she does it again, I will accuse you." Having settled that matter, he continued by explaining that our friends were not being released yet because he had not heard back from Mexico City. He then dismissed us.

Back in our favorite chairs, I asked Robin what "accuse you" meant. She thought it meant arrest or involvement with the *judiciales,* judicial police. She added: "Enough with the notebook, please. Rodolfo says *judiciales* beat up their suspects." (As if I needed further urging.)

We felt very discouraged by the time we took some fresh fruit to Oswaldo and Ricardo. The call to Mexico City meant that they were being checked at the national immigration headquarters. Perhaps our "pressure" was encouraging more official scrutiny of them than a simple deportation might have. Were we doing more harm than good? Even Ricardo, calm and positive yesterday, looked desolate when we told him they were being checked out in the capital. He tried to cover his concern with his easy sweetness. He didn't try hard. Oswaldo seemed bewildered, but took the news more stoically.

We assured them we'd return in the morning, but that we needed to call Jim, as well as meet with Rodolfo, to figure out what to do. It was becoming clear that the police did not intend to release them, but would wait us out. At this point, a normal deportation would possibly have been better, before a thorough investigation ensued.

As Robin explained to Ricardo and Oswaldo our most recent prognosis of what *la migra* would do next, we watched *"el maestro"* give his testimony to a typist. We didn't know what they thought of our connection with him; they never questioned any of us about him. Each night when we left, Ricardo and Oswaldo would be asleep on the office floor, a small victory for them, not having to enter the holding tank, only thirty feet away. They ate beans and tortillas with the other prisoners, but continued to sit off in a corner.

That night, we spoke with Rodolfo again and, after a lengthy conversation, in which he still would not commit himself to going to the *migra* office, he told us to take the morning flight out of Chiapas. In a rare departure from his obscure but very polite exhortations, he said pointedly: "Look, you're complicating this. Please leave!"

We felt torn. Jim's position was: never abandon the refugees. Rodolfo was telling us that we were intruders in a complex web of intrigue and danger that the underground Mexican church confronted daily. What complicated our decision was our uncertainty of the young men's fate: we suspected that Rodolfo would do nothing for them. Perhaps his advice was strategic—the good of the masses over the good of two individuals; protecting the capacity of the underground church to continue to help others. Or perhaps it was fear.

We called Jim, half-wanting him to decide for us, half-wanting him to give us his blessing on whatever decision we made on our own. Jim's approach to power confrontations, especially with the local *migra,* was clear and effective. If he had implied we should stay, we would have. (Jim didn't tell you what to do, an indirection that led me to mind-reading.) He implied no such thing; he seemed stumped, too.

Jim was preparing to leave with the ten refugees by bus. Incredibly, when he had been ready to try it before, there was a bus strike in progress. It was over within twenty-four hours, and he was now ready to leave the next morning. However, because he was not clear about our plans, and whether or not we could meet him in Mexico City, he made arrangements to take the Salvadoran family of five to a place outside Mexico City. Rodolfo had advised us not to attempt to conduct a group to the Texas border as long as our names or descriptions had been forwarded to the central office. That was not a sufficient reason to hold back, Jim said. He claimed the phone we were speaking on was "bugged," and "they" knew what we were all up to. Jim then cited a strange conversation he'd had with a "hotel employee" when he tried to place the call to us, an indication of their awareness of our moves. Both in the U.S.A. and in Mexico, Jim has consistently taken the position that the INS and *la migra* know about our "illegal" activities for refugees, and that we need not function clandestinely, because they already have all the information they want. I suppose I'm writing this story as proof of my faith in Corbett's philosophy: that the more publicly we can bear the message of the *campesino* survivors, and the more publicly we can tell what we have experienced at this moment in history—this moment of the crucifixion of the Salvadoran and Guatemalan poor—the more our people will respond, and the more our people will challenge our government.

In any case, the problem of Robin's and my making a decision was more logistical than strategic. Also, I was convinced that my *gringa* looks jinxed our moves. Robin was considered a Mexican by Mexicans, because of her dark hair and eyes, and small structure (five foot one inch). But a *gringa* with green eyes, auburn hair, alabaster skin, measuring five foot seven inches, cannot pass unnoticed. In spite of Jim's ability to avoid detection, regardless of his being a blue-eyed gringo, I still think I drew unnecessary attention to myself. Perhaps Jim, with his gray hair and ascetic countenance, looks like a missionary priest.

We didn't meet Jim in Mexico City. At the time I wrote this following our trip, I didn't know if Corbett had made it, but, given his track record and his skill, I trusted he finally swung past Peck Canyon checkpoint in Arizona, entered the back roads of the Sonora Desert, rolled past the strawberry cholla cactus still in bloom, maybe jabbed his thumb skyward just once in a small victory sign, breathed the sweet air of the desert, *his* desert, and sighed. He was home. He'd pushed the odds one more time. And he'd do it again, as long as it took.

The next morning, we entered the immigration office for the last time. A truck with fifteen refugees was just pulling in. For a moment we stood there watching the ritual—the refugees prodded toward the central processing section, then sent to the holding tanks. This one immigration center apprehended sixty a day! It was a fishing contest, but rigged. More like shooting fish in a barrel. Robin and I had traveled an hour by bus to Ciudad Hidalgo, to watch the refugee traffic. A half-mile from the *migra* patrol post on the bridge, a steady wash of persons crossed the Río Suchiate, the border river between Guatemala and Mexico. So porous is the border that *la migra* pays little attention to the flow. The daily quota of detainees is met; the others escape.

We hoped our departure would "normalize" procedures for Oswaldo and Ricardo. But I don't know. I remember Oswaldo's expression when we left, his dark eyes still bewildered, jaw tightly set below the high copper cheekbones. And Ricardo, still smiling, but fearful now, waiting. Waiting, without even Padre Rodolfo, whom he loved, whom he refused to telephone, so as not to implicate him.

Robin gave them the last of our money ($50) for bribes. A mere pittance. *La migra* wants $100 a head, for openers. We kept only what pesos we needed for a cab to the airport. Before we left, Ricardo took Robin's hands in his. It was a small act, a small gesture, but something to be cherished, something that symbolized more meaning than can be held by two hands, two hearts. Then he said: "Thank you, my *compañeras.*"

MEXICAN SANCTUARY

We had not been successful as "conductors" but other goals were accomplished. We had walked ever so briefly, and with our safety intact, the sorrowful road the refugees trod. We stood on the banks of the Río Suchiate and glimpsed the other side, the earth that cradles all the broken ones, the mothers and children who could not flee. We understood that the underground railroad has been laid step by step by *campesino* tracks, walking in the name of hope, making a new history with their feet.

If the U.S. sanctuary movement is to move more intensely in the direction of a liberation community, it must move closer to the fire that burns in Central America—a fire that burns away delusions about the cost of discipleship. The refugees have borne the flames; they wear the burn wounds of phosphorous and napalm. The clandestine church of Mexico is closer to the fire, closer to the hope.

Anyone who encounters the church of Chiapas, talks with refugee assistance workers from the diocese of San Cristóbal de las Casas, hears Guatemalan refugees testify to atrocities, looks into the eyes of mothers whose children were macheted or burned to death, will never be the same again—and will never again think of the sanctuary movement as a North American invention.

The daily practice of the clandestine church of Mexico in offering sanctuary to refugees more precisely matches the historical and spiritual experience of the exiles. The visible Mexican church, like the Mexican government, is an institution that appears to be refugee-supportive. But the fact of refugee support is to be found in the base communities, the church in solidarity with the oppressed, not the institutional church in solidarity with the Mexican elite. There are bishops who challenge this institutional church, bishops like Samuel Ruiz of San Cristóbal de las Casas, standing with the Mexican poor who have encountered and embraced the "refugee problem" along the southern border. The clandestine church of Mexico is very much alive in Chiapas, near the Guatemalan border, and in the many other church communities throughout Mexico that serve as refugee sanctuaries or underground railroad stations.

The clandestine church of Mexico harbors and transports not a few hundred refugees, as in the U.S.A., but thousands. A common Mayan bond helps forge this solidarity. The poorest of Mexicans invite Guatemalan Indians to put up *champas* (plastic lean-tos) on their tiny plots of land. Their solidarity is also fortified by a common faith in the God of the lowly, the God who dwells with those who suffer. "Our people may have only two tortillas," said Padre Rodolfo, "but they share one with their Guatemalan sisters and brothers. The poor are generous here; the middle class can't afford it."

Padre Rodolfo's courtyard is entered through a side gate along the adobe walls behind the church. From the outside of the church, one would never guess that the courtyard housed thirty Salvadoran and Guatemalan refugees. As we entered the courtyard, a rooster strutted toward the shade where a Guatemalan mother tickled a bamboo pole into the branches, tumbling a laughter of lime. *Los niños* clapped. On the rim of the courtyard, refugee men had built five huts, slicing branches from palm trees, asking forgiveness, as Indians do, for their machete strokes. In that garden it seemed that everything was kind.

Later that night the padre and Teresita sat to talk with Robin and me in the courtyard. We gathered in a corner near a well floating apples of moonlight. Rodolfo and Teresita talked half in a whisper so as not to waken the refugees. In another corner a vase of lilies and gladioluses, forgotten by the sacristan, drooped, defeated by the heat. The cool hand of night could not raise their heads.

Rodolfo explained his work for refugees. Thousands had passed through his courtyard since 1981. The basic risk is that refugees and their helpers will be considered subversives and put under surveillance.

"Even in here there could be 'spies,' agents from Guatemala." Rodolfo points to the palm huts, "but we have learned to spot them." Rodolfo is a short, dark man. His black eyes dart like small birds; the hands, almost delicate, gesture passionately. He is witty, *bien lleno de vida* ("full of life"). He offers a lesson in liberation theology:

> What Vatican II lacked was the concretization of the gospels that Latin America offered—the translation of the gospels that Latin America offered—the translation of Vatican II applied to Latin American reality. At Medellín it was the advisors, the peons, who shaped a theology of liberation. Even the *comunidades de base* [base communities] are a European phenomenon. You don't need to *make* community with indigenes. They are already a collective. It's the people from the city who don't have solidarity with each other.

Hours into the night the courtyard adobe walls turned silver, the purple bougainvillea was drenched in moonlight. Rodolfo became more serious:

In my country, if you work for refugees, you may "disappear." One priest was assassinated, although they tried to make it look like robbery. But those who found the body saw he had been tortured. Padre Cervantes Hippolito worked openly for refugees near the Guatemalan border in the diocese of San Cristóbal de las Casas. He was found with both thumbs tied behind his back, his head had been beaten with a statue. It was a kind of warning from Guatemalan agents that we're not to work with "subversives."

That same week, Padre Rodolfo spent two days in the mountains. While he was away, new refugees arrived to take the place of those who had left. The afternoon of his return, he approached a newly-arrived 4-year-old Salvadoran girl, his arms wide open to embrace her.

"Niña," he said, "welcome!" She began to sob. Terrified, she ran under a table where she crouched, locking her tiny arms in a tight grip around a table leg. For twenty minutes the child wept uncontrollably, despite the efforts of the Salvadoran women to calm her. She sobbed, her tiny arms trembling around the table leg, her eyes glazed over, seeing and reliving some terrible scene.

Rodolfo had gone to his room where Robin found him weeping. She asked why the child was hysterical. He replied tersely, *"Pregunta los pintos"* ("ask the soldiers").

When the child's mother, who had been doing laundry, returned, Robin asked what had been wrong with her child.

"Oh nothing," she said, eyeing her suspiciously. "Sometimes she gets upset."

It was clear the mother did not trust us. As the conversation continued, she explained that they were from a village near Chalatenango province and that they'd left El Salvador for economic reasons. It was a prepared response to tell North Americans what Salvadorans expected they wanted to hear. Only when Teresita came and told the woman that we were *"compas"* (trusted friends) did she explain that her daughter had seen soldiers slaughter their neighbors in a village massacre. The child was still terrified of men.

Late that night when we finally attempted sleep, I felt a heaviness—the burden Teresita and Rodolfo must carry. Three years . . . the anxiety of protecting, the edginess agent surveillance creates, the unbearable responsibility of another's trust. I didn't sleep. I was less worried about Teresita with her testy jabs at danger. But Rodolfo . . . I wondered how long the heart endures. What of the shopkeeper's family that hid Anne Frank's family . . . their burden of knowing. One year after our visit Rodolfo's kind heart, like a small brave bird in a storm that never broke, fluttered out. He died of a heart attack at 47 years of age.

WOMEN REFUGEES

It was not Rodolfo, disconsolate, unable to express the details of the refugee suffering, who would teach us. It was Teresita. She was the one who knew, who daily faced the psychic human wreckage washed across the Río Suchiate, dodging the rain of fire from Huey helicopters. She stayed with mothers numb with grief over children's deaths, talked them out of silent rocking back and forth, pulled them back into life with tortilla-making and a hand loom. She worked with children full of inextinguishable rage, some who beat their head against the courtyard wall if their mothers were out of their sight for more than a few moments. She confronted the child who did not speak, withdrawn into a seemingly impenetrable silence. She coaxed listless and traumatized children to help with the baby chick project.

We asked her about the journey of the women refugees. "Those ones, the silent ones . . . no one asks about them." Then she begins. It is an old story, a history of women and war, a story that is rarely told. Almost all the women are raped in their journey out of their country. "Those unaccompanied by males are open prey on the roads," she says. The women walk out of their countries, carrying one baby and trailing other children. Even when accompanied by male companions they are raped by Guatemalan or Mexican immigration personnel. All refugees must pay *mordidas* ("bribes") at each checkpoint. When the family's life savings are depleted, the men are beaten and then deported. But with the women there is always one more price to be exacted. Gang rape by soldiers is common. She finished with this story:

> The worst I saw was a young woman I found on the banks of the river. Children had found her first. Her thumbs were tied behind her back, a paper bag was covering her head. She'd been gang raped to unconsciousness the night before. Lying beside her on the river bank was her infant. We kept her with us at the church for a few months but she never recovered really. The spirit just breaks finally.

Teresita explained that the women rarely disclosed the fact of the rape to anyone, including their husbands. It is, she said, their great shame. For some of the young women, particularly from the city, there is more critical understanding of rape as a form of male violence. In fact, young women from El Salvador begin taking birth control pills before beginning their exodus, knowing that rape is almost inevitable. But for the majority of *campesinas,* especially Guatemala Indian women, the shame they internalize silences them forever.

There are other indignities, other shames, that mothers would endure, even choose, so that their children might live. Teresita drives us to the *zona roja* ("red zone") of the prostitutes of a large border town. It is a legalized zone. Single women with children and without any *mordida* money go into prostitution to support their children. According to Teresita, forty percent of the single women end up in prostitution. In addition to housing and a wage, the women receive protection from *madrotes,* men who live off women's earnings. Girls as young as twelve find themselves forced into prostitution.

We drove the seven blocks of the *zona roja* past rows of pink and orange adobe storefronts and two grand nightclubs. A slow breeze nudged a pink paper-mache cross dangling from one of the whorehouses. A few bedraggled children bounced balls in the tiny courtyard where others were cooking on grills over open fires. The children were not sickly looking. Their mothers' bodies had paid the ransom for their strong little bodies, their good teeth. But the price is high. Eighty percent of the women in the zone are from Guatemala and El Salvador. Having escaped death in their homeland, they now live in constant fear in Mexico.

Collusion between the town *policía* and the Mexican mafia creates an impenetrable ring of control around the women's lives. There were no steel bars, no guards to block entrances, as we drove through the zone. But for the prostitute we saw walking to the market and hanging clothes in the courtyard, the ordinariness was deceptive. Women are in prison in a *zona roja.* Attempts to escape can result in "disappearances."

Teresita told of a baptism Rodolfo performed for one of the prostitutes' babies. The woman came sheepishly and nervously to the padre's church. The baby's baptism would at least give her child salvation. From the prostitute's point of view the mothers of the *zonas rojas* have given their souls for their children's lives. For Central American women steeped in patriarchal religiosity expressed in simplistic sentimentality and violent moral choice, a *zona roja* choice means entry into the life of the damned. The fatalism of peasant ideology, buttressed by the dominant religion, functions to maintain a *campesino* class who believe themselves sinful and unworthy, and also keep women locked into demeaning, servant roles. Few if any of the prostitutes have been members of base communities, whose revolutionary potential derives from a reading of the gospels that discovers within them a new message of equality that shatters classist, racist, and sexist barriers. For the women in the *zonas rojas,* there is no critical feminist theology, no class analysis of the source of their suffering. What is left for them is a modest hope—that for their children there might be life. This alone gives them reason to endure.

As we left the *zona roja* and drove out of the city, bordered by mountains and jungle foliage, a town where we were the only Anglos, a huge billboard with a beautiful woman's picture read: "the blonde that everyone wants."

Teresita then took us to the Río Suchiate where clumps of *campesinos* stripped to underwear, their arms holding aloft shoes and pants, waded waist-high across the wide river. The traffic was continual within the shadow of a bridge where a *migra* official, with a rifle on his shoulder, stared indolently across the river to the Guatemalan side. It is all very peaceful, the placid river, the waders trailing silver ripples. But the placidness is as fragile as eggshell. An uninstructed Central American mixing in with the Mexican traffic, might make one error, a give-away sign—too many possessions piled on her head. . . . *Migra* rifles would instantly swing into aim, recoil, and pelt the river.

Teresita pointed toward a weedy rim of the bank. "There is where they found one woman," she sighed. She pointed toward a clump of trees twenty yards from the edge of the river. "She'd made it across the river, escaped a massacre where they'd killed her parents and sisters. But two days later she hanged herself." The peaceful trees belied the violence that stalks the border area.

Teresita walked downriver past the shanties where Mexican children dart and shriek toward the water. "Another pregnant woman delivered her baby on the river bank, alone. She lost consciousness and went into convulsions. When they found her a few meters from here, she was still alive but the baby had died of hunger. She was 'crazy' and wouldn't give the baby up, kept trying to give milk to the dead baby."

Teresita is a tiny woman with quick energy, her dark eyes direct, mischievous. She should be at a fiesta, the dancer calling others to the music, the tinkle of laughter. Why is she here?

"We all live under the same sky. I'm 100 percent indigenous. I've lived the suffering of the people. I haven't stayed behind. Jesus said to help the sojourner because he was one. Jesus became one with the suffering of the people."

GUATEMALAN INDIANS AND THE INTRIGUES
OF THREE GOVERNMENTS

Teresita's deepest sympathy is with the Guatemalan refugee. She implored us to "take American television to the Guatemalan camps to learn firsthand from the people." The television crewmen we accompanied had balked at the six-hour trip through the mountains, and they felt they had heard enough in Rodolfo's courtyard. After the first five refugees interviewed there, they thought they'd "happened upon" special refugees with stories of atrocities. After two days of testimonies they understood that the violence was pervasive, not exceptional. But now they were growing sickened, anxious to go home, away from the knowing.

We made contact with some nuns who ran a clinic an hour away from two of the camps. Then we began a journey into the mountains. The mountains are covered with lush foliage, emerald trees, and mossy chartreuse fields where gray ribbons of mist waft in fading sunlight.

Another "placid paradox." It was on that same mountain road, within a week of that journey, that Lupe Castillo and Margo Cowan of the Tucson Manzo Council rounded a curve on their way to the camps and came upon a death scene. Two Guatemalan soldiers were executing a Guatemalan catechist kneeling, thumbs tied, by the side of the road. The soldiers were too shocked to react. Lupe slammed the accelerator pedal to the floor. Margo's only comment was that she was sure they would have "disappeared" in an auto accident if they had been caught witnessing the incident.

Another paradox that sleeps in those remote steeps is that it is the terrain of a people—the Mayans—not of armies. Wild and inaccessible paths are trod by sure-footed goats and a sparse population. If Mexico ever has another revolution, that will be the terrain where the fire starts. It is why the Mexican government wants the Guatemalan refugees, with their ties to Mexican Mayans, out. It is why the Mexican government sympathizes with the Guatemalan government and its "problem" with the Guatemalan camps full of "subversives."

It is also why the United States government wants the Guatemalan refugees out, why it has advised the UN High Commission on Refugees to repatriate Guatemalans. It mirrors the right-wing domino theory—the fire that exploded Nicaragua into revolution, burned in El Salvador, and fanned into Guatemala, smolders in Chiapas. With the virulence of pyromaniacs, the juntas of these countries throw gasoline on the flames. They have never understood the nature of the fire.

We found the sisters' clinic—a courtyard encompassing pink bougainvillea and sheltering ten refugees. The sisters warned us that all foreigners were being kept out of the camps; entry would be dangerous. We pushed on. Although we were able to interview more refugees in another camp, our car broke down and a Mexican soldier threatened arrest or interrogation if we persisted. We left the car and the camp, rambling through the mountains in a *campesino*'s flatbed truck at 2 A.M. headed for Comitán.

The Kansas television crew had been able to interview Kanjobal Indians from the same group as the family in sanctuary in Concordia, Kansas. But we were unable to gather in-depth testimony, because a Mexican soldier detained us, threatening arrest. However, from the sisters and refugee *responsables* ("camp leaders") we learned about conditions in the camps and the politics of Mexican "protection." The camp we visited, Chupadero, was attacked by a 200-member Guatemalan military squad in summer 1984 and many refugees were killed. Refugees accuse COMAR (Commission for Aid to the Refugees) of complicity in the attack.

COMAR is a Mexican government relief agency that has joined with immigration officials to establish a *cordon sanitaire* around the camps, thus attempting to segregate them from the outside world. In addition to this isolation imposed on the fifty camps administered through the Mexican High Commission on Refugees, there is a geographic severance: the jungle camps are virtually inaccessible except by air or water. These camps, thick in the jungle, are where refugees have been driven, fleeing continual helicopter bombardment. For two years CARAGUA (Committee to Assist Refugees from Guatemala), a private relief agency, has worked the jungle camps. In 1983 spring rains flooded the jungle camps bordering the Lacantum River in the Montebello Lakes region. The resultant suffering of the war victims was singularly exemplified in one heartrending incident. A helicopter from a humanitarian aid group was sent to the jungle camp on a mission—to take out the treatable dying infants. But the first attempts of the helicopter at lift off were prevented by mothers who clung to the rudders, attempting to put their children into the cab. In some cases they simply placed the stricken children on the rudders.

In one of the larger camps, Puerto Rico (almost 25,000 refugees are spread out in the Montebello Lakes region), a refugee gave testimony about camp conditions to members of Plenty International, a U.S. aid group:

> There is not enough medicine, so the sicknesses continue. The body faints; it cannot stand it, and we die. All of this because of lack of food. Here we don't have the food we ate at home. Hard-working farmers, we

had fruit, sugar cane, corn, bananas, oranges, limes. We could take a break from working, and cut up some fruit to refresh ourselves. Then corn was eaten only in small amounts. But here, only dry grains and beans.

We live in fear. The Mexican authorities gave us a card good for two months, because of the change of government, they said. We don't have any assurance from their plans. Are they going to have us here or throw us out? How could it be possible for anyone to consider sending us back, into the ferociousness of a beast waiting for meat, to eat us? It is not possible.

We are afraid. We do not want to die. If our only offense is that we work and we eat, how can that be an offense? We all have a right to eat.[86]

In November 1982 another refugee testified to an American camp visitor about refugee treatment by Mexican officials:

It is easy for two young officials from Mexico City to dominate five-thousand Indians. "You! You Mayans! What have you been doing? What? You've got to work. What thanks do you give us for what we are doing for you? If you're not satisfied, you should go back to Guatemala." He says this to village leaders, as one would scold children. He conducts his tirade from a reclining position, stretched out over some bags of corn, as the leaders stand in front, hat in hand, waiting for some announcement as to when corn will be distributed. He is the nephew of the official who runs the local office of the Mexican Refugee Commission. Nearby is a thatched hut with seven tons of sardines, milk, cooking oil, beans, and corn that the Comité Cristiano has donated to the refugees. It has been there for some time. "You have no reason to expect that food," the young official continues. "If you want the food of the priests, go ahead, take it. Go on. But the priests won't be sending any more, and if you want to take their food, then don't expect to be coming back to us."[87]

In the summer of 1984 the Mexican government began relocation of some of the border camps deeper into the interior of Mexico. For refugees who have constructed life-sustaining infrastructures, relocation is difficult; for the elderly it is often fatal. It is not clear what objective the Mexican government has in carrying out these moves. Refugee assistance workers fear that it is some revised form of a rumored plan by Guatemala, Mexico, and the United States to create a model village program in the Guatemalan *altiplano* under UN supervision. Such a program would draw refugees back into Guatemala, thus "solving" the refugee "problem" for all three countries.

A model village under any auspices is an ominous eventuality. It is, in fact, the Guatemalan village pacification plan that refugees are fleeing. Under Rios Montt and Mejia Victores, the army launched a counterinsurgency plan to "win the hearts and minds of the people," especially the recalcitrant Indians of the highlands. In 1982 Rios Montt initiated his *frijoles, fusiles, y trabajo* ("beans, bullets, and work") program as a means of creating strategic hamlets, similar to those made during the Vietnam war. Starving peasants accepted the offer of food and work. The bullets came later, after the *campesinos* were indoctrinated into civil patrols. Civil patrols have become a paramilitary arm used to kill other, "uncooperative," peasants. *Campesinos* receive their bullets one way or the other. Either they use the bullets, as ordered, on neighboring villagers suspected of "subversion" or, if they refuse, they are branded "subversive" and the bullets are used on them. The proliferation of civil patrols in the countryside is due to a single motivating force: "kill or be killed."

A young Guatemalan told us his story. "Miguel" recounted that civil patrols marched into his village and, on orders from the military, murdered the adult males and slaughtered the women except for the youngest and most attractive whom officers ordered to be placed in one hut where they raped them before their throats were slit. Miguel escaped with some other young men and some of the dazed children they found wandering outside the town. Like the villagers of Parraxtut, El Parajito, and Pichiquel, where five hundred were massacred, leaving the towns deserted, Miguel's village stood in the highlands as a ghostly witness to the slaughter of its inhabitants. But Miguel's village still had some life; the mules, dehydrated and starving, began to bray. "At night you could hear the mules from our village crying throughout the countryside. Soldiers, disturbed by this sound, felt sorry for the starving mules. So they went up and fed them and released the animals." Miguel was neither angry nor sad; more empty. He still did not understand. "The mules' suffering touched their hearts."

Amnesty International has reported similar bizarre "kindnesses" by Guatemalan soldiers. After massacring most of one village, they returned to hand out toys to the children as part of a program that would demonstrate government concern for villagers. After the distribution ceremony the soldiers took to the village clinic all the men who came to the gathering. All that the villagers later found of these men were six bloody ears.

Government responsibility for these atrocities is not hidden. The dismissed former head of the National Police Detective Corps, Jesús Valiente Téllez, as well as President Lucas Garcia's vice-presidential running mate, Francisco Villagran Kramer, have testified that the killings are carried out from orders issued at the highest government levels and then blamed on "extremist groups from the left and right." In a transcript sent to Amnesty International, Valiente Téllez said he would return to Guatemala to "denounce those assassins who subjected our country to a bloodbath and tried to make governments around the world believe the guerrillas were responsible."[88]

The Guatemalan government rural pacification plan cannot be successful if the Guatemalan/Mexican border remains open, providing refugee escape. Additionally the government considers the hundreds of thousands of refugees in Chiapas camps as subversives prepared to support a general uprising in

Guatemala. For these reasons Guatemalan officials determinedly requested that Mexico order refugees returned, with Guatemalan government "guarantees" of amnesty for all repatriated refugees.

On July 11, 1984, a press communiqué was released by the diocese of San Cristóbal de las Casas accusing the Mexican government of persecution of refugees:

> Since the beginning of the month, the Mexican army and navy have encircled five thousand refugees in the Lacandona jungle. They are not allowing any food to enter the area. The limited food that the Guatemalan refugees still have is reserved for the children and the sick.
>
> On July 4, Mexican soldiers totally destroyed the Puerto Rico refugee camp and all the food found there. They also destroyed the rafts that the refugees had, so they cannot get out to obtain food. And they took from them all their tools and equipment for farming, without which they cannot survive in the jungle.
>
> On July 5, the Mexican military tortured and assassinated three refugees in the Ixcan camp. Their bodies were left on the landing strip. . . .
>
> The Guatemalan military, for its part, is on the frontier (only a few hundred meters from the refugee encampment). These refugees are encircled by Mexican and Guatemalan troops. The Mexican troops have threatened to maintain a circle of fire around the camp.
>
> The lives of five thousand refugees are endangered. If this encirclement is not broken within twenty-four hours, the refugees will begin to die.
>
> The refugees are asking for emergency food supplies. They are asking that representatives of the UNHCR in Mexico and Geneva, as well as of other international commissions, come and witness the terror that the Mexican military has unleashed. Many of the refugees who have been relocated to Campeche were transferred under conditions of terror and repression.[89]

Bishop Samuel Ruiz of San Cristóbal de las Casas, the great defender of refugees, has said:

> The camps on the border have become an embarrassment to everyone. The refugees have become pawns in the power games being played out in Central America. The model village idea and the dispersal plan are two of several scenarios that have been discussed by Mexico, the United States, and Guatemala. One way or another the border camps will be abolished, causing further suffering to the Indians, who, as in the past, will pay the steepest penalty for the political and social convulsions that are shaking our entire region.[90]

Ruiz has put himself and his co-workers at risk because of his unfaltering defense of refugees. He has confronted the collusion of three nations in violation of the human rights of refugees. His position and his courage both target him and protect him. He is so much a part of the lives of the suffering poor and dispossessed that he could, according to Victor Perera, a Mayan expert who visited the refugee camps, "rally three hundred thousand armed peasants in a matter of hours."

Perera tells of the arrest of Mercedes Ozuna, a student who worked as a volunteer in the camps. She was blindfolded and taken to a cell next to a university professor named Gustavo Zarote who had been tortured. Ozuna was questioned about the activities of CARGUA and about Bishop Samuel Ruiz. Her interrogators demanded that she reveal Bishop Ruiz's guerrilla contacts. Under prolonged torture Professor Zarote signed a statement saying he and Bishop Ruiz (they hardly knew each other) had conspired against the state.

Ruiz's public exposé of collaboration between the Mexican, Guatemalan, and U.S. governments for repatriation of Guatemalan refugees came months after such a plan was reported in the *New York Times:* "Reports from Guatemala last December said a repatriation agreement was being made a condition for acceptance of the regional peace proposals being put forward by the Contadora group consisting of Mexico, Colombia, Panama, and Venezuela" (April 21, 1984).

The same *New York Times* article reported the announcement by a Mexican official of a possible creation in Guatemala of "protected zones to receive repatriated refugees." He said the creation of such zones under an international agency such as the United Nations or the Red Cross would be a prerequisite to any repatriation.

Such use of international agencies in pacification/containment programs is similar to the Salvadoran government's attempted use of Red Cross workers as escorts of deported refugees to containment camps. The strategy to use international humanitarian groups to carry out plans that would militarize the "refugee problem" is clearly exemplified in the role the UN High Commission on Refugees unwittingly plays on behalf of the Guatemalan junta. Reporter Bill Lasswell stated that, "On July 5, 1985, the UN High Commission on Refugees returned refugees to Guatemala. They were relocated in 'model villages' and politically re-educated."[91]

An eyewitness, Vera Weinzettl, from Vienna, Austria, gave this account of the Campeche, Mexico, relocation camps:

Beside the hall were two wooden barracks. The hall was open and I could see that inside lay *thousands* of people on the floor. . . . It was such a depressing atmosphere that it reminded me of the strategic hamlets of Guatemala! They are both like concentration camps! . . . To me it is clear now that all the talk about integrating refugees into the population of Campeche is a fairy tale as macabre as the promises of the Guatemalan government saying that refugees can return to Guatemala without receiving any punishment but instead land. The land they receive is subterranean, it is their grave. . . . The refugee story in Campeche is that many of them will die just because of impossible living conditions.[92]

In further refutation of the Mexican government promotion of the move as *sought by refugees,* afraid and unwilling to live near the border, a July 1984 report in *Caminante* by the diocese of San Cristóbal states:

It is not true, despite what is being said on television, that the refugees go willingly. They cry as they go. It is horrifying to see tears of helplessness running down the cheeks of persons who were not daunted by the dangers of crossing the forest, who have stoically endured the hard life of the refugee, who in their many moves have seen their children and their elders die [July 1984].

These accounts testify to the great tragedy the Indians have suffered at the hands of those who seek their extinction or wish them out of the way. Faced with this genocide, the bishops of southern Mexico have issued a public declaration accusing Guatemala of murderous persecution. It is ironic that four centuries after a Spanish bishop earned the title "Protector of the Indians" because of his passionate defense of persecuted Mayans, another bishop—Samuel Ruiz—would have to carry on the same mission. Ruiz's diocese is named after that bishop—Bartolomé de las Casas. Bartolomé's defense of the rights of Indians began a tradition of witness on behalf of the oppressed in Latin America. It can be seen as the first embodiment of liberation theology. It was the same faith perspective that situated Archbishop Romero on the side of the voiceless and exploited. It is a choice that entails personal cost.

Where there is genocide, a great void in the world gapes open. It is a wound that many prefer not to believe, and so they remain blind, preferring senselessness to horror. Silence confirms that blindness and nurtures ignorance. A Ruiz or Romero, by virtue of their official church position, can puncture the silence, can echo the prophetic cry of the oppressed. In the case of Ruiz, his defense of the rights of thousands of Guatemalan refugees in border camps over and against the desire of three nations to "eliminate the refugee problem" has earned him the byname, the Mexican Romero.

Many Mexican church and relief workers—students, sisters, ministers, priests, nurses, doctors, technical assistants, catechists—have entered that void. They have attended the survivors in the camps; they have listened to the murmurs of starving children whose nightly cries are heard along the Lacantum River and farther into the jungle; they have remained present to the victims of atrocity; they have promised to tell the world about the hushed-up extinction of Indians. Those who have not turned away from their plight have been called, not by the void, in some perverse fascination with evil, but by their singular ability to endure—indeed, to have hope in the face of hopelessness. In their brushes with death they have borne witness to the meaning of life.

Romero and Ruiz are the creation of the poor and suffering masses. That was Romero's insight when he said, "It is a scandal to see the poor and the outcasts as saviors of the world, just as Jesus himself. But they, not simply by their suffering, but by their resurrected hope, will save us."

The United Methodist Church mandates its congregations to do justice and to resist the policy of the Immigration and Naturalization Service by declaring their churches to be sanctuaries for refugees from El Salvador, Guatemala, and other areas of the Caribbean and Central America. It urges the U.S. to follow the United Nations definition of refugees.

United Methodist Church
Book of Resolutions of General Conference, June 1984

5

CONSCIENTIZATION

You've beaten me badly
your brutal fist in my face. . . .
Now it's my turn
turn of the offended after years of
silence.

Be quiet
Be quiet

Listen

Roque Dalton

You shall know the truth and the truth will set you free.

Jesus of Nazareth

A Guatemalan Sergeant

WITNESS: A GUATEMALAN SERGEANT

(This Guatemalan ex-serviceman and his family
have been in sanctuary in Ohio.)

*"When I was fourteen and graduated from primary school, my whole class
joined or went to the military school. We went to the* Tigres Car, Zona de
Entrenamiento de Reclutas, *"boot camp." The* "Tigres Car" *means that our
job was to destroy whatsoever unknown person.*

*"We didn't know what we would be doing when we joined. Most of us joined
because we wanted to advance personally. In my case I dreaded the thought of
working 'by the machete'—working on my family's parcel of land. It was too
hard and too much suffering and poverty. I would do anything to avoid that.*

*"There were approximately a thousand in my batallion—all about my age.
About six hundred of them had been kidnaped by soldiers. They were picked
up in markets and forced into the army. Most of them were very ignorant,
illiterate. They didn't know what was happening to them. I remember that,
about fifteen days after I got there, one of them was not eating in a civilized
manner. One of our superiors kicked him in the stomach right at the table. His
stomach split open and he died.*

*"After six months of training, we were divided up. About two hundred of us
were sent to the* Escuela para la Caída, *paratroopers' school. I was there for
about a year. We learned parachuting, self-defense, torture, and how to kill
using a bayonet. I became a first sergeant almost as soon as we got there. I was
smarter than the others and learned quickly and knew how to organize others.*

We first sergeants were taught torture by U.S. soldiers and we in turn taught the others.

"The purpose of the torture and bayonet killing was to be able to kill and not leave traces that the military had done the killing. The torture had to leave no external traces on the body. We learned how to break bones, puncture lungs (which made bodies inflate), rupture or sever blood vessels so they would bleed to death. We learned how to electrocute using two needles and an outlet. We used this especially against professors and students. Our group was ordered to kill a hundred fifty students, which we did, one by one. We would catch them, bring them in, and interrogate them. Our main question was, Why are you against the rich? We were told they were and we really had no other information to gather from them.

"All but one of the two hundred of us graduated and we were sent to different military bases. I was sent with my group of forty-five to the Zona Tacapa. Our first assignment was to kill fifteen hundred campesinos from different zones in the area. We were given a list of names and told that these campesinos were buying and selling their produce through cooperatives, that they had refused to sell to the government corporation, ENDECA, from which the government made a lot of money. The other reason was simply that the campesinos were sitting on good land that either a military officer or a millionaire or the government wanted.

"For children four and under, we cut off their heads. For those five and over, we killed them by beatings but without leaving any external signs. We did this mostly to save ammunition. For those twelve and over, we tortured and also killed by beating. Some we put in a sack with insecticide called Garmesan. They would thrash about in the sack and we would open it. They would come out half-crazy and choking. We would eventually kill them that way. The man who ordered this sort of killing was Benedicto Lucas, brother of the president, General Lucas García, who was very expert in inventing methods of killing. He was the first chief of military police and still is.

"Sometimes we would kill a whole family. One of the men in my group became an expert at killing. He was elevated out of my group and made a colonel.

"During these two years, 1976 and 1977, we killed at least thirty-five hundred. We were the Primera Peletón de la Primera Compañía Fusilera, Base Militar Tacapa. *We killed the most of any.*

"My group was then sent to Quiché *in 1978, when General Lucas García was elected president. Our orders were to kill whole families. The reason why we killed is that we were told that the Americans wanted more communists killed, and if we did that, we would get a salary increase, better food, new shoes, and new helicopters. That was proof to us that the Americans were behind what we were doing.*

"I remember one case where the owner of a coffee plantation had killed the wife of one of the campesinos *who had six children. The owner then went to the man and gave him fifty quetzales to keep his mouth shut. One of the military police went and cut off the* campesino's *ear and six of his toes. One of my*

friends then killed the military policeman who did this—and killed the peasant
also because he was suffering and dying from the wounds. He put him out of
his misery.

"*My uncle then killed the six children. My uncle has since become professor*
of karate and chief of patrols of the National Police. Around the time of the
Mejia Victores coup in early August 1983, my uncle massacred two hundred
fifty persons in Quiché simply because he wanted their land. He is a wealthy
man and a big killer.

"*When my group arrived in Cotzal Quiché, we participated with five hun-*
dred other military police in a massacre of over five hundred persons. We killed
them in about twenty-five minutes. We were to destroy all cooperatives so that
only ENDECA would have the market and the land. We used sticks or clubs or
machetes. We continued this kind of killing. We were given lists and then we
killed. We didn't do any investigation, so there was no effort to convert the
peasantry from their communism. My soldiers didn't know what communism
was; they were uneducated. They were given instructions and were doing what
they were told. They wanted to live better and buy things at the military store.
They really never saw a paycheck, because it went for their debts at the store.
The courses they were taught must have been designed in the United States
because no one in Guatemala would have been capable of developing them. I
cooperated because I did not want to go back to living by the machete on the
farm.

"*I read the Bible all the time. It was dangerous but I didn't fear. Actually, one*
of the members of my group was caught with a Bible and he was shot. It was
against the rules to have a Bible. And he didn't even have a complete one. But I
had a captain over me and I had to be careful.

"*We killed whole families because many times it was the land that the*
military wanted, so it was necessary not to leave any heirs. Frequently we went
into a village posing as guerrillas and gave a talk. From a nearby private car
soldiers would notice who would cheer for us, and then other soldiers would
come and grab the guerrilla-sympathizers and either kill them there or on the
road. Sometimes we would take them to the base and kill them. We called our
gathering with the campesinos *a 'meeting.'*

"*Some coffee plantations are owned by Americans and they didn't like all*
this killing. They felt sorry for the poor campesinos. *But they couldn't do*
anything about it. They were not allowed to pay anyone more than $2.50 per
day. I remember one American plantation, Pollo Campero *(they raised chick-*
ens); because they paid well, the secretary of the plantation was burned alive.

"*I was in Quiché in 1978 and 1979, and then asked for a reduction in rank. I*
thought that the orders I was receiving were bad, stupid. I wanted to try to
convince the campesinos *to change. I didn't think what we were ordered to do*
made good sense. The reasons they gave I no longer accepted. I was now
smarter than those giving me the orders. I was married at this time, and my wife
really didn't believe that I was doing what I told her I was doing.

In late 1979 I was moved to another branch, the Policía Judicial, *which is*
part of the military police as well. I was still in Quiché. On my very first shift, I

was to receive seventeen heads from different patrols that had been sent out to kill campesinos and bring in their heads. They were put in bags and left in different parts of the city with notes on them using slogans from the different guerrilla groups. That was to give the impression that guerrillas did the killing. I remember that night because the patrols came in and one man, trying to impress my chief with his machismo, threw a head on the chief's desk—blood all over the place. The chief dug one eye out with his knife and smelled it; then he stuck it back in and threw the head across the room.

"My job, for a good part of the time, was to make bombs. It took about eleven hours to make one. Others then took them and put them in bridges, buses, certain places where peasants gathered. This had been carefully researched so that we knew when buses would pass by certain areas, etc. I was in charge of the men who took these out. American military were in and out, but they didn't teach us bomb-making.

"My uncle then offered me a chance for advancement if I would lead a massacre of the village where his wife's family lived and the one where my wife's family lived. I remember getting the list and seeing my mother-in-law's name on it. I decided I couldn't do it. I warned the family of my uncle's wife, but they didn't believe me. In fact they told him and he told my mother that he would find me, no matter what, and kill me. I told her not to worry. Later my uncle carried out his wish and massacred the whole family of his wife. I led the family of my wife and the other villagers into Mexico. My uncle bragged of having killed thirty-five hundred persons all by himself.

"Five months before this my daughter was killed. She was eighteen months old. She was playing on the curb in front of our house. A car pulled up and men got out. They machine-gunned some men on the sidewalk, killing them. A stray bullet killed my daughter.

"I remember one American who trained us in military school. One in my group would make fun of him for his broken Spanish. One day the American soldier got mad, took out his gun, and shot the soldier point-blank. He made a hole in his chest and a massive hole in his back. I remember his name, John Long.

"I knew Rios Montt, Lucas García, Arana Osorio. I ate with them, talked with them.

"I now hear the cries of children when I am walking alone. I remember those I just blew to pieces."

FROM TRUTH TO FREEDOM

After months of soul-searching and discussion, the Mission-Advocacy Committee of the Church of the Covenant, Boston, brought a proposal to a congregational meeting in late January 1984. The proposal was not to become a sanctuary church but rather to join the more than fifteen hundred churches that endorsed the concept of sanctuary in principle and provided supportive services to congregations that were sanctuary sites.

The proposal met substantial opposition and aroused a litany of fears:

potential criminal penalties, possible loss of tax-exempt status, harm to the building, reprisals against those who attended the church, cancellation of insurance, and jeopardy to the search for a new co-pastor. An additional negative argument was raised on the basis of an unpleasant experience resettling an Indonesian family twenty years earlier.

The intensity of fear was expressed in a letter from one parishioner to the pastor:

I want to go on record as being very much opposed to the Church of the Covenant getting involved in the sanctuary movement. If certain individuals wish to do so privately, that is up to them. But to commit the Church of the Covenant, I say a definite NO.

I feel very strongly about involving this church in illegal actions. We're in no position to be adding to our problems. With a budget which takes [all] our assets to balance, we should not siphon off any money which should go to keeping our operating expenses covered. Our very future may be at stake.

At the January meeting the motion was tabled. Many younger members, who had started attending the church in the preceding five years, wanted to have a vote called. Older, longtime members wanted it postponed.

Two months later, when the next meeting was held, half the congregation was angry it had taken so long and the other half adamant in opposition. As the session began, a woman expressed the opinion that the meeting was out of order because this was a "spiritual" body and sanctuary was a "political" issue. She quoted the Presbyterian *Book of Order* to substantiate her position. The pastor, Rev. Alice Hageman, ruled the topic in order. She referred to resolutions by the 1982 and 1983 General Assembly of the Presbyterian Church that encouraged local congregations to consider the act of sanctuary.

Martin, an usher in the church for forty years, began, his voice trembling, "We are all Christians, how can we be considering breaking the law?"

The discussion went on for an hour and the tone began to shift "from argumentation to testimony, from confrontation to witness," as Alice Hageman described it later. Members began speaking from their own life experiences and their experiences with sanctuary.

Newell, a composer, spoke of his decision to refuse conscientious objector status during the Vietnam war. When induction was ordered, he refused to appear. For five years he awaited arrest.

Doug, an Afro-American personnel officer, reminded everyone of the underground railroad of abolition times and the role of Boston churches in the shelter of runaway slaves. He felt that it was part of his own history, and had helped preserve the life of his people just as the new underground railroad was preserving the life of Central American peoples.

Larry, whose unwed daughter had recently given birth to a biracial child, acknowledged the anxiety of the congregation but testified that he had learned from his children that God does not always choose the moment we consider the most convenient to lay claim on our allegiance. The gospel is always disruptive.

Rosie, a poet, reminded the congregation that Martin Niemöller, the Protestant pastor interned in Nazi concentration camps for seven years, had died just the previous week. She quoted from him:

> In Germany they first came for the communists; I did not speak, because I was not a communist. Then they came for the Jews; I did not speak, because I was not a Jew. Then they came to fetch the workers, members of trade unions; I did not speak, because I was not a trade unionist. Afterward, they came for the Catholics; I did not say anything, because I was Protestant. Eventually, they came for me, and there was no one left to speak.

Ed, who conducted workshops on conflict-resolution, emphasized that what was happening was the voicing of disagreement on honestly arrived at positions. Ed looked directly at Martin, a staunch opponent of sanctuary, and said, "Martin, I love you a lot but I won't vote with you on this one."

After two hours of discussion, Alice asked for the final statements for and against. Martin, the choir director, said succinctly, "Compared to what persons in Central America now experience, we are being asked to risk very little."

There was a long silence; no one offered a statement of opposition. Finally, Newell, the former draft resister, said, "I want to speak on behalf of those who are not speaking. We are going to vote, one vote per person. I think it's clear how that vote will turn out. However, if we were to vote on the basis of number of years spent in participating in, caring about, and maintaining this congregation, that outcome might well be different. I want to acknowledge and express my appreciation for the efforts over the years of those who have made it possible for us to be here today making this decision."

The vote: forty-seven in favor, seven against, one abstention.

When the vote results were announced, everyone hugged each other. Those opposed did not change their minds, but neither did they go away. As Rev. Hageman said later:

> This was one of the most extraordinary spiritual experiences our congregation ever had. There was an extraordinary sense of power and energy in that gathering. People didn't argue abstract principles or recite brutal statistics. They simply testified from their own life experiences. The experience enhanced the commitment of those who participated in the process to each other as a congregation.[93]

A devastating truth had walked across the borders of the United States and into sanctuaries from coast to coast. It was a truth that, when accepted, shattered many of the myths and assumptions of its North American listeners and named the United States an accomplice in the violence of Central America. That truth, however, did not set everyone free. It is a long and difficult journey from truth to freedom. The way is fraught with doubts, denial, even betrayal. Many congregations chose to ignore it or limit it. Others did not want to admit or act on the full implications of stories like that of the Guatemalan sergeant. They preferred to think of sanctuary as Christian humanitarian aid that gave shelter and food to sojourners. Criticizing the U.S. government was too "political."

Raul and Alejandro, refugees in sanctuary in Detroit and New York, wrote their observations of the Anglo church and its difficulty to fully embrace the truth:

> Sanctuary as a Christian movement has to be a movement that tells the truth. Or are you afraid of the truth? Do you fear confronting the truth? You are working for charity only if you deny that a crime is being committed and that the guiltiest party is your government. To fall into the idea of sanctuary as merely an act of charity is to fail to make the historical response. The repression will increase as much in Guatemala as in El Salvador. The number of refugees will continue growing in large proportion and no one will be able to help them. All of us want to live in our countries without the danger of death. Christian love must not only be charitable, but must understand the roots of the problem.
>
> To continue sanctuary only at the level of charity is to be deceitful. It is to deceive and be at the service of the powerful. It is treason to the gospel.
>
> Our position is to speak as Christians, to point to the causes, to point to those who are guilty. To say the opposite is to be accomplices in the system of lies and repression.

But there were those who accompanied the refugees from Central America on the journey of truth. For them it was a conversion experience, a profound renewal of faith. It was also a process of conscientization, a process of deepening awareness of and closer identification with the peoples of Central America. This process began with the corporate struggle of communities of faith wrestling with the decision to declare sanctuary.

DECIDING FOR SANCTUARY

Massillon, Ohio, is a manufacturing town of about thirty thousand, known more for its great high-school football teams than for any social action. The congressional district has sent a Republican to the House every election since 1950.

The Central Presbyterian Church is a middle-class congregation that includes lawyers, retired military personnel, a federal judge, one person who was a legislative aid at the Pentagon, and another who did classified engineering work for the CIA.

The church went through a process of study of and reflection on sanctuary that lasted a year before voting. One of the moving forces behind this process was William Clarke, president of Hilscher-Clarke Company, an electrical contracting firm in Canton, Ohio. He is a member of Christ Presbyterian church in Canton who began a personal campaign to interest others in the plight of Central American refugees. He started with Congress, visiting Washington, D.C., but quickly found that refugees were not an issue there. So he went to the Ohio grass roots with his message.

One early summer night he went to speak at a Mennonite church in Tedrow, a small town in northwestern Ohio. About sixty persons gathered in the church and one man apologized for the small turnout, saying there would have been a lot more but the rest were busy in the fields. Mr. Clarke, a member of the Jaycees, starts all his talks the same way. "I'm a Republican, very conservative. I voted for Ronald Reagan. So I'm the last person in the world to be advocating civil disobedience." But by the end of the talk he is encouraging his hearers to counter the government's interpretation of the law. He admits he is a "conspirator" on behalf of Central American refugees. He says:

> We look down on those churches in Germany that allowed Jews to be rounded up after they knew what would happen to them. Now you know. If you believe that people are being tortured and murdered in El Salvador, and that we are supplying the guns and the bullets, then you know that we are standing behind the death squad member who has the gun and the knife.

Rev. Bob Hoover, pastor of the congregation, tried to sum up what was at stake:

> Breaking the law is something that is not in the character of these people to do, but they're doing it for deep humanitarian reasons. And when you have people out in the grass roots of Ohio saying that something is the matter, the politicians might be wise to listen.[94]

Elliott Abrams, the assistant secretary of state for human rights and humanitarian affairs, calls the sanctuary movement a "willful and casual violation of American law."[95] No one in the sanctuary movement would deny the willful part, but as for casual, there would be strong disagreement. The decision-making process in most congregations is long and thorough. The Central Presbyterian church took a year; most deliberate for months. Quaker meetings (churches) have gone through a thoughtful process of consensus. Quakers do not make decisions by majority vote. Instead they strive for a "will of the body." Consensus aims at unity. This does not mean that everyone has to agree equally. But if even one person disagrees strongly, it can block consensus and the body will not act until that person "steps aside" and agrees not to block consensus. Thus, if even one person in a Quaker meeting states that in good conscience he or she cannot support sanctuary, the meeting would not proceed with a declaration. This process always takes seriously the will of the minority and is anything but casual.

, Although every congregation creates its own process for considering sanctuary, a similar pattern has emerged. Usually a congregation has a committee look into the issues, define the problems, and then make a concrete recommendation to the church governing board. In deliberating about sanctuary an educational series is introduced giving background information on the history of Central America, the history of the U.S. intervention in the region, the scope and degree of poverty and oppression in the area, and the response of the popular churches of El Salvador and Guatemala. Many times Central American refugees or persons from other sanctuary sites make presentations on their experiences.

Invariably, the two greatest concerns are (1) the ability to meet the physical needs of the refugees, and (2) confronting the law. The first concern is usually solved by the generosity of the larger community. Some sanctuary churches spent no money at all to get the project started: donations of food, clothing, and money from sympathetic supporters were sufficient. Spanish speakers seemed to come out of the woodwork when it became known that a church was considering sanctuary. Doctors, dentists, lawyers all volunteered their help. Retired teachers and high-school students became English tutors. Space, too, was found in unlikely places. One church converted an old locker room; volunteer plumbers coaxed the showers back into operation. High-school seniors had wanted to use the space as a much-needed meeting room but they not only decided the refugees' needs were greater, they helped to repaint and decorate the rooms.

The second concern was more daunting. Confronting the government's interpretation of a law required a clarity and determination that went beyond housing and feeding a family. Fears were usually raised and the question of obedience discussed. "To whom are we obedient when there is an apparent conflict, God or Caesar?" "Where does our ultimate allegiance lie?"

Resistance

National law is neither as monolithic nor as sacred as those in power want the populace to believe. Law is dynamic, always changing, always being interpreted and reinterpreted, sometimes in contradictory ways. The law is often much more tenuous than the sturdy columns on halls of justice intimate.

Laws are written in the abstract but must be applied in concrete cases. Judges seek the "intent of Congress" but do not always succeed. For example, the Sherman Anti-Trust Laws passed by Congress to limit the power of the largest corporations were more often used against labor unions.

Right now Congress is passing new laws and the Supreme Court is striking down old laws. Every day lawyers go to court loaded with briefs to argue one interpretation of a law that is favorable to their client against an unfavorable interpretation.

Then there is the matter of selective enforcement and inconsistent prosecution. For example, the state enforces and prosecutes street crime more vigorously than white collar crime. International law and constitutional rights can mitigate or temper national law. International law, especially as used in the Nuremberg trials of Nazi war criminals, stipulates that obedience to superiors cannot justify crimes against humanity.

Ideally laws reflect justice, but history has witnessed some monumental exceptions. Slavery was once legal, and those who helped slaves escape were lawbreakers. The law kept women from voting and once Susan B. Anthony was arrested for casting a ballot. It was once legal to force blacks to the back of a bus. Authorities arrested blacks for drinking from "white-only" drinking fountains and the law upheld their convictions. Restaurant workers could legally refuse to serve blacks. All these actions, once legal, are now illegal, and most persons find these once legal activities morally disgusting. Congress and presidents did not initiate the changes of any of those laws—the people did. Protest and resistance changed those laws. Many times it began with the courage and conscience of one person, like Rosa Parks, who refused to move to the back of a bus, but eventually change depended on the thousands who joined together in acts of resistance to unjust laws.

Laws *should* reflect justice for all, regardless of religion, class, race, national origin, sex, or sexual preference, but all too often laws reflect the interests of those in power or those who paid to put them in power. Those in power want to elevate national law to ultimate or sacred status, but that is simply idolatry. Laws are not sacred, justice is. We worship God, not Caesar or the president.

Conscientious disobedience to unjust law or unjust interpretation of the law is not only biblical ("you cannot serve God and mammon"), it is as American as apple pie. The Boston Tea Party was an act of resistance. Henry David Thoreau wrote about the right of civil disobedience and its *duty*. Strikes, boycotts, sit-ins, tax resistance, massive demonstrations, aiding of fugitive slaves are all part of the history of the United States and were all at one time considered illegal activities by the U.S. government.

In declaring sanctuary, religious congregations, through deliberation and prayer, arrived at the point where they refused to bow down to the golden calf of secular authority. They opted for the law of God and divine justice.

Something Happens . . .

The moral decision of sanctuary has brought together faith and practice in a striking way that, at times, has yielded poignant moments of human compassion and justice.

About a week after a refugee family arrived at the Rutgers University Chapel in Piscataway, New Jersey, Henry Adkins, the pastor, received a phone call from the Rahway State Prison. He was told that someone would be there the next day. Taken aback, Henry responded, "Be here for what?" The voice on the other end told him they would be making a delivery. The next day a truck pulled up and unloaded an incredible array of toys including dolls and tricycles that looked brand new. In one section of the prison, lifers repair defective toys. One of them had seen the family arrive on television and organized other prisoners to donate the toys to them. Henry called the prison the following day and discovered that the man who had organized the donation was the first man in New Jersey history to be sentenced to life imprisonment for rape. He had such a long record that when Henry asked for it the administrator said it would be easier to read the New York City phone book.

In 1983, on a bright fall day at the Community Friends meeting in Cincinnati, Ohio, members gathered to hear the news about Sam Matthews. Sam was one of the first nonregistrants for the draft to be convicted and sentenced to jail. The community gathered in silence as Sam's father, Dr. Norman Matthews, sat beside Miguel, Jasmine, and Gabriela, three Salvadorans taken into sanctuary the spring before. Sam had grown up in the meeting (church) and was living out the deepest principles of the Quaker tradition. After Norman told how Sam was doing in jail, Miguel stood to speak:

> You should be proud that there is a young man like Sam in this community. The people of Central America are counting on people like Sam who will refuse to fight, who will refuse to kill us. It is people like Sam who give us hope.

Something happens to people in their encounter with sanctuary. On one level it is mysterious and inexplicable, a movement of the spirit. On another level, it is a shift of consciousness.

The process of sanctuary—the learning process and the wrestling with faith that occur before a declaration of sanctuary, and the conscientization that comes after a refugee family arrives—is a conversion experience. It is a change of understanding and a change of heart that leads to deeper commitment.

Conscientization is a process of critical reflection at deeper and deeper levels about how human beings live and die in this world. It invariably destroys old assumptions and breaks down mythologies that no longer explain reality because of new information. We all need to "make sense" of our world. We all construct a "worldview" or "ideology" that explains reality to us in a coherent fashion. Encounter with refugees, their story, and a more intensive study of the history and present reality of Central America have shaken the dominant worldview of many in the religious community.

At its best, what has been learned in sanctuary communities of faith is a vision of the reality of Central America from the perspective of the poor who live there. It means looking down dirt streets lined with shacks patched together with cardboard and metal signs. It means beginning to hear the Bible interpreted by those with an empty stomach, by those who have no guarantees that they will be alive tomorrow. The words of the Bible and the understanding of what is happening changes radically when viewed from this perspective. In the words of Latin American theologians it is seeing history "from underneath."

Latin American theologians talk of the irruption of the poor into history. That irruption has meant that the poor are forging their own history, becoming *subjects* of their own destiny, rather than passive *objects* used by others. They are also interpreting the world, articulating, after centuries of silence, a theology from "the underside of history."

That may be the only vantage point from which the original meaning of the biblical testimony can be understood. The story of faith was told from the perspective of slaves (in Egypt), the poor and most vulnerable (Amos, Jesus), captives (Jeremiah), a small, seemingly insignificant country (Israel), workers (fishermen), the marginalized (prostitutes, women), foreigners (Samaritans). In Matthew 25 Jesus says bluntly that whatever we do for the least of his brothers and sisters, we do for him. Therefore, the least, the lowliest, become the point of revelation of God in history. We can know God better through standing with and seeing the world through the eyes of the poor, the disinherited, the "insignificant."

Sanctuary at its best, then, began to view history and understand theology from the viewpoint of the most vulnerable. A reincarnation was happening. Just as God became flesh in Jesus, a common laborer, one of the most vulnerable, who was finally tortured and killed in his early thirties, so now were other "Christs" incarnated in the world. They too were being tortured and killed. They too were undergoing a premature death—not one person, but tens of thousands. These vulnerable "Christs" walked into one of the most insulated, insured cultures of the world where every possible contingency is planned for and covered with collateral safely tucked away.

The poor came into the midst of this culture without surplus, without even their daily bread. They came with nothing to fall back on save their hope and their faith in the struggle for freedom and dignity. They came as the least of society. And the churches would be judged by their response to them.

As parishioners met "Christs" in the form of poor refugees fleeing the violence of their countries (Jesus himself began life as a refugee fleeing the slaughter of the innocents of another imperial dictator), a twofold awakening happened. North Americans began seeing the world from the point of view of the poor. They saw history through the eyes of the dominated, the oppressed. They slowly gave up their First World perspective for a Third World perspective. Simultaneously, the Bible was read from the same perspective.

Those who opened themselves to sanctuary, opened themselves to a new historical, political, and theological understanding of the world as voiced by the lowliest in our midst. In general, this meant a shift from seeing the violence of Central America as just an aberration of a few "sick" torturers or ruthless dictators to an understanding of the systemic violence, the daily denial of life to the poor. There was also a shift away from calls for particularized reform to seeing the legitimate rights of revolution. And finally, the search for the roots of the violence led North Americans to see the complicity of the United States in the impoverishment and deprivation of the poor, a complicity that did not start with this administration but went back to the early nineteenth century.

THE PROCESS OF CONSCIENTIZATION

Violations of Human Rights

Although civilian men of all ages have been shot in large numbers by the Guatemalan army, women and children are particular victims; women

are routinely raped before being killed; children are smashed against
walls, choked, and burned alive, or murdered by machete or bayonet
[*Americas Watch,* Report on Guatemala, *May 1983*].

Atrocities committed against the peoples of Central America have shaken
the moral sense of many North Americans. The stories and facts of torture
have saddened, angered, and moved the religious community to action. It was
knowledge of human rights violations that first alerted many of them to the
situation in Central America.

From the North American perspective, "human rights" usually means
political rights or individual rights. Phillip Berryman has pointed out:

[Political rights] emerged from the British tradition and the French and
American revolutions, and were associated with the rise of capitalism as
the dominant mode of production. These rights are those of the individual and are aimed at protecting the individual autonomy and freedom to
pursue his or her chosen life goals.[96]

These individual rights, however, assume a certain level of class privilege and
freedom. They do not take into consideration economic rights such as the right
to work, the right to a stable means of livelihood and a fair wage. These are
more basic because their guarantee or denial can mean the difference between
life and death.

When North Americans speak of human rights they usually mean political
rights. This view of human rights, although culturally conditioned, has been
"universalized" by the United Nations. In many non-Western societies the
group and its welfare has a prior claim to the goods of society—prior to that of
individuals. In Western society the right of the individual to hold property
takes precedence over the right of all in society to have access to good health
care. In Central America, the denial of political rights is only the tip of the
iceberg. What difference does it make to *campesinos* that there may or may not
be freedom to pursue one's own life goals when they are without land, unemployment is at 60 percent, and their children are starving?

To begin defining human rights from the perspective of the poor, to view
society from their position, "from below," means seeing human rights in a
broader purview. Central Americans are now talking about the "rights of the
poor," the prior claim of the poor to the goods of society. They come first.

This reorientation also widens the definition of terrorism. Terrorism is more
than clandestine jails, electric-shock torture, and beatings. It is also a mother
watching her baby die in her arms from malnutrition, a young girl dying from
dysentery, a boy from malaria—deaths that are avoidable with a minimum of
fresh water, food, and basic medicines. All are avoidable, in short, with the
guarantee of a certain basic human right—the right to life.

Theologian Jon Sobrino, who has worked for many years in El Salvador,
tells what this understanding has meant to the Central American church:

Its defense of human rights has not been a defense of the liberal version of human rights—human rights as "civil" rights. It has been a defense of human rights in the most basic sense of the right to live and the right to the basic necessities of life. That is why the church has renamed them the "rights of the poor." Insofar as it could, it has demanded and advocated necessary structural changes on the social, economic, and political levels. It has fought for the organization of labor and of the common masses as a way of breaking oppressive centers of power and achieving a more humane and humanizing kind of power.[97]

Much energy in churches opposed to U.S. policy in Central America went into tying military aid to the elimination of human rights abuses. From the North American perspective, this was one way to contain the violence, and shock the U.S. citizenry into action. However, the certification process initiated by the Reagan administration "proved" that violence was decreasing. The proof was the decrease in the average monthly number of slit-throat cadavers found in the streets. This produced a new "body-count" mentality reminiscent of the Vietnam war. But it worked because the definition of human rights was the narrow North American one. From the point of view of the *campesinos*, even if all the death squads ended, the daily fact of violence and atrocity would remain.

North Americans usually understand torture and death squad violence to be the acts of an "extremist fringe" or "fanatics of the right and left." Many eloquent speakers denounce this "senseless" violence. But the testimony of refugees such as the Guatemalan sergeant at the beginning of this chapter and René Hurtado, former member of the Salvadoran treasury police, who has been in sanctuary in Minneapolis, paint a different picture. According to René, U.S. personnel conducted a course in intelligence for treasury police officers. It included training in "methods of physical and psychological torture":

First you torture him psychologically. . . .
When you are interrogating someone for the first time, you try to come across as a sensitive, decent person—not as a killer. . . .
But after using these methods for a few days or a week or two, you start getting tough. . . .
There are a lot of different methods of torturing a prisoner: cutting off pieces of his skin, burning him with cigarettes. They teach you how to hit a person in the stomach so he suffers a lot of pain but there are no signs on the outside.
There's a special torture room in the treasury police building. You learn how to give electric shocks. There are some very sophisticated methods of this kind of torture. There's a more sophisticated [machine] that looks like a radio, like a transformer; it's about fifteen centimeters across and it says General Electric on it.[98]

The torture of one human being by another is horrible, repulsive, almost impossible to believe—but it is not mindless. It is premeditated, strategic, scientifically researched for maximum results and taught, as René has testified, by U.S. military personnel.

It is the logical extension of other repressive measures to keep the majority from gaining their basic right to life. Torture and terror help to break strikes, intimidate agrarian unions trying to gain access to land, destroy indigenous leadership, and keep silent those who have the most to say. Maintaining control of many by the few is at the heart of the system in El Salvador and Guatemala. "When it is not possible to reconcile liberty and order," said Salvadoran Defense Minister Vides Casanova in a 1983 ceremony honoring the Chilean military attaché, "one should sacrifice liberty to order."[99]

And that system was set up by the United States in the early 1960s. Reporter Allen Nairn, in an exclusive report in *The Progressive,* writes:

Early in the 1960s under the Kennedy administration, agents of the U.S. government set up two official secret organizations that killed thousands of peasants and suspected leftists over the next fifteen years. These organizations, guided by American operatives, developed into the paramilitary apparatus that came to be known as the Salvadoran Death Squads.

Today, even as the Reagan administration publicly condemns the Death Squads, the CIA—in violation of U.S. law—continues to provide training support and intelligence to security forces directly involved in Death Squad activity.

[There is] a pattern of sustained U.S. participation in building and managing the Salvadoran security apparatus that relies on Death Squad assassinations as its principle means of enforcement.[100]

The specific involvement of the United States has included a wide range of activities. Providing surveillance equipment; providing information on individuals who were later assassinated by death squads; keeping the founder of ORDEN ("order") and other key officials on the payroll of the CIA; training Salvadoran intelligence operatives in methods of physical and psychological torture.

One senior officer of the Salvadoran right complained:

We learned our way of operating from you [the United States]. I studied in the Canal Zone. I studied in North Carolina. You taught me how to kill communists and you taught me very well. And now you come along and persecute my *compañeros* for doing their jobs, for doing what you trained them to do.[101]

The violence is neither mindless nor random. U.S. surveillance and intelligence maintains a systematic persecution of those who assist urban and rural workers to live, to gain their rights. The abuse of human rights is not an accident. It is state policy—a policy backed by the United States government, at the highest levels. Understanding the deeper connections between U.S.

policy and the violence in Central America prompted sanctuary congregation members to question other assumptions about Central America and the roots of the violence there.

Military Dictatorships

Most North Americans think of Latin American changes of government as a series of coups in which one military ruler overthrows another. According to the prevailing mythology, the area is unstable and Latin Americans do not know how to govern themselves. Following that reasoning, the military dictatorships are the source of violence. The solution, then, as the logic goes, is to elect civilian presidents. That is the "moderate" solution that will eliminate the "extremism" of the left and the right. El Salvador fits that model perfectly with Napoleón Duarte—a moderate civilian president with a North American flair for communication and the ability to speak fluent English. That is the view from the north looking south.

From the point of view of the *campesinos*, however, reality is quite different. For decades elections have been fraudulent. They only provide a thin veneer of legitimacy to long-standing military dictatorships such as Somoza's in Nicaragua or the military in Guatemala and El Salvador. For the peoples of Central America democracy and their elections have nothing in common. Real democracy is when the majority (and in the case of Central America, that means the poor) are in control of their own destiny. In a democracy the majority (in Central America, the poor) have control over their own lives. That means they have access to land, work, food, shelter, medical care, and schooling. It means they have ways to influence government decisions on a day-to-day basis.

Refugees from El Salvador are aware of a different reality from that imaged by the long voting lines and happy faces beamed at the U.S. populace during the Salvadoran elections in 1982 and 1984. They experienced firsthand the factors that made the election less than free. The media were censored and death threats were issued in the daily papers against even international journalists. In El Salvador the law stipulates that voters *must* vote. And there are threats hanging over those who do not vote; *cédulas*, identity cards, are stamped and if you do not have a stamped card, you cannot return to work. In a nation where right-wing and government terrorism has killed fifty thousand civilians, the atmosphere is one of fear and repression. Added to that was the fact that the ballot boxes were clear plastic, with soldiers standing guard by them. The ballots themselves were newsprint, making it impossible to register a blank ballot as a protest of the election. Candidates did not represent a true spectrum of the population, due to the history of assassinations of left-wing candidates (seventeen candidates were murdered during the electoral campaigns of 1982 and 1984).[102] Finally, according to *Washington Post* columnist Jack Anderson, in 1984 the United States through the CIA gave Duarte's campaign $960,000 and the National Conciliation Party $437,000. The National Conciliation Party is another right-wing Salvadoran party that helped

Duarte win by not aligning directly with D'Aubuisson and the ARENA (*Alianza Republicana Nacionalista*, Nationalist Republican Alliance) party. [103]

One of the first refugees taken into sanctuary, Albertina, the mother of five children, was in El Salvador during the 1982 election. When asked by reporters whom she voted for, she answered, "I and most of the people in my town voted for whoever we thought would kill us if we didn't vote for them."

As the sanctuary experience converted North Americans to the side of the poor, the old myths about moderation, civilian leaders, and military dictatorships gave way to a broader analysis of the roots of violence. They began to see that to posit military dictatorships as the root cause of violence in the region was giving too much credit to individual leaders without looking at the systems that they govern—or more accurately, that govern them. Patterns of landownership, pressures from the United States, prevalent types of cash crops, multinational lending institutions and their terms of trade, the role of the military and of local elites are all more determinative in a Central American country than who is president and how many voted for him in the last election.

More and more North Americans asked the question, Why are we always supporting the wrong side in Central America?

Institutionalized Violence and U.S. Involvement

When Pope Paul VI declared that development is the new name for peace, he was thinking of all the ties of interdependence existing, not only within nations, but also between them on a worldwide scale. He took into consideration the mechanisms that are imbued with materialism rather than authentic humanism, and that therefore lead on the international level to the ever increasing wealth of the rich at the expense of the ever increasing poverty of the poor [Pope John Paul II, Puebla, Mexico, January 1979].

As sanctuary congregations entered into the lives of the refugees in their midst, an awakening happened. In some measure, it paralleled the awakening of the Catholic Church in Latin America in the 1960s. White middle-class citizens of the United States were making new connections at deeper levels between the wealth of the north and the poverty of the south.

In the 1960s Catholic leaders in Latin America looked at the reality of their peoples from a pastoral perspective. They saw widespread hunger. They walked the overcrowded slums where paupers sold scrap paper and empty bottles to eke out a living in the shadow of modern high-rise buildings. They saw young girls sexually exploited, *campesinos* landless and exiled in their own country. They said funeral Mass after funeral Mass over the tiny coffins of children slain by hunger, dysentery, and pesticides. They wanted the major role of the church to be something other than administering the last rites over the demise of a people.

The theological proclamations that were heard at Medellín in 1968 (the

Second General Assembly of the Latin American Episcopal Council) and later came to be known as liberation theology were nurtured from the beginning by a pastoral love of and care for the people. Bishops, priests, and pastoral workers were studying the reality of their peoples, "the body of Christ," and then trying to respond in meaningful ways to their living conditions. They rejected the prevailing myths that served only to keep a people powerless. They rejected the fatalism that said poverty was their lot in life. They refused to call them "unfortunates," with the implication that it was luck or fortune that determined their status. Instead, they engaged in a critical social analysis aimed not at placating the people by promising a glorious afterlife, but striking at the roots of the problem. They said, "There is no peace without justice":

> We call this "violence" because it is not the inevitable consequence of technically unsolvable problems but the unjust result of a situation that is maintained deliberately. Each day it becomes more clear that the great problems of present-day Latin America are rooted mainly in the political, economic, and social system that prevails in most Latin American countries. It is a system based on the profit motive as the sole standard for measuring economic progress.[104]

This statement was from a document issued by more than nine hundred priests from Latin America at the Medellín conference. Poverty is violence—a violence that spells death. That was one of the conclusions at Medellín. The cause of that death is "institutionalized violence" (Medellín), "institutionalized injustice" (Puebla—the third general assembly of the Latin American Episcopal Council), the "permanent violation of the dignity of the human person" (Puebla). However it is phrased, the emphasis is on death as embedded in the prevailing power structures—death not shared equally by the whole of society. The many poor suffer so that the few wealthy can have better and longer lives.

Poverty is not only violence and death, it is sin—a sin against the children of God. That too was a conclusion at both Medellín and Puebla. It is not a sin of those who are poor; it is a sin of those who made them poor and keep them that way. Historically, colonial and commercial interests have pauperized Latin Americans. History speaks clearly of the manufacture of poverty. As sanctuary congregations came to know refugees as individual persons, they began to ask about the history of their countries. The Guatemalans particularly, by their beautiful weavings, demonstrated the heritage of a great people. Poverty was not indigenous to the peoples of Guatemala and El Salvador; it had been imported and imposed upon them.

The Mayans of Guatemala created one of the greatest civilizations known to history, producing impressive works of art in sculpture, ceramics, and architecture. They invented the concept of zero and plotted the movement of the stars with greater accuracy than any other civilization at that time. The general welfare of even the poorest was higher before the Spanish conquest in 1524 than at any time since. The Mayans supported a population at least as large as that of present-day Guatemala without the malnutrition and starvation of today. For the conquistadors, this new world was a frontier filled with riches, land, and slave labor that could be used for their own private accumulation of wealth. The wealth was acquired by selling goods in Europe. The system was directed toward a European market, ignoring the social and economic needs of the local population. Today that same system is still in place, but the market for Guatemalan coffee, cotton, sugar, beef, and bananas is now the United States.[105]

In El Salvador, too, the welfare of the people was better a hundred years ago than it is today. Peasants lived on communal land that provided their livelihood. The domination of the country by fourteen families—the oligarchy—can be traced back to the late nineteenth century and the "legal" dissolution of communal lands.

Laws passed in Guatemala at about the same time aimed at taking the land from those who worked it. It was, in a sense, a legal conquest. The indigenous Indians protested to Guatemalan President Lisandro Barillas about the loss of their land in the 1890s:

> You have ordered us to leave our lands so that coffee can be grown. You have done us an injustice. . . . You ask us to leave the land where our grandfathers and fathers were born. . . . Is it because we do not know how to grow coffee? You know very well we know how. . . . Are we not the ones who sow coffee on the *fincas*, wash it and harvest it? But we do not want to grow coffee on our lands. We want them only for our corn, our animals, our wood. And we want these lands where our grandfathers and fathers worked. Why should we leave them?[106]

The historical background was important for sanctuary churches to put present realities into a broader perspective. Sanctuary churches were not content with individual stories but sought to make connections and discern patterns to make sense out of those stories. Historical research was one way to do this. Statistical evidence also helped.

Statistics reflect a "total" conquest of the poor. In Guatemala the life expectancy in rural areas is forty-one years. Three out of every five children die before the age of five. El Salvador has the lowest caloric intake of any country in the western hemisphere. The average North American family spends more on groceries in one month than a Central American family earns in a year. The average rural wage, when seasonal work can be found, is $2 per day and the starting wage in a factory is $3 per day. Yet prices in supermarkets are similar to those in the United States, with eggs selling at 80¢ a dozen, milk 35¢ a quart, beans and rice 30¢ a pound.[107]

And the situation is getting worse. In the mid-1970s in El Salvador poverty was on the increase. Real earnings declined between 1970 and 1975. The most direct cause was the growing landlessness. In 1961, 11.8 percent of rural families were landless; in 1971, 29.1 percent, and in 1975, 40.9 percent.[108]

In Guatemala the situation was similar. In 1965, 42 percent of the population lacked the caloric intake necessary to sustain life and good health. In 1980 it increased to 80 percent of the population. The total earnings of the richest 5 percent jumped from 48 percent in 1950 to 59 percent in 1978. Needless to say, the earnings of the bottom 50 percent declined during the same period.[109]

The problem posed by landlessness is difficult for North Americans to understand. Landlessness in Central America means virtual slavery. When there is work at all, it is usually seasonal work only. Rigoberta Menchu tells what life was like without land:

> I should say that in Guatemala we Indians have no childhood. . . . Personally I started working for a living when I was eight years old, on the plantations of the large landowners on the south coast. I remember I started working because I could no longer bear the expression on my mother's face. She was always exhausted, picking coffee or cotton while carrying her newborn on her back, and my five brothers and sisters around her hungry. Since the children who don't work are not fed by the owners, she never earned enough. My wage when I started was twenty cents a day.
>
> When I was eleven, two of my brothers died on the plantations from malnutrition and sickness. We came from a cold region and the intense heat of the coast made us sick. One time I too almost died of fever.
>
> When my brothers died, my mother asked for permission to bury them, because our burial ceremonies are very important to us; but permission was denied. So she took a day off and returned to work the following day. . . . They fired us, and they didn't pay us for the fifteen days we had already worked.[110]

THE ROOTS OF INSTITUTIONALIZED VIOLENCE

We see the growing gap between the rich and poor as a scandal and a contradiction to Christian existence. The luxury of a few becomes an insult to the wretched poverty of the masses. This is contrary to the plan of the Creator. . . . In this anxiety and sorrow the church sees a situation of social sinfulness, all the more serious because it exists in countries that call themselves Catholic and are capable of changing the situation [Pope John Paul II].

The roots of institutionalized violence are most readily exposed through a case study of coffee. Coffee is representative of the world economy because it is the second most traded commodity on the world market. It is also the backbone of the Guatemalan and Salvadoran economy.

The following testimony of "José," a refugee in sanctuary, gives an insight into plantation life from the point of view of the workers. The Guatemalan army was hunting "José" because he was a catechist. The Guatemalan army had already killed five hundred catechists. Every day he worked in fear of being discovered. His identification papers had become illegible from sweat and rain because there was no safe place to keep them while he was on the plantation. Thus, he lived in double fear: he was a catechist and he had no papers, either of which could have meant his death. In a private interview, he explained:

You work all day from 6 A.M. to 4 P.M. It is a very brutal job and you only earn $1.50 a day to clear out the weeds around the coffee plants. There is no such thing as overtime pay. Coffee workers are transported to the *fincas* in cattle trucks. One hundred twenty-five people are packed into these trucks just like cattle.

Children on the plantation start working at age nine, just like my son. The children pick up the berries that fall on the ground. They are paid thirty cents for each basket they fill. The owners know that a child can barely fill up one basket in a day. Women do the same work as the children and are also paid thirty cents.

The first time you pick the coffee you only pick the mature beans. The second picking you harvest everything—both green and ripe beans. The collection point is about two miles from the coffee fields. When you fill one box it weighs 150 pounds. We had to bring the box over to the collection point. We would put a rope around our head to pull the box. Because it is the rainy season everything is wet. It makes it heavier because there is water in the box.

At the weighing at the end of the day the workers can be shortchanged. It's entirely up to the whim of the administrator. If there were a little bit of green coffee in a box, the administrator could discount the whole box.

There are also natural dangers. Fire ants and bees live in the coffee plants. Many workers are bitten when they shake the branches. There are also poisonous snakes. I once killed forty-five snakes while cleaning an area of twenty-one square meters. We all work barefoot or in sandals. My son was bitten by a scorpion and almost died.

On the majority of *fincas* there is no drinkable water. Everyone has to go to the river to wash clothes, bathe, and get water to drink. There are no toilets. If you have to do your thing, you do it in the coffee fields. The waste threatens the health of the women and their children. Many children die of worms, diarrhea, and viruses. There is no health care on the plantations.

If the workers have any shelter at all, it is a *galera*. It's a roof without walls. Sometimes three hundred people pack into that space. If it rains, the rain comes in. The workers and their families use cardboard boxes or banana leaves for mattresses.

A lot of people arrive sick, some with yellow fever. The *galera* becomes like an incubator for this disease. The food provided by the *finca* owner also does more harm than good. The owner says he provides us with food but they only provide six tortillas a day and a little beans—mostly badly

Conscientization

cooked. So, in exchange for providing food, you get bad health because you get organisms in your body. Many people get sick and die. Mostly children die on the plantations. Since the coffee plants are sweet, children chew on them. They get dysentery from the pesticides.

In the *fincas* we cannot complain about the low salaries, because complaining means death itself. In San Marcos hundreds and thousands of *campesinos* have disappeared for requesting a better salary in order to live, or even, at least, to eat a little better.

The institutional roots of violence are exposed when the relationship between wages and profits in the marketing of coffee is brought to light. The human cost of producing coffee is high for the workers—they pay with their lives. But their wages are very low. Just the reverse is true for the owners and the multinational corporations that eventually sell the coffee: the profits are high. In Philip Berryman's cost analysis of coffee production, the weeks of hand labor in the fields picking coffee bean by bean amounts to less than 10 percent of the total production cost and only 2.5 percent of the price paid on the international market. That means that when the U.S. consumer buys coffee at $2.50 a pound, $.06 goes to the workers. The money that is not paid to the workers goes to the plantation owners, the Guatemalan and Salvadoran governments, and multinational corporations.[111]

In order to picture this violence in clearer terms, it is important to see how each of these three uses the profits from the production and sale of coffee.

Landowner Profits

In addition to their own personal aggrandizement, landowners' profits secure for them a greater share of the national wealth and a more concentrated hold on the land. In Guatemala the richest 2 percent of the population controls fifty times the income of the bottom half. In El Salvador six large families (Guirola, Sol, Dueñas, Daglio, Samayoa, Romero Basque) among them own 71,923 hectares of land—equivalent to what is owned by 80 percent of the population.[112] The oligarchy of El Salvador, the fourteen wealthy families, has controlled the national wealth for decades:

There are fourteen of them. Their names are emblazoned outside the air-conditioned office blocks, the banks, the trading firms and insurance companies of San Salvador. They play golf. They give parties by their swimming pools. They join exclusive clubs. You find them . . . running every business and most of all the coffee industry. . . . They control cotton, cocoa, sugar, palm oil, phosphates, and livestock. They control cement works, transport, the sale of Coca Cola, mineral drinks, beer, and American cars. . . . This oligarchy runs the lives of three million *mestizos*.[113]

Archbishop Oscar Romero pinpointed the problem.

The cause of our problems is the oligarchy, that tiny group of families which has no concern for the hunger of the people, but in fact needs it in order to have cheap and abundant labor power to harvest and export its crops.[114]

Government Profits

The Salvadoran and Guatemalan governments receive enormous amounts of money from the sale of coffee. Guatemala does it through the steepest coffee export tax in Central America; El Salvador does it through a government agency, INCAFE, that buys, processes, markets, and exports coffee. A good portion of that money funds the military: in both countries it is the largest government expense.[115]

Coffee is also the most important way that Guatemala and El Salvador earn the foreign exchange money that enables them to buy imports. In addition to military hardware, many of the products bought with foreign exchange money include luxury items and manufactured goods. The governments, controlled by elites, import cosmetics instead of penicillin, cars for the few rather than buses for everyone.

Multinational Profits

The largest multinational marketer of Guatemalan and Salvadoran coffee in the United States is General Foods, the 39th largest U.S. corporation, with yearly sales in excess of the GNP of many countries. General Foods products include such household names as Jello, Kool Aid, Tang, and Minute Rice. In 1982, coffee (Maxwell House, Brim) accounted for 31 percent of General Foods sales and 22 percent of its profits.[116] Executive salaries, ranging in the hundreds of thousands of dollars, corporate expense accounts, and the stock options and other perquisites of top management personnel, are not included in profits: they are expenses.

When a group called the Campaign for Global Justice asked General Foods to stop buying Guatemalan and Salvadoran coffee, because of the gross violations of human rights in those countries, the company responded:

We feel that sanctions against foreign governments are appropriately instituted by government. Indeed, we can hardly imagine a situation in which a business corporation could claim competence to make such a political assessment on the basis of its own knowledge. Thus, we are reluctant to act as a prime agent of political change—a position that we believe conforms with the expectations of the American people regarding the scope of corporate activity.[117]

Their reluctance to act as a "prime agent of social change" does not extend to other matters. The chief executive officers of General Foods sit on the board of the Grocery Manufacturers of America (GMA). The GMA is a strong lobbyist in Washington and has opposed consumer protection legislation.[118]

The political and economic contradictions between North and South America become even more pointed when internal operations of a corporation like General Foods are looked at. One year recently, General Foods spent $180 million on advertising.[119] This breaks down to $342 every minute of every day during the year. This means that General Foods spent more in *two minutes* on advertising than a coffee picker will earn in a year of hard labor.

But the roots of institutionalized violence go deeper than one corporation or one export crop. Poet Pablo Neruda has called Central America the "most succulent . . . delicate waist of America." But it is a succulence that the overwhelming majority of Central Americans do not enjoy. Half of Central American agricultural land grows crops for export (cut flowers, frozen vegetables, cotton, coffee, bananas, beef), while the local population is starving.

U.S. corporations control virtually all production of Central American bananas. A United Nations study showed that only 11¢ of each dollar spent on bananas returns to the producing country in any form, even taxes. Beef production has dramatically increased in Costa Rica and Guatemala, although beef consumption there has dropped by as much as 50 percent. Much of the beef is exported to the United States.[120]

There is a myth in the United States to the effect that Central American countries are making good use of their natural tropical climate by marketing bananas and coffee, which have always grown there. The truth is they can grow a remarkable variety of crops including grains, high-protein legumes, vegetables, and fruits. In *Food First* Frances Moore Lappé states:

Latin America got along quite well without a single banana tree until the late 1830s. (The first banana did not arrive in the United States until 1866.)

What United Brands, Standard Fruit (Dole), and Del Monte call "prime banana land" turns out to be first-rate agricultural land—flat, deep soil, well-watered, suitable for a full range of crops.[121]

Seventy of the one hundred largest U.S. corporations do business in Central America. According to the U.S. Department of Commerce, for every dollar that U.S. corporations invest in Latin America, they get back three dollars in income. In 1979 that meant a rate of return of 19.6 percent on investment, whereas the international rate was only 7.6 percent. The Central American rate of return was higher than that in Latin America as a whole. The United States has had a trade surplus with Central America, although overall it has a trade deficit. The surplus has amounted to as much as $2.6 billion in one year. In addition, Central American countries have been "perfect" for labor-intensive assembly factories that employ mostly women who work for an average of $1.08 per hour. The average wage for similar work in the United States is $8.76, as of 1980. The elites of Guatemala and El Salvador, in conjunction with the military governments, attract these businesses through tax concessions, duty-free zones, liberal laws for expropriation of profits, and the guarantee of low wages through bans on unions or repression against organizers.[122]

"A TASTE OF EMPIRE"

We know very well that we are up against a Goliath, then we have to be clear that we are not fearing the strength of the enemy but the challenge that we have already accepted. And to be able to destroy that Goliath we have to gather more forces every day [Felipe Excot, Guatemalan refugee in sanctuary at Weston Priory, Vermont].

We battle not against flesh and blood but against powers and principalities [Eph. 6:12].

Refugee testimony and the weight of factual evidence propelled most sanctuary congregations into direct attempts at trying to stop United States intervention in Central America. It was the logical and theo-logical result of the conscientization process. But for some there was a final step, a further intensification of conscientization. They saw that even if U.S. intervention was stopped, there would still be an ideology, a spirit, behind that intervention that had to be eradicated. What was it in the culture, in the national mentality, that caused such intervention? Whose interests were really being served by intervening in the affairs of less powerful countries?

"Wee Shall Bee as a City upon a Hill" (Governor Winthrop)

Even from the first toeholds of Jamestown and Massachusetts Bay, the spirit of expansion and conquest became a way of life for the Europeans. That expansion was fueled by the desire for land, trade, and natural resources. James Madison intellectually rationalized expansion by positing that democracy can best exist in an "extensive sphere." And the church baptized it with the religious fervor of a "chosen people" called to "evangelize the heathen."

The decimation of the native peoples through European diseases and modern rifle power, the string of broken treaties, and the Cherokee "Trail of Tears" all attest to a drive for control that has become part of the self-understanding of what it means to be "American."

This control was never admitted as blatant self-interest but was always couched in righteous terms. John Adams spoke for a whole generation of early leaders when he described the colonial era as "the opening of a grand scheme and design in Providence for the illumination of the ignor-

ant and the emancipation of the slavish part of mankind all over the earth."
However, the founding fathers did not trust euphoria alone to set the stage
for building an empire. James Madison worked hard to institutionalize
this spirit of expansion in the Constitution. Thomas Jefferson, looking back
on two decades of life under the Constitution, said, "I am persuaded that no
Constitution was ever before as well calculated as ours for extensive empire and
self-government."

Justification for expansion included appeal to natural law, the guarantee of
a future reign of perfect justice, and the blessing of divine providence. In his
farewell address Andrew Jackson asserted that providence had chosen North
Americans as "the guardians of freedom to preserve it for the benefit of the
human race." This was the same man who had defeated the Seminoles in
Florida and driven the Cherokees west of the Mississippi in a bitter forced
march.

The Monroe Doctrine formally staked out the western hemisphere as the
domain of the United States. The thirst for more territory first annihilated the
North American native peoples and then set its sights on Mexico. The doctrine
that became known as Manifest Destiny legitimized, even moralized this
expansion. Manifest Destiny brought together an attitude of racial superiority,
business self-interest, and a belief that God had ordained the people of the
United States to control the affairs of the continent. The *Congressional Globe*
in 1847 reported this statement by a Maryland man: "We must march from
Texas straight to the Pacific Ocean. It is the destiny of the white race, it is the
destiny of the Anglo-Saxon race."[123]

The Mexican war became the first major action of that ideology. The light of
history has shown that the Mexican war was a war of conquest, pure and
simple. Even at the time, it occasioned protest, notably the tax protest of Henry
David Thoreau that led to his classic essay on the duty of civil disobedience.
North American civil disobedience has its roots in the subsoil of U.S. quest for
world domination.

God, race, and class were used to justify the war. Senator V. H. Johnson
talked of the Mexican war as the "high purposes of a Wise Providence," which
the United States could not refuse. The *New York Herald* said, "The universal
Yankee nation can regenerate and disenthrall the people of Mexico in a few
years; and we believe it is our destiny to civilize that part of the world."[124]

The Civil War was a victory for the industrial north. After 1865 the United
States changed from an agricultural to an industrial nation. In order to run that
machinery, the barons of industry needed rubber, tin, nickel, nitrate, manga-
nese, tungsten, and bauxite. They needed them and they wanted them cheap.
Those resources were not present in the continental United States, and Latin
America became one of the major "mines" where U.S. companies extracted
their raw materials. Later that region also served as a market for manufactured
goods, a source of cheap labor, and a prime spot for investment of surplus
capital. Right now the Caribbean region supplies the United States with 70

percent of its imported refined petroleum and 85 percent of the bauxite used in the production of aluminum.[125]

The 1890s saw a radical deepening of the ideology of Manifest Destiny that set the stage for present policy. That decade saw the end of the frontier, the final defeat of the indigenous population at Wounded Knee, South Dakota, and the first time U.S. industry produced more goods than the domestic population could consume. Manifest Destiny now meant overseas expansion, new markets, and the American flag flying over dozens of new trading partners.

Senator Albert Beveridge of Indiana summed up the prevalent attitude of that period:

> We will not renounce our part in the mission of our race, trustees under God, of the civilization of the world. God has not been preparing the English-speaking and Teutonic peoples for a thousand years for nothing. . . . He has made us the master organizers of the world adept in government that we may administer government among savages and senile peoples.[126]

The Spanish American War of 1898 was another war of conquest, but not only of territory. It was a war of conquest for the sake of an ideology that justified U.S. power in the western hemisphere. A *Washington Post* editorial in 1898 stated:

> A new consciousness seems to have come upon us—the consciousness of strength—and with it a new appetite, the yearning to show our strength. . . . Ambition, interest, land hunger, pride, the mere joy of fighting, whatever it may be, we are animated by a new sensation. We are face to face with a strange destiny. The taste of Empire is in the mouth of the people even as the taste of blood in the jungle.[127]

Teddy Roosevelt ("speak softly and carry a big stick") heralded in the period of "gunboat diplomacy." That term is being used again to describe the Central American foreign policy of Ronald Reagan. It is important, then, to understand the roots of that original policy.

For Roosevelt, the "Rough Rider," the first of the White House cowboys, one issue was manhood.

> When great nations fear to expand, shrink from expansion, it is because their greatness is coming to an end. Are we still in the prime of our lusty youth, still at the beginning of our glorious manhood, to sit down among the outworn people, to take our place with the weak and craven? A thousand times no![128]

Behind the tough talk, though, was hard money. United States control of the Panama Canal was the biggest but not the only instance of its regional domination. When Nicaragua began negotiating loans with England and Japan, the United States helped support an insurrection there, sent its own customs officers to collect revenue, and backed all of it up with the U.S. Marine Corps.

Roosevelt's 1904 corollary to the Monroe Doctrine shows how blatant commercial self-interest was always couched in moral terms:

> Chronic wrongdoing or an impotence which results in a general loosening of the ties of civilized society, may in America, as elsewhere, ultimately require intervention by some civilized nation, and in the Western Hemisphere the adherence of the United States to the Monroe Doctrine may force the United States, however reluctantly, in flagrant cases of such wrongdoing or impotence, to the exercise of an international police power.[129]

How "reluctant" Roosevelt actually was to use force is questionable. As assistant secretary of the Navy he had said that the "great masterful races have been fighting races."[130]

The United States certainly was never reluctant to use force. From 1793 to 1895 the United States made 103 armed interventions in the affairs of other countries.[131] In the first three decades of this century, U.S. presidents sent troops to Central America and the Caribbean twenty-eight times.[132] The U.S. Marines occupied Nicaragua almost continuously from 1912 to 1933 when they trained the infamous National Guard of Anastasio Somoza to take their place.

But U.S. intervention, then and now, cannot be written off to the whims of a macho president. William Howard Taft followed Roosevelt and said in 1912, "The whole [western] hemisphere will be ours in fact as, by virtue of our superiority of race, it is already ours morally."[133]

In the 1920s, under the Coolidge administration, the Evart doctrine justified U.S. intervention in the internal affairs of Latin American countries to protect the foreign holdings of U.S. nationals. A memo in 1927 from Robert Olds, undersecretary of state, put it succinctly:

> We do control the destinies of Central American nations and we do so for the simple reason that the national self-interest dictates such a course. . . . Until now Central America has always understood that governments that we recognize and support stay in power, while those we do not recognize and support fail.[134]

Franklin Roosevelt coined the phrase "Good Neighbor Policy" in the 1930s to describe a "new" way of treating the countries to the south. One of those "good neighbors" was Anastasio Somoza, dictator of Nicaragua. Roosevelt said, "Somoza may be a son of a bitch, but at least he's *our* son of a bitch." Somoza bragged that he always voted with the United States in the United Nations.

What the "Good Neighbor Policy" ushered in was a time of "surrogate control" by the United States. Instead of sending in the Marine Corps every time there was a disturbance, thus causing domestic protests at home, as was the case of the Marines in Nicaragua in the 1920s, the United States supported dictatorships that created "stability." That stability was profitable for U.S. business interests but costly to the peoples of Central America. Dictator Maximiliano Hernández Martínez of El Salvador massacred thirty-two thousand peasants in 1932. Somoza murdered Augusto Caesar Sandino in 1933. Jorge Ubico, dictator in Guatemala, outlawed unions and kept wages low, offered tax shelters to corporations, and severely repressed dissent.[135]

Thus, in the 1930s and 40s intervention took on the guise of neighborly cooperation. That worked well as long as strong armed military men carried out the wishes and needs of the Empire. But when the people overthrew the dictator (as in Guatemala in the 1940s) and elected someone who represented the needs of the majority, "neighborliness" gave way to "anticommunism" as the basis for state policy.

Manifest Destiny has never died, it just changes guises from time to time. Sometimes it is rapacious and overt, other times subtle and hidden, covered with a veneer of civility. It goes underground at times in CIA covert operations; at other times it is as blatant as flotillas and contras. Always, though, for the peoples of Central America, it is deadly.

The CIA, in conjunction with the United Fruit Company and the Eisenhower administration, overthrew the duly-elected government of Jacobo Arbenz in Guatemala in 1954. John Kennedy's covert operations to overthrow the government of Fidel Castro in 1961 ended in the Bay of Pigs debacle. Lyndon Johnson sent twenty-five thousand Marines to the Dominican Republic in 1965. Henry Kissinger, Richard Nixon, ITT, and the CIA conspired to overthrow the duly-elected government of Salvador Allende in 1973 in Chile. Chile up to that point had enjoyed uninterrupted democracy since the turn of the century. Since 1973 it has suffered through the uninterrupted dictatorship of Augusto Pinochet who suspended the Constitution, dismissed the Congress, and declared a state of siege with the suspension of most civil rights. In the wake of the coup Pinochet detained, tortured, and killed hundreds of Chileans. One of the victims was Victor Jara, the brilliant folk singer who was a leader of the "New Song Movement" that was sweeping through Latin America. He was standing in the soccer stadium, detained with hundreds of others, when soldiers told him to sing and play his guitar. He sang and played. The soldiers crushed his fingers and taunted him to continue to play. He kept singing until they shot him down. This is Manifest Destiny from the south looking north.

The most recent act of conquest by the United States was the invasion of Grenada. The justification was "to save American lives and interests." That is the same reason given by the State Department for the Marines to land in Buenos Aires in 1852, in Nicaragua in 1853, in Uruguay in 1855, in Hawaii in 1893, in Nicaragua in 1894 . . . and so on, for a century and a half.[136]

Closer to the truth are passages from the memoirs of General Smedley D. Butler who headed many of the military interventions of the United States in the early part of this century. He spent thirty-three years in the Marine Corps rising to the rank of major general:

> During that period I spent most of my time being a high-class muscle man for Big Business, for Wall Street, and for the bankers. In short I was a racketeer for capitalism. . . . Thus I helped make Haiti and Cuba a decent place for the National City Bank to collect revenues. . . . I helped purify Nicaragua for the international banking house of Brown Brothers in 1909–1912. I brought light to the Dominican Republic for American sugar interests in 1916. I helped make Honduras "right" for American fruit companies in 1903.[137]

The Reagan administration is not an aberration in an otherwise just history. It stands in direct line with one hundred fifty years of U.S. domination in Central America. Perhaps the language is less subtle than we have grown accustomed to hearing or the firepower more awesome than we realized, but the same ideology—Manifest Destiny and the building of an economic empire—underlies the aggression.

CONFLICT AND THE CALL TO CONVERSION

North Americans generally try to avoid conflict. At times, sanctuary churches participated in this avoidance—when they eloquently decried the violence in Central America but refused to denounce the role of the United States in creating that violence. Some congregations stayed away from "political" issues because they did not want to alienate other members of their congregations. Fear of divided congregations was always uppermost in the minds of those who introduced the concept of sanctuary into their community of faith.

That viewpoint, however, makes the faulty assumption that the world and North American society, and even their church, are in fact unified. But they are all deeply divided. To fail to recognize this is to embrace a half-truth.

Violence does not grow rootless in midair. The process of conscientization uncovers those roots and places them in their proper historical and present-day context. The megastructure of the technological North runs not only by oil and coal, but by the fuel of human sweat and blood from the South. There is a cause-and-effect relationship between them. The affluent life of some is due to the large-scale exploitation of others. It is not that some happen to be rich and others poor. Some are rich because most are poor.

When God asked Cain, "What has become of your brother?," God was not searching for the fact of his death but for its cause. "What has become of your brothers and sisters in Central America?" To answer that they are dying is not good enough. Cain murdered Abel. The Roman government, aided and abetted by the religious establishment, crucified Jesus. Central Americans are asking us to name and stop their killers.

Conflict is a fact in Central America. Silence or denial will not change that fact. Communities of faith share a vision of a new earth, "where the lion and the lamb lie down together" and where there will be "no more violence in all of my holy mountain, so says the Lord." Many in the North American religious community assume that the way to achieve that unity is to act as if it already existed. They play down differences or relegate justice to a gray foggy wasteland where only years of study will ever produce clarity. Unity, in this scenario, is akin to neutrality—a view that is neither realistic nor biblical.

The Old Testament prophets knew the impossibility of compromising with injustice. "Let justice roll down like waters, and righteousness like an ever flowing stream." The biblical witness calls not for accommodation with injustice but repentance and conversion, a complete turning around. The sinner is called to conversion and in the United States that means changing sides and joining with the poor in their struggle for life.

Authentic unity comes through telling the whole truth. Unity will be achieved by spotlighting divisions, not by hiding them. The religious community joins the poor and calls the rich to conversion. That call is both verbal challenge and historical action. Repentance and conversion are not easy. Paul had to be struck from his horse and blinded before he stopped persecuting the early church. Radical conversion involves "shaking the foundations." Unjust economic structures will have to be dismantled, imperial policies struck down. God called Jeremiah to prophesy, saying:

> Behold, I have put my words into your mouth,
> See, I have set you this day over nations and other kingdoms,
> To pluck up and to break down,
> To destroy and to overthrow,
> To build and to plant [Jer. 1:4–5].

The prophetic charge is to overthrow the barriers to new life. Conflict between rich and poor, between owners and workers, is the oppressive reality of Central America right now. The poor did not create that conflict; they are only asking for justice and the creation of a new order.

The cry that is rising higher and higher from the peoples of Central America is *Basta*—Enough!

There is a limit to the number of times a people can bear taking a tiny coffin to a remote graveyard. Violence has been embedded in the flesh of the poor for decades—the stooped backs; the burning in the eyes and throat from pesticides; the constant abdominal pain from drinking contaminated water; the ache of muscles pushed to the limits of human exertion to earn not enough food to feed their families; the premature deaths at forty of parents who should live to be seventy or more. And beyond that, the mockery, the daily indignities of being treated as subhuman, and the constant fear of losing employment or land or home, or sons and daughters. Life-and-death conflict has been embodied in the poor for centuries. Periodic revolts have taken place in the past—nearly one every generation since the Spanish conquest in the sixteenth century. We are living through another, and we are being asked by the struggling peoples of Central America to choose sides.

Solidarity with the poor is not easy. Choosing sides can make us feel uncomfortable. As Gustavo Gutiérrez says:

> Perhaps what most shocks the Christian seeking to take sides frankly and decisively with the poor and exploited, and to enter into involvement with the struggles of the proletariat, is the conflictual nature of praxis in this context. Politics today involves confrontation—and varying degrees of violence—among human groups, among social classes with opposing interests. . . . It is equally hard for those who with all the good will in the world confuse universal love with a fictitious harmony. But the gospel enjoins us to love our enemies. . . . This means we have to recognize the fact of class struggle and accept the fact that we have class enemies to combat. There is no way not to have enemies. What is important is not to exclude them from our love.[138]

Juan Hernández Pico, a Central American theologian, writes that entering into this conflict is not only just, it is a revelatory act—a self-revelation on the part of God:

> *The conflictive reality in history of a struggle between good and evil, between justice and injustice, being waged by the poor in our countries* (and by those who have taken up their cause despite their own class origins) *is a* locus theologicus *where God is breaking into history.*[139]

Obviously, for those whose class position is structurally contradictory to the cause of the poor, such an invitation is a call to conversion. It is an invitation to join in the struggle for life.

Theologians sometimes interpret conversion as solely a change of heart, an internal process that dramatically changes the person. Such an interpretation makes conversion highly personal, even mystical. But the conversion that the poor demand of us goes beyond such an interpretation. In the encounter with refugees, and through them the encounter with the peoples of Central America, conversion becomes a drastic change in the world as well as the person. It calls for a change in the sinner *and* in the forces that perpetrate sin.

Testimonies of refugees, historical analysis of U.S. involvement in Central America, and a clearer perception of the roots of institutional violence have propelled sanctuary congregations into a collective conversion process. It is a conversion to the side of the poor, spiritually and historically. It requires the heart but also the hands and feet.

Even in the traditional sense, conversion is a radical break. It is a break from a past life of sin and a turning toward a new life of solidarity. Sin is separation from God and neighbor. It prevents formation of the natural communion of all. Gustavo Gutiérrez writes:

Conversion implies that we recognize the presence of sin in our lives and our world. In other words, we see and admit what is vitiating our relationship with God and our solidarity with others—what, in consequence, is also hindering the creation of a just and human society.[140]

Conversion leads to reunion. It necessitates a decision to join the poor in their struggle for life. Invariably that choice precipitates a for-and-against stance and an unmasking of de facto conflicts. For conversion involves a choice *for* life and *against* death, *for* the poor and *against* those who uphold structures that perpetuate poverty. Conversion is unauthentic if it is content with halfhearted commitment or halfway reform. It demands a change of the whole person and the whole situation that causes death for the many and luxury for the few. It calls for a complete turning over of the self and the world—that is, revolution. The unity of all humankind depends upon turning the present world upside down.

Conversion begins by hearing the truth and believing the almost unbelievable. It begins, as it did before with sojourners in Egypt and Galilee, by speaking out against the truth of oppression and proclaiming a new kind of liberation. Conversion continues by rejecting classist and racist privilege and embracing vulnerability by standing on the side of the other sojourners, from Guatemala and El Salvador. Conversion is not a once-and-for-all act; it is a daily decision. In the end, it continues only by making solidarity a life stance and by allowing hope to inspire revolutionary acts of religious faith.

Be it resolved that this [General] assembly urges Unitarian Universalists' active support of those Unitarian Universalist Societies and other religious communities which offer sanctuary to El Salvadorans and other Central American refugees.

Unitarian Universalist Association
General Assembly, June 1984

6

FREEDOM'S COURSE:
THE ABOLITIONIST MOVEMENT
AND THE SANCTUARY MOVEMENT

In my country
freedom . . . is also a skin of courage.
They can hit us again
and again, believe me, they can.
[But] you will always *win* freedom.

Otto René Castillo

There are a thousand hacking at the branch of evil
to one who is striking at the root.

Thoreau, 1858

Alicia

WITNESS: ALICIA

"My 16-year-old sister, 17-year-old brother, and I left El Salvador in December 1980. I was a catechist with the Catholic Church in the capital, involved with the base communities. What we did was to learn the Bible according to the time we were living, trying to understand the exploitation and injustice and poverty and misery. And we would go around and teach the Bible, especially in the countryside, and we would try to raise the consciousness of the people: why the exploitation, why the injustice, why there were no schools for their children. We would go to the poorest community in that area and we would try to collect clothes for them.

"In 1979, the situation of killings by the government became more open. It was decided that church communities were against the government because we worked with the poor. We had a great relationship with the poor. We started to hear rumors that the security forces were wanting to come into the church, kidnap the padre, and kill him. We immediately became afraid of meeting. One day, he was celebrating Mass and they shot him. A little while later one of my co-workers was kidnapped where he worked. We never heard from him for months. When he finally showed up, we hardly recognized him. He was very skinny and had signs of torture. He related to us how they had put electric shots into his ears and nose and to his eyes, and how they had put a rubber mask with some kind of chemical (I think it was lime), to provoke suffocation, while the interrogators asked quesitons like 'Where do you keep the arms?' and 'What are the names of the people in your group?' and 'Who are the communist priests who are teaching the people revolution?' He fainted from so much

torture that they threw cold water on him so he would wake up again. They tortured him several times.

"[Prisoners] were not allowed to use a bathroom so they had to do their necessities in their clothes. In the prison where he was kept, someone had written on the wall with his own excrement, 'God, someday you will see inside this prison and you will help us.'

"The priest thought that he was dead and the security forces thought he was dead. He was taken away in a truck but he didn't know where. He was left in the countryside. When he recovered consciousness he was in the house of some campesinos who told him how they had found him in the field and how the dogs were smelling him. The vultures were flying around him ready to eat him. And that's how he showed up at the church to tell us that we shouldn't meet again. He couldn't remember if he had given our names while he was being tortured.

"One day I was told that the security forces came to my house asking for me by name. It has happened to so many people; when they come for you like that it is because they want to [make you] disappear. So I went away to my hometown to try to hide. There lots of people were being killed. There were things I had never seen before, like bodies in the streets, or in a trash dumping place where people went to search for their relatives. There were dogs walking around with parts of human bodies in their teeth.

"One day when the curfew was set up we heard shots, but we didn't open our doors, because if you saw something you would get killed. One day we heard shots in the middle of the day. We ran into our neighbors' house and the whole family had been shot—the mother, the 17-year-old son, and the father. We found the bodies of the mother and son embracing each other. Another son who had been there told how the soldiers said that they had to die together. Their 16-year-old daughter was raped in the house and then they drove her away. The next day she showed up in the town; she had been raped many times. Another friend of mine who was a student was taken out of the bus and 'disappeared.' Another student friend of mine was killed. In that town everyone was so afraid because we were being killed in the schools—the teachers, the nuns. Everyone closed their doors at five o'clock and nobody would open them.

"We decided to leave El Salvador before we were killed. Some relatives of mine were threatened by the security forces. We had a brother in Mexico who wanted to help us. We went to Mexicali. One friend of my oldest brother was going to try to help us cross the border. We started to walk one night in 1980, through the fields. It was very cold and windy. The wind hurt our faces. We didn't have warm clothes. We walked and walked that night. There were planes of the Immigration Service flying all around; they would illuminate the whole area and we would run and throw ourselves on the ground to hide. There were some rocks where we were hiding. We couldn't go onto the highway, because the Immigration vans were driving back and forth. Finally, I think it was four or five in the morning, we ran onto the highway and got into a friend's car.

About three minutes later we were stopped by the Immigration and taken into an Immigration van and asked where we were from. We explained we were nationals. They took us to the Mexican border. We were left there.

"We tried to cross again that night. We took a different way this time. But this time it was through a field filled with cactus. When we threw ourselves to the ground we had to withstand the pain of the cactus spines. There were no trees or rocks to hide behind. So this time we would run when the plane came over. But a big plane lit everything again and we ran into some aqueducts. But some people were already hiding there and there was no room for us. We were all arrested. Again they took us to the Mexican border.

"So a third time we started to walk at night. This time, to get away from the lights, there were some branches that we threw ourselves over. They were all full of thorns. My brother was bleeding from his lips. My oldest brother was there to help us but he was so cold that he kept trying to find the dry grass and throw it over us. The three of us were holding each other to keep warm. I was digging with my feet in the ground where we were waiting to cross the strip of highway. When my brother said, 'Let's go,' I had unconsciously made a pretty deep hole. I had buried my shoes in there and couldn't find them. I had to run over the cactus barefoot. It was difficult and again we were caught. Without my shoes and the way my hair looked after such a night, I looked crazy. We were full of thorns and dried leaves.

"It was six o'clock in the morning when we were returned to the Mexican border. The Mexican officals were standing outside their headquarters. Of course, we looked like thieves. We caught their attention. They said, 'Come here, where were you going?' We said we were Mexicans but they told us we didn't look like Mexicans. They took us inside their headquarters and asked us many questions about Mexican customs. We did not pass the test. There were so many things I did not know about Mexico. So they said we were not Mexicans and the Americans could not deport us to Mexico. They called the U.S. agent and said that we had no country to be deported to. The Mexicans refused to take responsibility for us. The Americans got really upset that we had lied to them and told them we were Mexicans. From that moment we were treated very badly by the Americans.

"They took us to their headquarters. My English was very bad at the time, so they brought Chicano immigration officials to ask us questions in Spanish. They called us vulgar words, saying we were prostitutes. They almost hit us in our face because we kept saying we were Mexicans. They kept interrogating us. They forced us to sit and stand up, and searched all of our clothes, even trying to search our inside clothes. They tried to find the labels where the clothes had been made. We had taken all the labels off because we had been advised to do that by some Mexicans. Since my sister and brother did not speak, only I spoke, they decided to separate us. We were lying, so we all said different things.

"It was raining and they took my brother outside to the patio. They took his clothes off. They hit him and tried to stick their fingers into his eyes. They pulled his hair and made him sit down and stand up. They pushed him back and

forth between two agents. They brought my sister and me out and told us that if we didn't tell where we were from, they were going to throw my brother down and jump on him. My brother was so skinny. He was bleeding. I couldn't stand it anymore so I said, 'Stop it. We are from El Salvador.'

"Even now I feel something inside, in my throat. I couldn't believe what I was seeing. I thought the Americans were moral and that they didn't treat people like they do in my country. I had respect for them, but I couldn't stand to see them doing what they were doing to my little brother. After that we were taken to a toilet room which was very dirty. They locked us there and we slept there. The next day we were taken into another room. They took our pictures and showed us pictures of others who had been deported to El Salvador. I knew that the government of El Salvador believed if you left the country, it meant you were against the government and they would punish you if you returned. I kept asking them why they wanted the pictures. And they said that they wanted to make sure that we were not going to come back.

"They gave us some forms that I didn't understand. They wanted us to sign them. For some reason I knew I didn't want to sign anything that I didn't understand. After having been tricked that way, I didn't want to sign. So they took our hands by force and signed, not even a signature, just scratches. We were put into a big room with a lot of Vietnamese. When there were enough to fill the plane, we were put on a plane.

"When they were making us sign, I told them that if they sent those pictures to El Salvador, we would be killed. I was trying to tell them why we left. They said if we wanted to survive, we had to go back and fight for our lives. They kept laughing at us and telling us that we had given them a great show of lies and that we were good actors.

"I felt like jumping out of the plane. My brother and sister begged me not to, because they said I would be shot if I tried. I didn't jump out because there were no windows.

"Finally, we went back to El Salvador and nothing happened to us there. We went back to our hometown and many of the people who we had known since childhood were no longer there. Some had 'disappeared,' some had been killed. One of my relatives had been killed by the death squads while working. One of my uncles had been threatened and had been taken to the police to be tortured, but because he had a connection he was released.

"We put enough money together and we decided to leave El Salvador again. This time we made it because we crossed with a smuggler. My brother paid him $3,500. That's how we came to the United States."

LEGAL OR ILLEGAL: AN IMPORTANT QUESTION?

Many of the parallels between the original underground railroad and its modern version are inspirational. Inherent within both movements, however, are contradictions: stories of betrayal and of the naivety of "conductors." In doing research for his article on the underground railroad, historian Charles Blackson, whose great-grandfather escaped to Canada on the underground railroad, discovered that "spies of both races abounded, ready to sell out escaped slaves." The full scope of infiltration of the current "railroad" will be discovered only in the future. Even now, however, a problem for border assistance centers is the presence of "refugee plants." "Plants" are offered deals by INS border agents for information on other refugees and North Americans aiding them.

Conductor Naivety

Many abolitionist conductors believed that freedom and justice would cascade down like water if whites would courageously stand on the side of the poor and oppressed on the issue of slavery. They believed the abolition of slavery would bring about black liberation and overcome white supremacy. Arguments among abolitionists erupted over the strategies and tactics necessary to accomplish abolition and liberation. For instance, Francis Wayland in the *Elements of Moral Science* argued that "slavery could be peacefully eradicated only by changing the mind of both master and slave, by teaching the one party the love of justice and the fear of God and by elevating the other to the proper level of individual responsibility."[141] But, such an argument, by calling for gradualism, supported the slave-owning class. William Lloyd Garrison was feared by the south because he demanded abolition immediately. On the issue of abolition of slavery, he said:

> I will be harsh as truth, and as uncompromising as justice. On this subject I do not wish to think, to speak, to write, with moderation. . . . I am in earnest—I will not retreat a single inch—AND I WILL BE HEARD.[142]

Both abolitionist tendencies, however, focused primarily on the moral necessity of ending slavery. Historian Vincent Harding, in his account of black history, *There Is a River*, claims that the white abolitionists did not understand that although slavery had ended in the north, the undergirding forces of "white supremacy, economic exploitation, and fear were firmly in place, offering troubling intimidation of the future of an American society in which all legal slavery would eventually be destroyed" (p. 119). The white abolitionists did not understand the political and economic structures that would carry systemic white control into the next century, spawning by the 1960s such dashed hopes that a black nation would confront a white nation in the civil rights movement. Not long before Martin Luther King, Jr., was assassinated, he had begun to point to the fundamental structural inequities that kept blacks oppressed. Moreover, he had linked the oppression of blacks and an international extension of racial/economic exploitation of Third World peoples in his opposition to the Vietnam war.

According to historian Howard Zinn:

> Slavery itself was ended not because of an upsurge of moral resentment in the North, or an insistence on the principle of freedom by the federal

government. It was ended because the political and economic interests of the slaveholders clashed with the Northern politicians and business interests to the point of war. Expediency, flavored with morality, brought emancipation, and only after prolonged, unrelenting pressure on Lincoln by abolitionists.[143]

As the abolition movement grew, conflicting positions within it intensified, leading, as in the case of William Jay, to a deeper understanding of the roots of the slavery question. Jay, who was head of the New York Anti-Slavery Society, resigned his position. He had begun to see the struggle to abolish slavery as demanding a deeper and more precise understanding of the causes of black oppression.

> We commenced the present struggle to obtain the freedom of the slaves. . . . We are now contending not so much with the slave holder of the south about human rights as with the political and commercial aristocracy of the north. . . . Politicians are selling our Constitution and laws for southern votes. Our great capitalists are speculating, not merely in lands and banks, but in the liberties of the people. We are called to contemplate [something] never, I believe, before witnessed—the wealthy portion of the country striving to introduce anarchy and violence in a calculation of profit.[144]

Within the black abolitionist movement splits also occurred. Most black abolitionists, distrusting the writers of the Constitution and noting their own disenfranchisement in that document, believed the Constitution virtually upheld slavery. Frederick Douglass, the black abolitionist and statesman, however, believed the Constitution was not meant to protect slavery, but that slavery was an aberrant system of lawless violence. Again, historian Vincent Harding interprets the Douglass position as a tactical move but one that was unrealistic, given attempted federal legal attacks against black abolitionist vigilance committees. According to Harding:

> Douglass, who tended at times to back away from the grim political realities, seemed to suggest that black men and women could oppose slavery and the Fugitive Slave Law without really challenging the federal government and the power of the American state. . . . Douglass tended dangerously to dissociate the institution of slavery from its roots in the racist, exploitative American society. Such a point of view could well leave him unprepared for the time when the institution might be destroyed without the roots having been seriously affected.[145]

Similarly, within the sanctuary movement a split developed over the goals of the movement. Would opposition to U.S. intervention in Central America be too polemical a goal? While this debate continued among white middle-class sanctuary leaders, the refugee community continued to beg for the solidarity of the North American community, asking in particular that North Americans act to stop U.S. government involvement in Central America. Like black abolitionists who understood that the roots of the problem of racism were systemic, Central American refugees argued that North Americans should uproot the continued cause of their exodus.

Antonio, a refugee in sanctuary in Madison, Wisconsin, said:

> The direction of the sanctuary movement should be to know more the direction of our people and advance more the protest against the American government, to form small groups to conscientize the American people, to take to the streets in demonstrations, to speak out publicly.

Another refugee, Francisco, in sanctuary in Washington, D.C., said:

> I believe that sanctuary should help from the point of view of humanitarianism, but also carry out the respect for human rights and the problem of intervention in Central America, and take a position before those facts. . . . Solidarity is something real and concrete that must be felt and touched. Already our people receive so much moral solidarity of words and pamphlets. What is necessary is action and material aid.

The refugee insistence that the sanctuary movement declare its opposition to U.S. intervention in Central America was made even clearer during a Presbyterian conference on sanctuary when the refugees in attendance formed their own work group and declared to the conference that stopping U.S. intervention should be the primary goal of the movement. As Linda, a Salvadoran refugee in sanctuary in Philadelphia, said, "We want to go back home. We want El Salvador and Guatemala to be sanctuaries."

Different Views, Different Conditions

Within the sanctuary movement, different stages of discernment have led to different strategies or goals in a particular community or region. At other times differences were the result of geographic dissimilarities. For instance, groups in border states have emphasized the need for direct services, as well as evasion services. In southern Texas refugees have drowned in rivers and died in train accidents. In Arizona and California many have died in the desert. As Sr. Darlene Nicgorski reports, "I've found Guatemalan families huddled in desert areas of Arizona without protection and with babies dying of malnutrition and malaria." The vast majority of refugees will not enter public sanctuaries, either because they are too traumatized or because they seek anonymity in order to protect others back home. Border refugee assistance groups are doing advocacy work for thousands. Only a few hundred of them travel the underground railroad to public sanctuary.

In the spring of 1984 the Tucson group called a meeting to deal with different strategies emerging within the sanctuary movement, occasioned by the arrest of refugee assistance workers. One of the fundamental arguments put forth by Dan Sheehan, Stacey Merkt's lawyer, was that Stacey had violated no law but was in full accord with the U.S. Refugee Act of 1980. Accordingly, many sectors of the sanctuary movement, particularly Tucson, insisted that sanctuary workers appropriate this new legal understanding of themselves and their movement. Such a position changes the original articulation of sanctuary as involving a willingness to break the law of the land. Other segments of the movement argued against characterizing the stance of the movement simply as law-abiding. They agreed that what the underground railroad and the sanctuaries are doing is indeed legal, in accord with the Refugee Act of 1980, but inasmuch as the Reagan administration was falsely interpreting that act, and inasmuch as the administration represented the power of the state, offering sanctuary amounted to breaking the law, or at least acting against the "official" (although illegal and immoral) interpretation of the law. A compromise of sorts was reached: sanctuary participants could define their work as law-abiding (whereas the U.S. government was in violation of the law) *and* warn new participants, especially as regards railroad conducting, that their participation would involve defiance of government interpretation of refugee law. In other words, new sanctuary workers needed to be told: you are not breaking the law, but you could get up to fifteen years in prison!

Even on this issue there are some vague parallels with the abolitionist era and the original underground railroad. For instance, was it important for abolitionists to argue that their aid to escaping slaves was legal? The Fugitive Slave Law was unconstitutional; it was later repealed by Congress. Nevertheless, any abolitionist aiding or abetting a runaway was subject to prosecution. Government use of law, even good law, to serve the interests of specific groups is not resorted to only by a very conservative government, such as the Reagan administration. A fundamental issue then, as now, is the moral right of the religious community to break civil law in fidelity to a higher law.

On the day that John Brown was hanged for his leadership in the Harpers Ferry rebellion, Thoreau gave a public address, "A Plea for Captain John Brown," in which he posed five questions that defined the problematics of this dilemma:

> Is it not possible that an individual may be right and a government wrong? Are laws to be enforced simply because they are made? Or declared by any number of men to be good, if they are not good? Is there any necessity for a person's being a tool to perform a deed of which his better nature disapproves? Is it the intention of lawmakers that good people should be hung forever?[146]

Critiquing White Abolitionist Zeal, Critiquing Ourselves

Though splits existed within the white abolitionist movement, different overall ideas inspired both abolitionists and sanctuary workers. For the white abolitionist the existence of slavery was a moral transgression of such magnitude that the very soul of America was in jeopardy over its continuation. Many white abolitionists would endure imprisonment and in some cases death in their effort to signal the moral intention of some whites to stand against the violation of human dignity that slavery represented. Similarly, North Americans horrified by INS deportation policy are willing to go to jail to confront it. The challenge to both positions comes, as always, from those at the bottom of the social pyramid, those directly affected by that policy and aided by solidarity undertakings. Vincent Harding reflects on the motivating ideals of the white abolitionists:

> No one could deny the personal courage and self-sacrifice of such [white abolitionist] men as these, and the women who worked by their side. Relentlessly, often at the cost of fortunes, families and friends, they crisscrossed the nation lecturing, preaching and agitating the anti-slavery cause, facing white mobs that were sometimes murderous. But by the same token, no one among them would have doubted that their movement and its national and state organizations were meant to be white, under essential white control, and for the healing of a white-defined nation. . . . To a large degree, most white abolitionists saw slavery as a dishonor to their vision of the real America—the democratic, divinely-led, essentially just America. For almost all of them, slavery was a sin against God, an obstacle in the way of His kingdom's establishment in an otherwise fair land.[147]

What the white abolitionist movement did not see was that America was, essentially, a slave society. So, too, sanctuary members are struggling even now with respect to U.S. foreign-policy decisions—not as occasionally resulting in moral compromises, but as consistent policy decisions with no other goal than North American self-interest.

Moral preoccupation with the healing of the sinful white nation is a danger to which white abolitionists succumbed and with which the sanctuary movement is struggling. The conversion of the Anglo church and religious community cannot supercede the concrete moral/solidarity claims of the peoples of Central America. Thus, although true conversion takes place in the encounter between the refugee and the congregation, thinking of that encounter event as the *only* sacramental moment of such religious work fails to uphold the holiness of actions that flow from such an encounter. These "next-step" solidarity actions involve the terrain of political advocacy and the mundane sphere of nitty-gritty organizing. These spheres have to be acknowledged by the movement as aspects of building the kingdom. The sanctuary movement must more and more widen an understanding of religious work from narrowing confines to understand building a resistance movement as a religious task. This transformation involves an ever deepening conversion process.

Such a commitment will save religious persons from preoccupation with *their* religious conversion, so that their actions will be less witness *to* and more advocacy *for* a struggling people. Thus the goals of self-determination that Guatemalan and Salvadoran refugees uphold would become goals that inform the sanctuary movement. In other words, the sanctuary movement would be *accountable* to the refugees as representatives of a people on the move, struggling for human freedom. Without this accountability the sanctuary movement is in danger of setting its own moral agendas, accountable to its own reading of the Gospels and Torah, and subject to the same historical errors that white abolitionists made.

Accountability to the poor of Central America shifts the sanctuary agenda from the accountability of a specific congregation to a specific refugee, to accountability to a national movement for a people's struggle for liberation. Without such a criterion for direction, the sanctuary movement remains a confused expression of moral values. The spiritual impetus of such a movement, although religiously and aesthetically attractive, fails to connect with the aspirations of *el pueblo* whose agenda is more demanding than ours. The struggle of Central Americans, like the struggle of black abolitionists, is a struggle at the depths of history, a struggle for hope and life itself. Vincent Harding notes the difference in the black abolitionist struggle and the white abolitionist struggle:

> The struggle in which the black abolitionists were involved was at once more personal and more profound. They were fighting against slavery but also, and more importantly, *for* the enslaved people. . . . The freedom, dignity and self-determination of black people was central to the struggle. Even when they were most confident about the coming of a society of justice and brotherhood in America, these black abolitionists knew . . . the transformed society would have to be hewn out of the American experience as a new creation extending in depth and meaning beyond anything that white men and women—or blacks—had ever known before.[148]

To remain morally and politically accountable to the struggling poor of Central America grounds the North American faith response in the depth of history, which reveals God's presence. Such accountability should proceed from the critical reflection of the religious community, in the light of Torah, illuminated by a gospel addressed to the least of history. It should entail a dialogical process between sanctuary workers and Central Americans.

The need is not for either group to control goals or direction of the movement but for collaboration and mutual accountability. Should not the first act of trust and confidence come from those who have had access to power? North American congregations and leaders need to make their faith option concrete. They need to seek the collaboration of Central American refugees at the decision-making level, otherwise such an option remains abstract. Antonio (in sanctuary in Madison, Wisconsin) has said, "We must play a role in the direction of the sanctuary movement because we are an essential part of sanctuary and we must give a message to the American people and so work together." Francisco, in sanctuary in New Jersey, considered refugee involvement at the decision-making level "an urgent necessity":

> The refugees should have the right to a voice and a vote in the decisions of the sanctuary movement. To guarantee this it is necessary that representation exists in finding direction of the movement. We are the active part of the work of denouncing through our testimony.
>
> I will mention some of the impediments that don't permit the refugees to be listened to:
> (a) we don't possess legal status;
> (b) we don't know English well;
> (c) too much outspokenness shown by some refugees at raising the problems of our country;
> (d) the narrowness that exists in some sanctuary churches believing that refugees only should limit themselves to their own testimony.

Some refugees have criticized sanctuary organizers locally and nationally for not using them enough. "I have not come to your country to sit on my hands," said a Guatemalan refugee in sanctuary in Dayton, Ohio. "My criticism of the sanctuary organizers is that they have not given enough direction to the local church communities, have not challenged those communities to organize more opportunities for us refugees to speak. I want to speak more and more."

Without a collaborative and mutually accountable decision-making process, the sanctuary movement could repeat the errors of white abolitionists who wanted to be savior-advocates for blacks but who did not see themselves as accountable to blacks:

> Since many white abolitionists assumed that they were to be the saviors of the American society and its black underclass, they often treated their black co-workers with patronizing disdain at worst (or was awestruck idolatry the worst?) or at best as almost equal but clearly subservient allies of their white-defined cause.[149]

As refugees in sanctuary recovered from an overwhelming sense of thankfulness for being safe, they became more honest about how they felt about treatment from the host congregations. At a Presbyterian-sponsored conference on sanctuary, a refugee in sanctuary in Minnesota said, "We don't want you to treat us like we were your pets." Two others from upper New York state wrote to sanctuary organizers that "the great majority of the members of the church still maintained their racism." In their case, the refugees were never consulted about upcoming plans and the congregation went so far as to tell them when they could take a shower.

Much of the refugees' frustration at not being involved at a decision-making level nationally was due to the fact that the sanctuary movement had no organizational process for decision-making. At the 1985 national sanctuary convocation held in Tucson, after the arrests of forty-nine refugees and sixteen North Americans, a regionally-based representative structure was created. It involved representatives from North American sanctuary communities and refugee representatives. That national meeting provided the Central American sanctuary refugees a first national opportunity to meet with each other and raise their concerns. One of the most emphatic presentations to the national sanctuary assembly was the plea of the refugees to North Americans to continue their resistance to U.S. policy in Central America. Unfortunately, many refugees from the midwest and east coast were unable to attend for fear the INS would arrest them en route.

By 1985, chastened by the seriousness of government attacks on the movement, with leaders being driven away from margins of safety and closer to the vulnerable, hunted positions of defenseless refugees, the sanctuary movement embraced refugee input. The movement was deepening, moving closer to refugees, not simply as conscienticizers, but as *compañeros* in a joint struggle.

Before offering a final comparative analysis between the abolitionist movement and leaders, and the sanctuary movement and leaders, it is important to acknowledge a limitation. Although there are parallels that have struck us in researching the abolitionist era, we offer this framework tentatively, recognizing that different historical conditions, national interests, and liberation struggles do not allow perfect comparisons. Our intent is to put forth an analysis that might challenge the sanctuary movement to deepen its self-understanding and open the horizons of its solidarity practice.

EXTREMISM?

Within the white abolitionist cause there were leaders who were considered extremists. William Lloyd Garrison, Wendell Phillips, and John Brown are considered fanatical extremists by most modern historians. The dilemma for many abolitionists was to remain activists *and* legitimate their position by distancing themselves from extreme abolitionist positions.

Garrison, for instance, went so far as to burn a copy of the Constitution before thousands, calling it "source and parent of all other atrocities." Wendell Phillips considered the pietistic silence of the American church in the face of slavery, collusion with the demonic.

Historian Zinn questions the charges of extremism:

Did they help or hurt the cause of freedom? Did their activities bring a solution at too great a cost? The real question is: Can moderation ever be an effective tactic for sweeping reform? It is often thought the agitator alienates potential allies by his extremism. Lewis Tappan, the wealthy New Yorker who financed many abolition activities, wrote anxiously to

George Thompson, the British abolitionist. "The fact need not be concealed from you that several emancipationists so disapprove of the harsh and as they think, the unchristian language of the *Liberator* [Garrison's journal], that they don't feel justified in upholding it." The American Anti-Slavery Society . . . was [similarly] concerned lest others be alienated.[150]

There is some parallel between differences within the sanctuary movement and accusations of extremism leveled at abolitionists like Garrison who demanded abolition of slavery immediately, not gradually. It is true that the government has not been successful in labeling the sanctuary movement "extremist," because of its broad grass-roots church base and the evident desperation of refugees. However, the sanctuary movement itself must still grapple with its fear of the label. On the one hand, the movement must not become isolated, cut off from its base in the religious community. On the other hand, government pressure through arrest and infiltration seeks to compromise the movement, demanding it legitimate itself against charges of extremism. Such pressure can result in confused or compromised tactics. For example, the tactical argument that resists stating a political goal such as stopping U.S. intervention because not all the churches and synagogues are conscienticized, sets the conversion of the North American religious community as a priority over the liberation cause of Central America. Salvadoran Marta Benavides, an ordained Baptist minister, has said, "Our people can't wait for your religious community to be converted. We are dying. We are at war. And whether you acknowledge it or not, you too are at war and must choose sides."

Rev. Benavides has voiced the urgent claim of Salvadoran refugees that the North American church unequivocally choose sides. After the indictments of the sixteen, Marta Benavides exhorted the national sanctuary convocation to "not be afraid. Each one of us is political. Even when we choose to be neutral we are being political." The tactical arguments of some sanctuary leaders, that the goals of stopping U.S. intervention will alienate some congregations newly considering sanctuary if it is publicly stated, fails to acknowledge that *not* stating such a goal will alienate Central American refugees. The sanctuary movement must declare itself and accept the consequence of alienating some persons.

The strength of the sanctuary movement is its popular grass-roots religious appeal and its capacity for conversion. When the *Wall Street Journal* published a long article on sanctuary and mentioned its fervent support by Bill Clarke, a wealthy conservative Republican from Ohio who felt called by the God of the poor and suffering to risk arrest, many were convinced the movement had "arrived" as strong, broad-based, and, by virtue of its political pluralism, less vulnerable to accusations of extremism. But the dilemma of choosing sides, as a political-faith option, de facto leads to accusations of extremism simply because unequivocal choices will alienate some religious persons. Archbishop

Romero said, "In a society that is divided, it is likely that the church will be divided too."

The North American church is already divided. To mitigate the determination of religious persons to openly state opposition to U.S. policy in Central America, even for tactical reasons of broadening and diversifying and building popular support, is to risk diluting the force of that position and to allow "liberal" elements the opportunity to "reconcile" the "extremists" and the more moderate/reasonable tendencies. The result of such reconciliation within the churches is compromise and a divided movement limping its way toward confusion or retreat.

The Churches and Abolition

During abolitionist times churches made unequivocal denunciations of slavery and recommended that all Christians work to abolish slavery. But the clamor of the southern clergy with its political strategy to gain greater control of national assemblies resulted in equivocated and morally compromised moderate positions by the mid-1800s. The General Assembly of the Presbyterian Church had, for instance, vehemently condemned slavery in 1818, but by the mid-1800s the northern and southern Presbyterian Church was divided. The head of the southern branch, Dr. Thornwell, linked abolitionism to atheism and communism. He clarified the sides to be chosen:

> The parties in this conflict are not merely abolitionists and slave holders—they are atheists, socialists, communists, red Republicans, Jacobins on the one side and the friends of order, regulated freedom on the other. In one word, the world is a battleground, Christianity and atheism. The combatants and the progress of humanity is at stake.[151]

The tendency to brand radical faith positions within the religious sector as communistic or nonreligious is prevalent even within the sanctuary movement, and not only as an outside accusation (the State Departement has accused sanctuary leaders of being simply political organizers) but as a fear within the sanctuary movement that religious persons would become political activists.

Similar to the Presbyterian initially strong proabolitionist position, the Methodists also were strongly opposed to slavery at first. But at a general conference in 1836, southern Methodists won their proslavery argument and circulated a pastoral letter advising the clergy to abstain from discussion of slavery and chastising proabolitionist northern ministers and underground railroad conductors. The split in the Methodist Church resulted in the organization of the Methodist Episcopal Church South. In 1845 a similar split over the issue of slavery took place within the Baptist Church, resulting in separate organizations for both home and foreign missions.

In his *The Negro People in American History*, William Foster claims that:

The Catholic Church remained intact [undivided] all through the civil war, a militant pro-slavery organization. . . . Some of the upper class Jews were not to be outdone by their Christian brethren when it came to profiting from slavery.[152]

Such political ruptures within the churches of the abolitionist era reveal the institutional churches as a reflection of the classist and racist divisions of society at large. Choosing the side of the oppressed and poor will lead to a confrontation with the government and with those who identify their economic and political interests with the powerful and controlling sector. Such an assessment appears simplistic, immoderate, and unnecessarily (tactically) polemical to many within the religious sector. But why? Howard Zinn's historical analysis of North American society offers a clue to these fissures within church bodies. Zinn claims that charges of immoderation and extremism are charges raised by the liberal position against both conservative and radical positions. According to Zinn what has been left out of historical analysis of the history of abolitionism was American liberalism as collaborator, by acquiescence or default, with American racism.

American Liberalism vs. Biblical Justice

American liberalism was most idealistically expressed in the American Revolution and its principles in the Declaration of Independence. North Americans who fought a revolutionary war against imperialistic Britain in order to establish the right to national self-determination would, within the same century, uphold a principle of national expansion that would suppress the rights of others to self-determination. Arthur Weinburg, in his study *Manifest Destiny*, states that "America's natural right to territory essential to its security must override the right of self-determination of its inhabitants." After the revolution, American leaders, full of idealistic zeal for principles of liberty ensured by democratic liberalism, were determined to teach these ideals to savage or enslaved nations. This national mission was our "manifest destiny" ordained by Providence.

Expansion was so rationalized that it seemed at the outset a right, and soon, long before the famous phrase itself was coined, a manifest destiny. Moral ideology was the partner of self-interest. . . . The alchemy which transmuted natural right from a doctrine of democratic nationalism into a doctrine of imperialism was the very idea of manifest destiny which the doctrine of natural right created.[153]

This moral and political ideology justified the conquest and appropriation of native American Indian lands, Hawaii, the Philippines, Puerto Rico, and half of Mexico. It justified forming a protectorate over Cuba. It justified Marine invasions in Haiti, the Dominican Republic, Nicaragua, and Panama.

Democratic liberalism in practice contains certain contradictions codified in national law—for example, the U.S Constitution, which guarantees the rights of all men, though initially denying basic human rights to women, native American Indians, the propertyless, and blacks. Liberal democracy is compatible with moral righteousness and a gospel upholding the dignity and rights of all, even those most disenfranchised. The problem is the liberal willingness to compromise principles for tactical or strategic goals. Gradualism, for instance, has been the tactical and strategic position of white liberalism on issues of human rights for others, from the abolition of slavery to the affirmation of women's rights.

Modern liberals hold to three basic assumptions, in a more sophisticated fashion than our forefathers who saw our nation as the godly savior of backward heathen nations.

1) Liberals believe there is a middle ground in national and international power conflicts. This assumption is attractive to religious persons who truly desire peace and who see disruptive conflict as antithetical to the ideal of a loving community of brothers and sisters. The assumption is that legitimate neutrality is possible.

2) Liberals blame victims for "excesses" in their response to repression. Religious liberals do not blame victims for resistance to repression, but they criticize them for responses that seem too violent, too abrasive. They want victims to find a loving (middle-ground) response.

3) Liberals distrust the masses. For liberal religious persons there is genuine love for the poor and oppressed, but a fear that they need experts who can give them theological or political directioning. White male clericalism is given disproportionate authority and power.

For liberals within the sanctuary movement there has been a willingness to acknowledge conflict and even a willingness to choose sides by harboring refugees and risking arrest. But the extent of this solidarity is an individual prophetic witness (either personally or with an individual congregation). Solidarity becomes an individual faith choice and a willingness to pay the price of the choice of such faithfulness. But this position stops short of confronting the role of the U.S. government openly, or, more importantly, of building a movement capable of stopping U.S. intervention. It also fails to adhere to a revolutionary faith that demands lifelong resistance to U.S. structural oppression domestically and internationally. Such a religious task appears to the liberal as a political option that, by virtue of its radical stance, has lost its rootedness in religious tradition.

It is not so much a failure of heart that is the liberal characteristic; it is a failure of imagination and historical analysis. The faith stance of the liberal stops short. Central Americans, unencumbered by the U.S historical liberal tradition (enmeshed rather by feudalism within the grip of neocolonialism) understand the wider context of their historical struggle. Now, as in abolitionist times, oppressed national racial groups (in particular, blacks) recognize that humanitarian assistance that does not struggle against the roots of oppression will not lead to liberation, though it might raise hopes for a time.

The sanctuary movement is primarily based among white middle-class churches and synagogues whose most progressive expression is liberal. Conversion to the side of the refugees, the prophets from a martyred church, is a faith conversion that demands a critique or realignment of one's political stance. Only naivety would fail to discern that a conservative government, such as the Reagan administration, would be alienated from a church that challenged the status quo and opted for the side of the poor and oppressed in Central America and for refugees in our midst. What is less clear, however, is how far should such identification with *el pueblo* go before charges of extremism emerge from all sides, even from friends? Dare we risk alienating too many?

Once the journey of conversion has begun, there is no criterion for deciding the next step except faithfulness to the God of Judaism and Christianity, who is the God of all humankind, calling us to solidarity with the least. According to theologian Robert McAfee Brown, such a choice is a subversive act:

> So here is the point at which a significant identity crisis will continue to confront white middle-class Americans: do they find their true identity in terms of nation, race and class, or in terms of their larger identity which their religious community offers them? . . . How revolutionary are middle-class people really going to be? . . . My own feeling then is that if white middle-class churches are going to do no more than reflect (in pale fashion) the values of the culture around them, they do not really deserve to survive; that they are going to have to look long and hard at where their allegiances lie, and then make some basic choices in the near future. The choices, if properly made, will place the churches in jeopardy, for they will involve tremendous risks with no assurances of success.[154]

Brown goes on to note that such options on behalf of the oppressed will not increase church membership but may indeed drive away many who feel they share the name of Christian. Some may even turn violently against such a church but at least "they will no longer do what they presently do—ignore it."[155]

What the sanctuary movement has offered the Anglo church is an opportunity to live a radical faith by sharing in the risk that such commitment demands. But the risk is precisely a faith risk and a political risk—a risk necessary because of political power that is unjust. If the analysis of the roots of structural oppression is shallow, the response of the sanctuary movement will be shallow. If the faith stance, informed by a precise analysis of the roots of structural oppression, is deep, then a truly revolutionary faith will be born.

A final but noteworthy fear that liberals harbor is that their faith motives, construed as too political (meaning, aligned with Central Americans involved in liberation struggles), will lead to accusations of communism. Such a fear leads to tactical decisions to distance themselves from social elements, other solidarity groups, politicized refugees, and the like, who might "taint" the individual or group. Religious liberals, unlike conservatives, may not be personally afraid of such "red-baiting," but they decide tactically to *legitimate* themselves as religious, before governmental or institutional pressure is brought against the movement. When this tendency emerged within the sanctuary movement in 1984, Rev. Gil Dawes, a sanctuary pastor from Iowa, faced it head on:

> "Ain't nobody here but us religious folks, boss!" This is the kind of self-defensive cry that delights the IRD [Institute for Religion and Democracy] and other right-wing forces. Their goal has long been to drive a wedge between liberals and the left, and between religion and the left. If they can intimidate liberals into silence, or at least get them to separate themselves from those further left, and at the same time monopolize the public use of religious myths and symbols, then the left will be isolated from the body politic, and the right will control the body politic.
>
> If the sanctuary movement goes down the path of separating within itself those of "religious" orientation from those of secular, or "intentional" motivation, it will have done the work of the oppressor for him. Those whose policies cause the oppressed to seek refuge in the first place must divide the opposition before they can conquer. If we think they will stop once they have destroyed secular resistance and honor the "religious" conscience of those who resist "in faith," then we will naively do their divisive work for them.
>
> To say in any manner, "Ain't nobody here but us religious folks, boss," is not only bad political strategy, but also bad theology. It is to cut the left hand of God off from the right hand of God! It is to say that unless you use traditional religious language and follow established religious style, you are not doing the "work" of God in human history. It is to divide not just the sanctuary movement and other movements for justice and peace, but the Body of Christ itself. As Jesus observed under similar circumstances of conflict, his followers are not necessarily those who say "Lord, Lord," but those who do the will of God on earth. They are not to be known primarily by what they say they believe in, nor even by whom they believe in, but by what they do. In a broader sense, to break solidarity with those whose deeds meet human needs, though stemming from different motivational presuppositions, is to theologically break the unity of God's new creation in formation.[156]

Charity or Liberation?

Before the national sanctuary convocation was held (and historically marked by the multiple arrests), the themes of biblical justice/American liberalism were being debated. Though local groups would use other language to name the different categories, the movement was struggling to define itself and its motives, to validate itself as religious. Members of the movement were intuitively (and at the border, consciously) anticipating the next move of the government. The thematic differences that had emerged prior to 1985 might be characterized as charity or liberation, Matthew 25 or Exodus. With the arrests, the movement eliminated the *or* and substituted *and*. Persecution levels, clarifies, and deepens. The government helped the movement to synthesize, to develop a wholistic political and theological understanding of itself, its purposes.

Addressing the desire for legitimacy, and the debate over the labels "political" or "religious," Sr. Darlene Nicgorski wrote this statement for *¡Basta!*, a sanctuary newsletter of the Chicago Religious Task Force, which went to print just before the indictments:

> We cannot "legitimate" our involvement with refugees—it is impossible. As we begin to walk with them, some of the marginalization, oppression, and repression will come to us. . . . The message of the prophets from the South is often hard for us to hear—we who love so much and live in a sense of righteousness and with the illusion of power and control. The spirit is moving in the church, but it is now a movement from the South to the North. Again it comes in forms hard to recognize—another language, culture, experience. It is all changed—what appears to be religion is politics, what appears to be political is faith lived in the public forum. Sanctuary is one of the clearest ways the North American church has to identify with the spirit, life, and the future. In solidarity with those struggling, we are asked to risk the traditional concept of church—peace and neutrality. Do we know where this leads? Do we trust that this is not just another North American white, middle-class, male, clerical, paternalistic program of compassion trying to seek approval of the institution or is it something we do in solidarity with the church of the South—with the thousands suffering in the camps in southern Mexico, in the church camps in San Salvador, or with those hiding in the mountains of Guatemala? The refugees in public sanctuary are following the saints of Latin America—they are the voice of the voiceless. Can we love them, join in their struggle? Love cannot stand back [Jan. 1985].

The leadership had to answer some fundamental questions as leaders faced the courts of Caesar. It took little speculation to surmise that government arrests would continue. The government would expand the witch-hunts by charging many within the movement with conspiracy. Or the government would call up special federal grand juries to take on the movement nationally in a final bid to disrupt it. Since most sanctuary workers would refuse to cooperate with a grand jury probe, they would be jailed and thus "out of the way" for some time.

In any of these scenarios the assumption was that more legal arguments lay ahead. As the movement affirmed its legal right and moral duty to continue to be a covenant people, acting in solidarity with the poor and oppressed, how would its members define themselves as religious persons? Surely their lives and deeds would speak louder than their words. But unless they interpreted what "religious" meant, they would allow government lawyers to set a legal interpretation of it. And that definition would be as narrow as the eye of a needle. The intention of the government would be to prove they were not religious, but only political—"political" meaning that they intended to criticize the foreign policy that is at the source of the refugee exodus. Thus, government witch-hunts would "burn" those who had the least evident claim to presence in the religious sphere—namely, (1) those who were not professional religious (clerics); (2) those not directly affiliated with a church; (3) those less able to articulate biblical exegesis; (4) those who were not "practicing" members of a church or synagogue; (5) members of solidarity groups who identify with persons of spiritual values.

Would all who struggle for justice and peace in Central America, those who have identified with the sanctuary and refugee assistance movement, fall under the religious rubric or only those who "talk the talk"? Would they be judged religious persons by affiliation, creed, dogma, or by their actions? Latin American theologian Hugo Assman suggests that the unique contribution of Christians to the struggle for justice lies only in prophetic stance and actions:

> Confessional fidelities don't have in themselves a prophetic significance. All professional and ecclesiological internal criteria for an improvement, a historical improvement of Christian charity in the world, are not sufficient for prophecy.[157]

Nicaraguan theologian Juan Hernández Pico states that those who are faithful to the God of history may be those whose motivating convictions stand outside religious categories:

> [In the revolutionary process] seeing people die for others, and not hearing any talk from them about faith in God being the motivating factor, liberates Christians from the prejudice of trying to encounter true love solely and exclusively within the boundaries of faith. It also helps to free them from the temptation of not considering a revolutionary process authentic unless it bears the label "Christian."[158]

Responding to these concerns at the convocation, Mary Ann Corley of the Chicago Religious Task Force and the American Friends Service Committee said:

> The selected religious themes which are emphasized in our legal and political struggles will also instruct the depth and breadth of our religious imagination and practice. The themes of the Central American church are liberation, Exodus themes, the themes of the North American church are charity. Liberation without charity is only a power struggle. Charity without liberation is only self-serving pietism. But when charity is truly

effective it acts to stop the deprivation of charity, entering a struggle for liberation.

When we quote Matthew 25 claiming before courts our moral duty to feed the hungry, clothe the naked, and shelter the homeless, will we risk challenging the root causes of people's hunger, nakedness, and homelessness? Will we name that cause (for example, U.S. foreign policy) and act to change it even if in so doing we do not fit the government's definition of religious? If not, our "charity" will remain unbiblical, ahistorical pietism aimed at ministering to timeless refugees who are without concrete historical, political, moral claims on our lives.

The Conference of Major Superiors of Men, USA, gathered in National Assembly, acknowledges and endorses the work of the Sanctuary Movement in our country on behalf of Salvadoran and Guatemalan political refugees. We applaud and encourage especially the 150 churches and synagogues which have opened their doors as havens for these strangers and pilgrims among us. We pledge our support for the Sanctuary Movement.

(Catholic) Conference of Major Superiors of Men
August 1984

7

BREAKING INTO HISTORY WITH SOLIDARITY AND REVOLUTIONARY HOPE

Because at each nightfall
though exhausted from the endless inventory
of killings since 1954
yet we continue to love life.
What keeps us from sleeping
is that we have been threatened with
Resurrection.

> *Julia Esquivel*

Our people will never lie down. If they shoot us, our children will
stand. Our struggle is invincible. History has taught us revolutionary patience. Our enemies have only hunger for personal gain—we
hunger for life.

> *Secundino Ramírez*
> *Salvadoran Human Rights Commission*
> *Coordinator*

Photos by Marc PoKempner

Don Jesús and Abuelita

WITNESS: ABUELITA AND DON JESÚS

(Abuelita and Don Jesús are Salvadoran refugees
who have been in hiding in Chicago.)

Abuelita's once red hair has turned light gold, and her eyes are cloudless even at seventy-seven. Her real name is Angela but the Salvadorans call her Abuelita, "little grandmother." Her light coloring is unusual for a Salvadoran. Sitting next to her is her brother, his hands grasping his knees stiffly, his grainy face a deeply carved block of ebony. Don Jesús's black eyes dart like clarinero *birds, following his sister's gestures.*

She begins the story hesitatingly, her voice looping upward then dropping into tones of sorrow. She plays her life's music muted, understated like a sad ranchera. *There is little crescendo even when she counts the number of her family killed by the Salvadoran military. "Thirty were killed and five disappeared," she says simply.*

Ashland Avenue traffic plays a counterpoint to the Spanish radio station blaring from a store below Abuelita's apartment. This space of her remembering is cramped, vacant. Her granddaughter's white teddy bear, pinned with a valentine heart, teeters on a ledge above the couch. A plant on the windowsill and some yellow plastic flowers relieve the room of despair. From the chilly street, a dull light swarms on the gray rug. There are no trees near Ashland and Division, which is five thousand miles from Abuelita's village of Suchitoto and its mango *and* cieba *trees, singing* tortolita *birds, and dawn spilling rivers of gold in the village shadows.*

Abuelita never leaves her apartment. It is not the weather, nor her lack of English, that inhibits her. It is la migra *(immigration officials), the possibility that the INS might deport her back to El Salvador. She fears* la migra *even though her intention is to go back to El Salvador before she dies.*

"On the radio I hear of opportunities for senior citizens but I know they are not for me. . . . Sometimes," she says, patting her couch, "I lie here most of the day thinking, remembering. It is lonely. Sometimes Zoila (she points to her teenage granddaughter, cooking in the kitchenette) looks in to see if I am still. . . ." She does not finish. Then she smiles, shrugging.

The smile turns into a chuckle as she picks comical memories from her long years. "I came to this country on inner tubes," she says, shaking her head. "The 'coyotes' my daughter paid took us across the Río Bravo *(as Mexicans call the Rio Grande) floating on inner tubes pulled by ropes. We hid behind shrubs in the dark, afraid of the bark of dogs. Finally we made a run and made it."*

Angela was seventy-five years old when she made that run. She laughs now, recalling the careless, greedy "coyotes" who led her in, and then the conversation drifts to the elections in El Salvador. Abuelita is still amused. "I was in El Salvador during the 1982 elections. The armed forces said, 'If you do not vote, we know you are guerrillas.' Therefore, everyone voted. Even the dead came to the polls. For example, my brother who was in the States six years—he voted. The living and the dead voted in El Salvador."

She opens her photo album, a ritual familiar to those who know her, to intrude upon her memories, the silence of her two rooms. "This is my son, the mayor of Suchitoto." She points to a thin man surrounded by five children. She tolls each child's name.

"The soldiers took them from a car in the center of our village—my son, daughter-in-law, three of their children, and four friends. Their car was later found burned in the mountains."

I ask why, so obvious a question, so naive to Salvadorans.

"Reasons do not matter," she says. "They started picking up the priests first, then professors, then students, finally all of our young people were considered subversives. My son Miguel was one of the first because as mayor he protested the beating and jailing of the priest, Padre Palacios."

Miguel was the father of Abuelita's granddaughter Zoila, who fled the country and came to Chicago, as Abuelita did, as Don Jesús did, all separately. Next to die was Abuelita's brother Salvador, who had witnessed a shooting and brought the injured man to a hospital. The next day the guardia *burst into the tiny house and took him. "Two bullets," she says, the hands resting in her lap, exhausted or defeated. "Sixteen days later he was found in San Martín village. He was in bad condition." An understatement. Don Jesús clarifies: their brother Salvador was tortured before he was shot to death.*

As Abuelita speaks, her granddaughter Zoila passes through the room. Perhaps Zoila remains in the kitchen because the tiny room is overcrowded. Or it may be that she can't bear to hear the story again.

Abuelita begins the tales of the others but then gives the floor to Don Jesús. She sinks back on her small couch lost in her thoughts. She shrugs again. "So old, such memories. I'm happy when he comes." She touches Don Jesús's knee. "Then we laugh together."

Don Jesús doesn't laugh. He seems perpetually weary, his placid expression that of a farmer, a man of the land. He smiles rarely, furtively, soon regaining his stoic weariness. In the hollows above the bony cheeks, Don Jesús's eyes stare placidly. He seems half-present at the conversation, as if he were waiting for someone, something else. He seems surprised, sardonic, at being interviewed.

He begins matter-of-factly where his sister left off. But Don Jesús remembers it more fully, more purely.

"When I would leave my little village in a truck with watermelons, I went by other villages and I saw bodies in the street. By a river I saw vultures eating bodies left on the banks. Near La Bermuda there were twenty-eight bodies. I don't remember exactly, because I have seen so many. I saw dogs walking with people's arms in their jaws.

"It was the family of Don Alfonso Alas that they killed first. The only crime of Don Alfonso was that he went to church. Don Alfonso's wife was pregnant when the guardia came to their home, so we always say they murdered nine persons even though it was four adults and four children. Don Alfonso's other crime was that his wife was a catechista. My wife also was a catechista and taught the children in church. She was threatened with death. They said she was teaching communism in church. [After the threats] I sent her to the United States—not long after that people from my village began to disappear."

Don Jesús fingers some small snapshots of his son but does not show them yet. Behind him, perched on a chipped end table, sits a ceramic Spanish puppy, woeful and cuddly.

"Beyond the town strewn bodies were eaten by dogs. It was because we could not bury the corpses or be considered suspect."

He remained in El Salvador after his wife came to the United States. "Soon guerrillas came to my house and asked for weapons. I said I had none; the national guard of Guazapa took my pistol. The guerrillas searched my house anyway. The guerrilla in command asked me to check to see if anything in my house was missing. I told him it does not matter—I have nothing to lose. But he insisted, explaining the guerrillas should never take from the people."

Don Jesús becomes more animated, more openly proud of this encounter. He finishes, explaining that the guerrilla leaders warned him to hide whatever he might have because they expected the army to come to the village soon.

The guerrillas were right. Two weeks later, on Christmas Day, 1981, as full piñatas *awaited the squealing children's blows, the army came. As the soldiers encircled the town, the songs of* Navidad *broke off. The entire village was marched in stone silence to the soccer field and ordered to lie on the ground. "I remember the old women trying to lie down quickly." Before nightfall the army put everyone in a line and called out the men aged fifteen to twenty. The mothers watched as their sons were tied and thrown into trucks. They bit their hands, muffling cries.*

At 10 o'clock the next morning, another thirty men were selected. After the truck swung down the road toward Chalatenango, the villagers were released. Two days later they found most of the men assassinated near a local river. Later, when the children spotted army trucks approaching the village a third time, all the young males bolted, like startled deer, into the countryside. By then the soldiers were taking men of any age and gathering them into groups of thirty. Don Jesús was one of the last.

"But I must have been the thirty-first and the transport truck only fit thirty, so they released me. I was lucky."

He does not dwell on this act of fate, its meaning or irony. He is more enmeshed in his villagers' story, as if all were one, all the individual details of triumph or defeat part of the same violated tapestry.

Still shocked, he recalls the final violation. "The fifth time they came to town they went to our health clinic and took out some of the sick. I knew two of the young women they killed." By now Don Jesús had lost family and he had lost his small plot of land to the Government Land Reform Program. In order to install a hydroelectric plant, the officials had confiscated peasant properties. The "agrarian reform" novelty was that they offered payment. Don Jesús's farm was over twenty acres, with a barn, livestock, and a house—almost middle-class by Salvadoran standards. Engineers valued the property at $24,000 U.S. He was offered $2,000—almost the exact amount he owed city hall in property taxes. Don Jesús refused to take the money. "Keep it," he told the lawyer from city hall, "so that your robbery is complete." Nevertheless he accepted payment later. He needed the money to move to a government relocation village in Chalatenango named, ironically, El Dorado, "the gilded."

It was in El Dorado that the old man—landless, penniless, with family members scattered or dead—finally faced a hard decision. In order to live, he would have to leave the land he had worked for forty years and say goodbye to the campesinos *who greeted him as Don Jesús from Suchitoto. The incident that made up his mind was an encounter with a Salvadoran military commander in Chalatenango.*

"The commander asked me if I would become a member of a death squad. I said why? To kill subversives, he said. But the subversives are not killing the people, I said. Besides I am old. I want my hands clean, not stained with the blood of anyone.

"Then the commander accused me of being a subversive." Don Jesús throws up his hands, spreading the knotted fingers. " 'But commander,' I said, 'it is my belief that the subversives are those that kill the innocents.' "

Don Jesús made ready to leave. He had his cédula *(ID) altered and began his journey. On the way to San Salvador he froze when his bus was stopped by police at the first checkpoint. He suspected his name was on their list, and he hoped his new "village of origin" would throw off these investigators. It worked. He made his way to California, far from the land that holds his only son and so many of his family in its dark bowels.*

Don Jesús points to a painting of his son Miguel Angel, and his son's lover María Alicia. Shortly after he arrived for our interview, Don Jesús remembered this portrait and returned home to retrieve it. It was as if somehow we could believe the worst if we saw their youthful innocence. In the painting both youths are looking off and smiling, as if at a future of their dreams. They were students at Colegio Orantes in San Salvador when Miguel Angel decided to order a painting for his campesino family. The couple had lived together two years, working and studying, when they were picked up. Miguel Angel was taken off a bus. A friend found his mutilated body on a street that leads to the Mariona Prison. His body was in parts, his head in a garbage can. María Alicia's body was found near Soyapango. The friend notified the Salvadoran Human Rights Commission, which sent a letter informing the family of their deaths.

Don Jesús begins a litany of the family dead, with his sister nodding at each name. "Sonia, who was eighteen years old, my nephew Antonio assassinated at twenty-five, Modesto murdered at seventy, my cousin Enrique. . . ." The list rolls on and the old man's eyes redden, his woody fingers tremble. He does not use the neutral verb "died" in his narrative. His defiance is made clear by his choices: "assassinated . . . murdered." He ends by telling of his most recent loss.

"Only months ago they killed my grandchildren in the village of Copapayo—their mother, their mother's mother—all. The oldest child was thirteen. The youngest, fifteen months." Don Jesús grips his knees and squeezes again and again. "It was the Atlacatl Brigade [a U.S.-trained Salvadoran military battalion]; they came by land and air. They bombed three villages, killing four hundred. Even though President Magaña said the people killed were subversives, I know they were civilians. I know those villages: Copapayo, San Nicolas, La Escopeta."

I ask how he feels about North America, knowing U.S. advisors trained the killers of his grandchildren.

"The U.S. government is not good. Here they do not want us. If the INS could find me, they would deport me back to El Salvador. I am afraid of the U.S. government, but the American people, the common people, are good people. When I was in Los Angeles, I worked with the Refugee Committee of Santana Chirino Amaya and North Americans came to demonstrations with us." (Chirino Amaya was a Salvadoran refugee deported against his will from Los Angeles and later found beheaded in El Salvador.)

I ask him why he agreed to be interviewed and photographed though knowing the INS might recognize him and pick him up. He sits forward on the couch, and for the first time the old campesino finds my eyes.

"It is my obligation to tell the truth. Like Archbishop Oscar Romero, I must speak out. Romero was assassinated because he told the truth."

A buelita later has decided to return to El Salvador. Even with the promise of spring, she was leaving el Norte, leaving the cold, leaving Ashland Avenue. She was going home. "I want to die in El Salvador," she said. "I am from the village of Suchitoto."

LIFE ISSUING FROM DEATH

As Don Jesús says, "It is my obligation to tell the truth." In this book we have tried to tell the truth from the point of view of the peoples of Central America. That truth lives in spite of U.S. administration lies to discredit it and U.S. government attempts to deport and indict it. Public sanctuaries and refugee communities have harbored that truth, sometimes publicly, more often clandestinely. Mexican priests have been clubbed to death with statues while passing that truth along, and poor Mexican families have kept it from starving by sharing their last tortillas. It lives, in order that we may hear it, through the death and sacrifice of thousands.

The truth came to us as it always has—in prophets, babies, as refugees fleeing the Herods of this world. And the powers that be have reacted to the truth of the people as they always have—by slaughtering the innocents.

It should not surprise us, then, that those in power try to kill or silence the truth. Neither should it surprise us that the truth lives in spite of the powerful.

As Raul, a member of the Baptist Church in El Salvador and now in sanctuary in Detroit, says:

> A faith in God keeps me struggling, which revealed itself in the most difficult moments of my life. It is a faith that makes itself real to the extent that I do something for the sake of my people. And in the people I meet the love of God.

Raul himself was in Mariona Prison in San Salvador for seven months. He was released, but like so many that are released, he had to hide by sleeping in a different house every night. Church persons helped him escape to Mexico. In Mexico City he applied twice to the U.S. embassy for political asylum. It was denied twice. He was in the process of obtaining asylum from Holland and Canada when he heard of the sanctuary program. He decided to go into sanctuary and risk being deported instead of the safety of another country because, as he says:

> On the first day when I was tortured I prayed to a God I had not prayed to before. I promised that if I got out, I would dedicate my life to God. I wanted to go into sanctuary to tell the truth about the situation in El Salvador and try to help my brothers and sisters who are still suffering.

The peoples of Central America have brought us two truths. One is a story of brutality and death, the other a story of hope and new life. Hope lives in the midst of atrocity. Hope lives when all logic says that it should not. By purely human calculation, fifty-five thousand deaths in El Salvador should result in despair, hopelessness, surrender. It has not. The force for life only grows stronger.

As Pedro and Silvia, refugees in sanctuary in New York, say, "In El Salvador the unquenchable struggle lives on. . . . The deaths of more than fifty-five thousand show that we must struggle at all costs for a country more just."

Or as Ana, a refugee in sanctuary at the Riverside church in New York City, replied when asked how she maintains her hope in the midst of such atrocity, "I want to tell you that this is something that is constantly on our minds. If we were not Christians, we could not do it."

The peoples of Central America have denied death its triumph. Their resistance to death is coupled with an affirmation of life and the future. They see in the eyes of their children the possibility for a new heaven and a new earth. The biblical vision lives side by side with the simple hopes of indigenous women of Guatemala:

We share dreams, common hopes for the right to live, to develop, to be truly Guatemalans. Our hope is that tomorrow our dignity is respected not as objects for tourism, but respected as human beings. We hope that discrimination will be destroyed, that our *trajes* [woven clothing] will be respected, that the women will not be sterilized against their will. We want one day to live in our houses, make our weavings, mold our pottery without being killed.

Their words remind us of a passage from Isaiah:

For behold, I create new heavens and a new earth;
No more shall there be an infant that lives but a few days. . . .
They shall build houses and inhabit them,
They shall plant vineyards and eat their fruit. . . .
They shall not build and another inhabit,
They shall not plant and another eat. . . .
They shall not hurt or destroy in all of my holy
mountain, says the Lord [Isa. 65:17–25].

In Central America the vision of a new earth has begun to materialize. It is a vision of hope whose simplicity and tenacity confound the powerful and inspire the powerless. Hope lives as does truth, by the sacrifice and solidarity of thousands. Hope lives in the sharing of a last tortilla as profoundly as in the clandestine breaking of the eucharistic bread or the sheltering of a refugee.

The sanctuary movement has brought that hope to live among us, but it has asked something of us—our solidarity. As Raul, in sanctuary in Detroit says, "Solidarity is doing all that we can to stop the suffering of others."

We end this book, then, with reflections on solidarity and revolutionary hope. We reflect on what we have already done in order to understand what yet we must do. What must be done is clear: to put an end to the suffering of others and work to create a new earth and a new people.

SOLIDARITY

Biblical Roots

"I shall be your God and you shall be my people."

Solidarity as a word does not appear in the Bible. As a practice of faith, however, it captures the essence of the Judeo-Christian tradition. The Bible is a multithousand-year story of Israelites trying to maintain solidarity with their God and with the poor. When that struggle succeeds, slaves go free from bondage, captives return from exile, the blind see, the poor are fed, the sojourner is welcomed, and knowledge of God fills the land. When attempts at solidarity fail, denial and betrayal, apostasy and heresy are the result.

Solidarity is the essence of the covenant relationship between God and Israel and the covenant is the essence of faith in the Old Testament. The prophets extend the stipulations of the covenant to include the poor. And the birth, ministry, and death of Jesus are signs of God's new covenant, God's new solidarity with the world.

Solidarity is a sacred act. Today it is used more in a secular context but its roots are religious. When the Hebrews groaned under slavery in Egypt, they cried out and God heard their cries. God knew their suffering under bondage and remembered the covenant with Abraham. God acted with the oppressed in their liberation as a way of upholding and sealing the covenant relationship. "I will be your God and you will be my people" are the words that describe the covenant relationship. Liberation is the act that seals the covenant and makes it binding. Solidarity is the modern equivalent of that covenant bond made with God.

When God first called Moses to lead the people from bondage, he balks and gives excuses. But God promises, "I will be with you." That is the basis of the relationship of solidarity. It is not paternalism or pity; it is working shoulder to shoulder in the act of liberation. As one Central American refugee has said, "Solidarity is total identification with the suffering people." In Exodus that total identification is expressed by God, "I have seen the suffering of my people." To be in solidarity with the people of Central America, the North American religious community must say, "We have seen your suffering and we will be with you."

God and the people were bound together in a dynamic covenantal relationship—a relationship of solidarity. That covenant carried with it certain stipulations—what each partner in the covenant promised to do to maintain the covenant. To be in covenant means that each partner has certain responsibilities. It means there are promises to keep. So it is with solidarity.

The Old Testament prophets extended the meaning of the covenant and solidarity to the doing of justice. Hosea rails against the nation of Israel:

> Ephraim is an oppressor trampling on justice. . . .
> At Admah [*or:* like Adam] they have broken my covenant. . . .
> Gilead is a haunt of evildoers
> marked by a trail of blood [5:11; 6:7, 8].

Hosea uses the phrase *daath Elohim* ("knowledge of God") again and again.[159] In Hebrew, "to know" is something more than intellectual awareness. Knowledge involves the whole person, for to know, at times, referred to sexual union between love partners. At times knowledge meant entering into the life of the other, an empathy and identification that required the whole person, not just the mind. Knowledge for Hosea and the Israelites meant a profound awareness of the other. In Exodus we read that God saw the Israelites in bondage and "knew" their suffering. In this case, "to know" connotes a deep emotional bond with the people. In contemporary terms, the Hebrew "to know" can best be translated "to be in solidarity with." Thus, the Exodus story reads, "God saw the Israelites in bondage and was in solidarity with their condition." The same is true when Israel is told, "You shall not oppress a stranger, you *know* the heart of the stranger for you were strangers in the land of Egypt" (Exod. 23:9). "To know" means to have total identification with the stranger, to have in one's own heart the heart of a stranger. Therefore, we can translate it, "You shall not oppress a stranger, because you are in solidarity with the stranger, for you were strangers in the land of Egypt."

For Hosea knowledge of God is the basis of relationship with God: "For I desire steadfast love and not sacrifice, knowledge *(daath)* of [solidarity with] God, rather than burnt offerings" (6:6).

Amos adds another dimension. For him solidarity with God means solidarity with the poor:

> For crime after crime of Israel
> I will grant them no reprieve,
> because they sell the innocent for silver
> and the needy for a pair of shoes.
> They grind the heads of the poor into the earth
> and thrust the humble out of their way [2:6–7].

The poor have a special place in the relationship between God and the people. God calls Israel to justice and solidarity with the poor as one of the promises exacted to keep the covenant in effect.

Jeremiah combines both Amos and Hosea by saying that knowledge of God depends upon treatment of the poor. Jeremiah prophesies before King Jehoiakim, a petty dictator who has had a magnificent palace built with forced labor:

> Woe to him who builds his house by unrighteousness
>   and his upper rooms by injustice,
> Who makes his neighbors serve him for nothing
>   and does not give him his wages. . . .
> Did not your father . . . do justice?
>   he judged the cause of the poor and needy;
>   then it was well.
> Is not this to know Me?
>   says the Lord [22:13, 15, 16].

For his blunt truth Jehoiakim ordered Jeremiah arrested. Jeremiah made knowledge of (solidarity with) God dependent on justice to the poor. To know God is to pay fair wages to coffee pickers and not build grandiose haciendas at the expense of *campesinos*. And to know God is to refuse to participate in international structures that maintain oppressive poverty.

The birth of Jesus, the incarnation of God into the world, is the paradigmatic act of solidarity. God so loved the world that God took human form. It was total identification with the human condition, total solidarity with human history. God embodied love in a stable in the midst of the most imperialistic empire in the world, and from the very beginning Jesus had to flee the excesses of secular power. From the beginning Jesus was a threat to the established order and so had to flee the death squads of the Roman government. Jesus began life not as one of the elite but as a refugee, homeless, living on the run. Thus, the love of God for the world meant very specifically solidarity with the persecuted, the fugitive, the outcast.

Jesus' ministry was a continuation of that solidarity with the outcast—embracing lepers, eating with prostitutes and other social undesirables, using foreigners like the hated Samaritan to give Israel an example of moral excellence.

In the parable of the Samaritan, one of the most important of his ministry, Jesus shows what is morally good and who one's neighbor is. Traditionally this parable has been interpreted as an example of concrete charity. But Jesus adds several twists that probably shocked his Middle Eastern audience and made the point of the story much more than mere charity.

First of all, the Israelites hated Samaritans. To the audience Jesus was addressing, Samaritans were not simply foreigners, but were less than human. It would be like telling the story today with a Methodist bishop and a corporate executive passing far on the other side of the road, whereas a Marxist-Leninist from Central America stops and takes care of the wounded man. When Jesus asks at the end who is neighbor to the wounded man, North American listeners would have to say "the Marxist-Leninist." But after that shock, there is a deeper meaning to the story that only those familiar with the Jericho road would understand. The road to Jericho was treacherous with robbers and killers hiding on the side or feigning injury and then jumping up to rob those who bent over to help them. Therefore, what the Samaritan (Marxist-Leninist) did was not simply an act of charity. He entered into the danger of the road by risking being robbed himself. He risked sharing the same fate of the one he was trying to help. It was more than charity, it was an act of solidarity—and that is what Jesus is trying to tell us is love of neighbor.

Jesus asked solidarity of his disciples. He asked them to drop their nets and follow him. He asked them to stay awake in the garden and stay with him to the end. But Peter denied him. At that point solidarity would have meant saying, "Yes, I know that man, I am with him. I believe in liberty for captives and setting free those who are oppressed. I believe in standing against secular authority when it means idolizing the Caesars of this world and their laws. I agree with Jesus that the poor and outcast have a prior claim to our allegiance, and I will stand in solidarity with them rather than betray their cause." But Peter only said, "I do not know that man."

Before we are too judgmental of Peter, we have to realize that same question is daily asked of us, the question of solidarity with the peoples of Central America. Jesus wanted his disciples to stay awake, but they fell asleep, kept their distance, denied knowing him. It is not uncommon to sleep through crucifixion. What percentage of the church is sleeping right now through the crucifixion that is happening in Central America? To what extent are our responses guided by fear of what may happen to us if we are really in solidarity with the people? In that way we are not so different from Peter. The choice for us is the same: Are you with this man (this people) or not? Yes or no. Solidarity or betrayal. There was no neutrality for Peter, there is none for us. What begins with Jesus' simple call, "Follow me," leads to the demand of faith to stay with him to the end, the ultimate act of solidarity.

"The greatest love that one can show is to lay down one's life for a friend." That is solidarity. It is symbolized in the Eucharist as Christ said, "This is my body broken for you." But the full implications of those words come through only when the Eucharist is seen in its proper context. That celebration is embedded in the Passover event, that act of liberation when God stood in solidarity with those who suffer. The breaking of the bread and the pouring of the wine are fundamental symbols of the new liberation event, the new covenant, the new solidarity with the poor, the outcast, the oppressed.

The crucifixion of Jesus was the logical consequence of a ministry of solidarity with the powerless. Those who enter into solidarity with the poor share the same fate as the poor. Part of that fate is being accused of subversion. The religious leaders brought Jesus before Pilate, charging him with "subverting the nation" and "causing disaffection among the people" (Luke 23:1-3). It is the same charge that the Salvadoran and Guatemalan governments bring against those who feed the poor and care for Central American refugees.

Just before his crucifixion Jesus chose to move his ministry forward rather than stagnate or retreat. He could have stayed in Galilee, which was not occupied by Roman troops, where it was safe. He chose to go to Jerusalem, the occupied city, seat of religious and secular power. He told his disciples, "We are now going up to Jerusalem; and all that was written by the prophets will come true for the Son of Man. He will be handed over to the foreign power. He will be mocked, maltreated, spat upon" (Luke 18:31-33).

Today in Latin America and North America Christians have the same choice between Galilee and Jerusalem, safety or risk. In the Rio Grande valley of Texas, to be in solidarity with undocumented refugees, to even drive them three blocks to the bus station, runs the risk of arrest, indictment, and possibly fifteen years in prison. Jack Elder, director of Casa Romero, faced just that. His wife Diane has faced the same hardship and difficult choices:

> So now here I am, with four small children dependent upon me, and Jack facing a fifteen-year jail sentence (if convicted). Some days I look at what is going on around me and I think I must be crazy to be doing what I am doing. But I have no choice, not really. Life is so simple for me now—things really *are* white and black. It is only our frail human egos which fill in the shades of gray. God calls us to two things really—obedience and love. We can serve the cause of truth or untruth, justice or injustice, the cause of right or wrong, morality or immorality.

Diane and Jack, Stacey Merkt and others who daily risk arrest along the Texas/Mexico border work from Casa Romero, named after Archbishop Oscar Romero of El Salvador. Romero came to see, after opening himself to the testimony of the poor, those same choices between justice and injustice, safety and risk. The poor converted Oscar Romero as shades of gray neutrality melted from his life, and he too took the way to Jerusalem.

He was shot a few days after he called for the Salvadoran military to lay down their arms and stop killing their brothers and sisters. He, like Jesus, was subverting the established order. He sided totally with the persecuted and in that choice he renounced the protective privileges of his class and office. Near the end, when the death threats became more numerous, he refused personal bodyguards. He refused to have personal security that his people did not have. "I must continue to be as vulnerable as they are." In that decision he became one with the poor, the ultimate act of solidarity.

Jesus leaves little doubt that his life and ministry is not just something to admire and remember from a distance. Solidarity is not just for messiahs and saints. "If anyone of you wants to be a follower of mine, you must leave self behind and take up your cross and come with me. Those who care for their own safety are lost, for those who want to save their lives shall lose it and those who lose their lives for my sake will save it."

Two Nicaraguan *campesinos* who were part of the Solentiname community, the contemplative community started by Ernesto Cardenal, reflect on those passages:

> Oscar says, "I don't know. . . . I'm very ignorant, but it seems to me that life and love are two things that are alike or maybe the same thing, I don't know, and so to love is to give your life for others, while to try to save your life selfishly for yourself is not to live."
>
> William adds, "And this business of giving your life for the sake of

others doesn't have the sense of physical death but also of living for others. That's also a way of giving your life. Your life already belongs to others, so the life you give gets lost. It's not your life anymore."[160]

Solidarity, then, is a crossing over from a living death to authentic life. It is a crossing over to the side of the persecuted:

> Do not be surprised if the world hates you. We for our part have crossed over from death to life; this we know, because we love our brothers and sisters. The one who does not love is still in the realm of death, for everyone who hates his brother is a murderer. . . . We know what love is: that Christ laid down his life for us. And we in our turn are bound to lay down our lives for others [1 John 3:13–16].

That is biblical solidarity.

Taking to the Road

Felipe Excot, Guatemalan refugee in sanctuary at Weston Priory, Vermont, said, "Charity is giving someone a dollar to go buy food; solidarity is going with them to share the dangers of the journey."

Solidarity means taking to the road. As poet Antonio Machado writes, "There is no way; the way is made by walking." Solidarity invites us to go and do—to walk the road to Emmaus and encounter the Christ on the road and recognize him fully in the breaking of the bread, a shared meal.

Solidarity is taking the road out of bondage, leaving quickly, as in the exodus, before the bread even has a chance to rise. Liberation is sometimes sudden or not at all. It is a life-and-death decision; delays only increase the deaths. Solidarity is not in equivocation or moderation; it is found on the road. It is made not by talking, but by walking. The clandestine Mexican church does not deliberate for months whether to help Guatemalan refugees; it does not ask the cost even though church workers know they risk death. Their only questions are "How many can we help?" and "How long will it be until we are caught?"

In walking alongside, we discover God. We who are safe—with a safety bought for us by the sweat and blood of our sisters and brothers to the south—are being called out of our safety to walk the treacherous Jericho road. The peoples of Central America are calling us out of our safety to run headlong into the possibility of danger because that is where the "least" are—in the midst of death, witnessing to the triumph of life.

In the midst of creating that bond of solidarity the word *compañero* is born. It has no direct English translation. To translate it "comrade" is too stiff, to translate it "companion" too colorless. It can mean anything from spouse to co-worker. Embedded in it is the meaning of common work and shared life, walkers making their way by walking.

To be a *compañero* is to have passion for those close to you and equal passion for the building of the new earth. Its root is in *con pan,* meaning "with bread." Our *compañeros* are the ones with whom we break bread, the unleavened bread of the exodus from bondage in Egypt, the eucharistic bread of the liberation from death.

As one Guatemalan revolutionary now in exile in the United States has said:

> There is something wrong in the United States. In Guatemala, even when our lives were constantly interrupted by crisis, being called at 2 A.M. to help a *compañero* out of danger, there was a wonderful feeling of life. Even when we faced death, at the end of the day we were just thankful for being alive. Here in the United States there is not that sense of struggle, that sense of urgency, that sense of life.

National Solidarity

The biblical faith does not call only for individual solidarity or even solidarity between communities of faith. Nations are also called to solidarity with the poor. In Matthew 25, which in many ways sums up the effects of Christian solidarity with the poor, the teaching is quite clear:

> When the Son of Man comes in his glory, and all the angels with him, then he will sit on his glorious throne. Before him will be gathered all the nations, and he will separate them one from another as a shepherd separates the sheep from the goats. . . .
>
> Then he will say to those on his left hand, "Depart from me, you cursed, into the eternal fire prepared for the devil and his angels, for I was hungry and you gave me no food, I was thirsty and you gave me no drink, I was a stranger and you did not welcome me, naked and you did not clothe me, sick and in prison and you did not visit me. . . ." Truly, I say to you, as you did it not to one of the least of these, you did it not to me [Matt. 25:31–46].

This passage is usually interpreted on an individual basis. But when Jesus makes it clear that the *nations* stand before the Judge, the whole meaning of the passage changes. The question then becomes, "Is your nation so ordered and governed that the hungry are fed, the naked clothed, the homeless housed?" Do the political and economic structures of the nation allow for the "least" to be fed, housed, and clothed? The parable of the last judgment, by calling the *nations* together, focuses on salvation as a question of structural justice. It makes it clear that not only does Jesus call individuals and communities of faith to solidarity with the "least," but also that he calls nations to that same relationship with the poor. God calls the nation itself with its foreign and domestic policies, its laws and customs and economy, to justice and righteousness. Individual salvation may well depend on the nation and its ability to be in solidarity with the oppressed.

Solidarity is the most appropriate word for the religious community because it describes in concrete terms what faithfulness means in our time. Faith is not a matter of adhering to a set of prescribed rules or reciting a creed. Faith lives in the strength of the bonds created between us and God, and between us and the poor. Solidarity describes an attitude, a relationship, but also historical action. It upholds the dignity of victims by merging with their lives, identifying with their cause as if it were our own. Thus, it is a relationship of equality that seeks to know God in the doing of justice to the least. It is neither cheap nor easy, because it requires a crossing over from death to life, the kind of costly discipleship that emerges from the best communities of faith in times of crisis.

REVOLUTIONARY HOPE

What the refugees have brought to North America is a liberation gift—they have brought us revolutionary hope. What the popular church of Central America has bequeathed to the world, but most of all to its own people, is an irreversible hope in history. History, Gustavo Gutiérrez says, the poor know is theirs. Their hope is a fundamentally subversive act. The military rulers of Guatemala and El Salvador cannot kill it off, torture it to death; they cannot bomb it into oblivion. In El Salvador they have failed, after fifty thousand murders, to eliminate insurgent hope. They cannot make hope die in the Guatemalan highlands, even after the military offensive in 1983 of genocidal proportions.

The obdurance of revolutionary hope is what enrages dictators . . . they cannot explain its persistence.

The following was written by a North American church worker in a refugee camp near the Honduran border:

The pervasive presence of children is a striking reality of the camps. They dominate everywhere, in the processions, around the manger scenes. These camps are truly a world of children. It seems that the adults are here simply to take care of and provide for the children. The dominant motive in the lives of the refugees is to be the servant of one's children, of the next generation.

Perhaps this is because here in the *campamento* [the child mortality rate is so high.] The doctors say they die from a combination of factors: malnutrition and susceptibility to diseases, especially diarrhea and pneumonia. During the first month here, two children died every day. Still hardly a day passes that a child does not die.

It is a common sight in the early morning to see the carpenters in the *campamento* hard at work building a coffin. Each day measurements must be taken to determine the size of the coffin, depending on whether the child to be buried is an infant or five years of age.

I have seen children who have died, and I have been to the cemetery to bury them. I have been with children near death. I can still remember a tiny child who suffered from severe malnutrition. Unable to feed him intravenously, his mother fed him during the night from an eyedropper. By morning he was dead.

I remember another time when I could hear a group of women in a nearby tent singing quietly in chorus; it sounded much like early morning prayers in the *campamento,* with one leading and the others repeating. I asked Consuela, "What is that singing?" "It's the child," she said. "The child is dying." She invited me to come with her, and we made our way to the tent and entered. Nine or ten women were gathered in a circle around the mother of the child. A single candle burned. Between the verses of the song the anguished cries of the mother filled the air.

And there in the center was the child. His eyes were open and expectant, as if overcome by the whole spectacle before him. His mouth, too, was wide open, but he did not cry. The mother was unable to take the child in her arms, so she covered her face with her hands and rocked back and forth. One of the women marked the sign of the cross on the child's forehead while the child looked at us fervently, as if expecting an answer.[161]

The church worker ends the narrative by claiming that hope is born again, given in newborn life. The refugees are certain that hope is given to the poor of the earth "this night as it was two thousand years ago in a stable in Bethlehem":

We [North Americans] experience this word of hope as the living unity among us and the hope of liberation for El Salvador in history. We feel all this profoundly when we take hold of the rough and expressive hands of the *campesinos,* worn by labor with the machete and the grinding stone. We feel this hope as we raise our hands together to give expression to our faith.

This capacity of the Central American peoples is not an expression of stoicism but a grasp of life priorities, a sensibility chastened by raw encounters with death. Their trust in history is both audacious and humble but not romantic. It is a hope that is lucid and realistic about human cost—in life and death they accept the anonymity of *el pueblo.*

In Bolivia Luis Espinal, who was killed a month after writing the following, affirmed a love for life in the context of death:

The faithful do not have a vocation to be martyrs. When they fall in the struggle, they fall with simplicity and without posing. . . . Life ought to be given by working, not by dying. Away with the slogans that create a cult of death! . . . The revolution calls for human beings who are lucidly conscious; realists who have ideals. And when the day comes when they must give their lives, they will do it with the simplicity of someone who is carrying out a task, without melodramatic gestures.[162]

Like the fallen Espinal, North American Carroll "Carlos" Ishee had appropriated the Central American sense of revolutionary hope. Ishee was a guerrilla fighting with the Farabundo Martí National Liberation (FMLN) forces when he was killed in September 1983. This is an excerpt written in the midst of battle, after a period of casualties for the FMLN:

> I was reading Che's message to the Tricontinental recently, an exercise worth the effort on a periodic basis. If you don't remember it begins with the following excerpt of José Martí—"Now is the time of the furnaces and only light can be seen."
>
> In the extremely outside chance that the turn of events prohibits our reunion, I want you to know that I am prepared for the prospect, no matter the form. I see light.[163]

We spoke in October 1984 to a friend of ours, Jim Feltz, who is a priest working in the parish of Paiwas in the Zelaya region of Nicaragua. Contras had killed thirty of his parishioners; most had had their throats slit. We asked Jim about the morale of the people—what do they have hope in? He sounded weary:

> Those who have put their hope in the revolution have become defenders of the life of the people. They are the ones willing to join organized projects for health, our pig farm collective, the adult literacy program, our *comunidad de base* groups, the militia. They are the *campesinos* who have to walk a day's journey out of the rain forests, sloshing through the mud to pick up vaccines, be trained in inoculation so they might return to their villages to inaugurate health campaigns. But if they join projects, if they become delegates of the word or catechists associated with the church or government programs such as health or education, they become targets the contras will kill. The people who are most committed, they are the ones who are dying. Even if you believe in an afterlife, you have to believe that the kingdom has to start here. So you don't want to invite people to be slaughtered. . . . In a way their hope is a blind hope. It is the same as the hope the Sandinistas had before the triumph, that the people would respond, would rise up. This time it is the *campesinos* of the rain forest of Zelaya.

Following are statements of two of Jim's parishioners after a contra attack that included mutilations and decapitations. Susana Castro, mother of ten children and the widow of Emiliano Perex Obando, a lay minister slain by contras, expressed this confidence:

> My husband's blood was not spilled in vain. It is enriching the land and the new life that we poor people are leading. . . . People feel more human now. After all that has happened, I would say that we now have a firm grasp on our future. No task force is stronger than the God of the poor who is with Nicaragua.

Carmen Mendieta, the Paiwas coordinator of AMNLAE, the women's association in Nicaragua, believes that:

The future of our children is at stake. Therefore we women have to fight in any way we can. We are going to create a new cooperative for making bread. We will do all sorts of things and they won't make us give in.[164]

Birth of a Revolutionary Church

These women are the new voices of the popular church that has emerged from the silence of the institutional church that colluded with oppressors. This is a revolutionary church, a church that has incarnated itself among the poor. It is a sign of hope for the world because death has not overcome it.

Maryknoll priest and minister of foreign relations of Nicaragua, Miguel D'Escoto, describes that church of the poor born and martyred during the Nicaraguan revolutionary war:

I remember that one day late in the evening I came to a camp where some combatants of the revolution were sitting in the grass under a tree having a conversation. They saw me coming and asked me to celebrate the Eucharist. I had no bread or wine, but I was able to respond to their request to "give us some uplifting words from the gospel of our Lord."

As I talked I noticed that one young man was fidgeting and seemed very uneasy. Finally, I said, "Hernando, it looks to me as if you want to say something."

"You are always talking about the Lord," he replied. "Who is this Lord? The Lord People?"

"No, not the Lord People," I answered, "although he is identified with the people and is the Lord of many."

At this point an older man broke in, "Father, don't be upset with this young *compañero*. He is a good boy, he's just very revolutionary and has gotten himself confused by reading a book written by that Spaniard."

"What Spaniard?" I asked.

"Karl Marx."

No one laughed, and the man continued, "I don't know how to read. But I can tell this little fellow who the Lord is, because my grandfather used to tell us about him."

At that everyone hushed, because they knew that the older man's grandfather had been a lieutenant with Sandino. The man continued, "I don't want to brag, but I remember what my grandfather said. He said it was all in the book—the Bible. There it says that God is the father of all of us and that Christ is his son and is both God and man. We are all brothers and sisters, and we must be willing to give our lives for one another.

"So that's why when I was at home in my little town near Honduras and we heard on the radio that we must go to free our people, all of us Christians knew that we were supposed to be willing to risk our lives. And so we went in obedience to the Lord.

"My father died three months before the triumph. He knew he was dying, because his heart was getting bigger and bigger and this was making it difficult for him to breathe.

"I was living clandestinely at the time and couldn't visit him. But I heard that a bomb had been placed in his house, and it exploded where he usually sat. Somoza's people were looking for me, and after the bomb exploded, thirty-six armed men came and threw my father to the floor and demanded to know where I was.

"After the men left, my father called me because he was afraid that news of this event would weaken me, make me worried. And he said, 'I want you to know that your mother and I wanted to call and tell you not to worry about us, because no one can really kill us.' This is a new understanding of death: they can shoot our bodies but they cannot kill us.

"And he said, 'Don't be afraid yourself to die. I am praying with your mother one more rosary.' (By now they were up to about six, because for everything that I got involved in he was praying another rosary.) I am praying with your mother that you have the Christian guts to accept Calvary, if that is what the Lord wants."[165]

Resurrected hope is indeed a hope that, like the phoenix, rises from the ashes, a fire that death cannot extinguish. Fear of death is overcome by love of the people. Courage is less a personal attribute than a social gift—the fruition of a decision, a commitment to be faithful to a people to the end. As María, a Salvadoran catechist has said, "We cannot avoid suffering and death, but we can choose freely and consciously the side of our poor and oppressed people. In this way we live scripture, which says, 'No one can take life from me, I myself give it freely' " (John 10:18).

Central American Women: Sacrament of Revolutionary Hope

Such faithfulness forges a nobility and dignity of spirit that overcomes the banality of torture, rape, and death. Such was true for Sr. Victoria de la Roca from the district of Esquipulas in Guatemala. After months of torture by Guatemalan soldiers, she was brought out for execution by firing squad. Weakened by cancer she was dragged into the yard clothed only in bed clothes. She faced her killers knowing the young soldiers' ritual was to gang rape the women before their execution. Standing before the leering soldiers she raised her voice and said, "I supported the cause of the people because I loved peace." Then she flung open her robe, saying, "I am a consecrated religious who has been faithful to the people, to her vows. Come forward and do what you will." Not one soldier moved, except to raise their rifles for her execution. Even in the teeth of death this frail and dying woman would snatch victory as her last act of defiance and dignity.

Too often the revolutionary legacy of the women of Central America is martyrdom. The women, left with the care and protection of the children and elderly in refugee camps or half-abandoned villages, remain the voice of the voiceless.

But if the locus of God's action in history is among the poor and the oppressed, then it is the women of Central America, triply oppressed, who most fully express the suffering and resurrected hope of the God of history. The *indígena*, the ladina woman of Guatemala, the exiled Salvadoran woman, the women cotton pickers of Chinandega bracing for bomb attacks—all these women, tenacious as the forgotten wildflowers clinging in the rocky crevices of the highlands, are the blooming presence of God in the blood-drenched earth. These are the "weak ones" whom Julia Esquivel has said are the ones who are a particular source of revelation:

> I praise and bless you God . . .
> Because you have revealed to the poor and little ones
> What you kept from the wise and learned.[166]

A North American Lutheran pastor who visited a refugee camp in El Salvador tells another story of the valor of the weak ones. This story is indicative of the source of hope that Salvadoran women are to their children. National Guard soldiers entered the camp looking for Alfredo, one of the teenage boys. But the mothers locked arms and formed a circle around the boy. The *guardia* used rifle butts on the women, knocking them to the ground. But as the circle was penetrated the children of the camp ran to their mothers' places, locked arms, and held their circle of protection, bracing for the blows. Seeing the tiny circle, the *guardia* turned away. The beaten mothers, the weak ones, had won.

It is the woman refugee, like a tree rooted in soil moist with her people's blood, who uproots herself, snapping off the tender links of village life to journey into refugee camps, into exile, into liberated zones to save life, to struggle against death. Even in exile she is the rooted tree from whom others will go forth and return. Until she is cut down she will unobtrusively remain "home" and root the community.

She is the one who will construct the social fabric of communal life, even in a wilderness. She is an *arbol fuerte* ("strong tree"); the sap of the people's life runs in her veins. She is God's hidden promise of hope in the uprooted and exilic community. She is the organizational and communal backbone of the refugee camps in Honduras, El Salvador, and Mexico. The woman of Central America is a sign of hope, the incarnation of God's presence. Even when the world falls apart, she holds.

Womanly life as an embodiment of resurrected hope was exemplified by the women cotton pickers of Chinandega, Nicaragua. In 1984 the women had seen some of their hopes realized in the construction of a small infant day-care and preschool program for their children. We visited the tiny school, situated in the midst of chocolate-brown cotton fields that extended as far as the eye could see. These barren fields had once been orchards that extended to the mountains bordering Honduras, but under Somoza the fields were leveled to cultivate cash crops. As a result there was no shade for miles and miles. We understood what a fulfillment of maternal hope the small children's center represented when we asked the cotton pickers what they had done with the infants while they were picking before the revolution brought them this center. The women, who gathered at the center doorway in order to speak with us, looked away as if embarrassed. "We did all we could," they said, "we put the babies by the side of the fields, with a small sheet. But if the snakes or rodents came, we could not protect them. There was no means."

In the midst of this conversation with the mothers, an old woman, whose deeply lined face was shaded by a straw hat, edged through the crowd. She had walked in from the fields when told that North Americans were at the center. I've never forgotten her challenge. With exquisite patience she said this to us:

Why would your country wish to harm us? We are only a small nation, not even the size of one of your states. Nevertheless, your leaders will send the marines again as they did in Sandino's day. But this time they will have to spill every drop of blood of Sandinismo in this country. Because now the children will remember for us, even the youngest understand, *patria libre o morir* (a free homeland or death).

Then she sighed and without pause concluded:

They say Sandino said, "Even if I don't live to see the people's triumph, I'll know because the little ants will crawl in the earth to tell me." Well, I think if the little ants are making their way to Sandino now, they are saying, "Sandino, there is trouble, its *them* again . . . but don't worry it's *us* again . . . *el pueblo.*"

The American Lutheran Church recognizes that giving public sanctuary is a local decision. . . . It reminds congregations of the biblical call to care for the sojourner and stranger in our midst and commends those congregations which seriously pursue justice and compassion for any person who seeks safe haven amongst us. Such commendation is equally proper whether a congregation chooses to offer public sanctuary or finds other ways to be faithful to the call of the gospel in ministering among undocumented persons.

American Lutheran Church
12th General Assembly, October 1984

Appendix 1

OPEN LETTER TO UNITARIAN UNIVERSALIST CONGREGATIONS

Unitarian Universalist Association/Unitarian Universalist Service Committee

January 23, 1985

Dear Minister or President of the Congregation,

The Unitarian Universalist Association and the Unitarian Universalist Service Committee are writing to all our congregations in the United States about the sanctuary issue. We are holding a news conference today to urge Congress to investigate the recent Federal government actions against Central American refugees and religious people of many denominations.

We are proud that 22 of our congregations have gone through the soul-searching process of declaring their religious society a sanctuary for those who fear persecution upon return to their native land. Our congregations, from Massachusetts to California, from Texas to Minnesota, have been among the leaders of the more than 160 congregations of all denominations which are proclaiming sanctuary.

This is consistent with the Unitarian Universalist Association General Assembly resolutions of 1983 and 1984 to "support and encourage those societies which give sanctuary to Salvadoran and Guatemalan refugees and recommend to all our societies a serious searching of conscience on this issue." At last year's General Assembly in Columbus, Ohio, the General Assembly went on record in support of the specific legislation, HR 4447 and S 2131, sponsored by U.S. Rep. Joseph Moakley (D-Massachusetts) and U.S. Sen. Dennis DeConcini (D-Arizona). This legislation called for a three-year suspension of deportation of Salvadoran citizens, and our General Assembly urged that this legislation be extended to Guatemalan refugees. The legislation will be introduced again in the coming weeks.

Sanctuary is a complex issue. But it is a human rights issue, a moral issue, an issue that is close to our souls as U.S. citizens. We sing of "this land of liberty." We are, indeed, a nation founded by refugees fleeing political or religious persecution.

The United Nations High Commission on Refugees reports that over half the Central American aliens it has interviewed would be entitled to refugee status in the United States. Yet the U.S. Immigration and Naturalization Service, since passage of the

Refugee Act of 1980, has granted only 1.5 percent of the applications for refugee status to these peoples.

In contrast, other nationalities have been treated differently. In 1983, the Congressional Research Service reported in its Issue Brief 83119, 71% of Iranian refugee applications for political asylum were approved, as were 62% of Afghan refugees, 28% of Ethiopian refugees and 27% of Polish refugees. In that same year, only 2.4% of Salvadoran refugees were approved for political asylum; 1.5% of Guatemalans; and 5.3% of Haitians.

The U.S. Immigration law [8 U.S. Code Sec. 1101 (a)(42) (A)] defines a "refugee" as "any person who is outside any country of such person's nationality . . . and who is unable or unwilling to return to, and is unable or unwilling to avail himself or herself of the protection of, that country because of persecution or a well-founded fear of persecution on account of race, religion, nationality, membership in a particular social group, or political opinion. . . ."

That is a good law. Apparently, it is not being upheld. We are urging the President to review the current policy of deporting these people who are refugees (as defined by American law) and of prosecuting the religious people who are giving them sanctuary. We are joining the many people who are calling for a Congressional investigation into this situation.

We urge the Administration to heed the decision of the U.S. 9th Circuit Court of Appeals in California. In a Dec. 19, 1984, ruling in the Bolano-Hernandez case, the court ruled that an alien, seeking asylum because of fear of political persecution in his home country, need not present independent corroborative evidence of a specific threat to his life. The court also ruled that an alien's right to remain neutral in a civil war can be "political opinion" within the meaning of the Immigration Act.

It is incumbent upon all of us to become informed on this issue of human rights.

Some of the ways your society can do this is by providing time during your service to a member of the congregation or your community who has special knowledge or interest in the issue; by distributing this letter to the local news media with comments from a member of the congregation; by having the accompanying article by John McAward printed as an "opinion article" or a letter to the editor in the local newspaper.

You may want to give public support to those of all faiths who are providing sanctuary, by joing in interfaith activities. To find out who in your area is providing sanctuary, contact the Chicago Religious Task Force on Central America: (312) 663-4398. Or contact your Congressional Representative through letters . . . and urge a Congressional investigation of the situation.

It is an urgent matter.

The Rev. Dr. Eugene Pickett,
President, Unitarian Universalist Association

Dr. Richard S. Scobie, Ph.D.,
Executive Director, Unitarian Universalist Service Committee

25 Beacon St., Boston, Mass., 02108-3497

Appendix 2

RELIGIOUS LEADERS' AFFIRMATION OF SANCTUARY MINISTRY

We, representatives of religious and ecumenical bodies in the United States of America, reiterate our support for the ministry of providing sanctuary to Central American refugees fleeing war and violence in their home countries.

Despite the recent apprehension of over 60 Central Americans—men, women, and children whose lives are once again endangered by the action of the federal government—and the threat to imprison 16 U.S. citizens who support these people, we proclaim our belief in the moral rightness of "sanctuary." It will flourish as long as hope, love, and a belief in the ultimate authority of God live in the hearts of our people.

' We give thanks to God for those who have fearlessly chosen to follow God's call to "give shelter to the stranger among you" (Ex. 23:9) and decry the persecution of them. They are not criminals but persons of deep religious conviction who are also upholding deep-seated United States tradition and international treaties to which the U.S. is signatory. Our nation has accepted to provide asylum or refuge to persons who cannot return to their country of origin because of fear of persecution for reasons of race, religion, nationality, or membership in a particular social group or political opinion (Refugee Act of 1980). It is tragic that the conditions again exist that brought the "underground railroad" into being more than a century ago, so that, as persons of faith, we have felt called to respond in a similar manner to safeguard the lives of those who flee terror in their lands.

Sanctuary is not a building. It is not one man or one woman or 16 of them. It is a response rooted in faith and nurtured by prayer and conscience that has captured the hearts of tens of thousands of persons across the country. It is a sign of hope and compassion that is springing forth from an ever-growing number of faithful every day. To prosecute those who have shown leadership in this ministry will not bring it to a halt but rather is likely to swell the ranks of those who will stand firmly in their place.

Today, as our brothers and sisters suffer persecution for their willingness to respond, we encourage our congregations and the public at large to increase their response with greater vigor:

—to attend to the needs of Central American refugees;

—to provide resources for the defense of those who now face prosecution;

—to work for an end to the policies of violence that have forced so many to flee;

—and to press our government to grant Extended Voluntary Status to them and to cease its harassment and intent to prosecute workers and participants in the sanctuary movement.

We rejoice in and pray for those who may face trial for their actions. We celebrate their commitment. And we stand firmly alongside those whose witness to faith is given through involvement in the sanctuary movement.

Rev. Anthony Bellagamba, I.M.C.
Executive Director, US Catholic Mission Association

Dr. Arie Brouwer
President, National Council of Churches

Sr. Margaret Cafferty, P.B.V.M.
Executive Committee, Leadership Conference of Women Religious

Rev. Ronald Carignan, O.M.I.
President, Conference of Major Superiors of Men

Sr. Joan Chittister, O.S.B.
Prioress of Benedictine Sisters of Erie

Sr. Mary Lou Kownacki, O.S.B.
National Coordinator of Pax Christi USA

Mercy Administrative Team
Sisters of Mercy of the Union

Rev. Dr. Robert Neff
General Secretary, Church of the Brethren

Dr. Avery D. Post
President, United Church of Christ

Rabbi Alex Shapiro
President, Rabbinical Assembly

Mr. Richard Sider
Secretary for Central America Programs
Mennonite Central Committee

Mr. Ronald G. Taylor
Executive Director, Board of International Ministries
American Baptist Church in the U.S.A.

January 23, 1985

Appendix 3

COMMENTARY ON THE ARIZONA INDICTMENTS

*Jeffrey Haas**

In January 1985 the U.S. government brought a seventy-one count criminal indictment against leaders of the sanctuary movement from Arizona and Mexico. Count 1 of the Phoenix indictment charges sixteen sanctuary workers with being part of a "conspiracy" to bring "illegal aliens" (refugees) into the United States, and to "harbor, conceal, and transport them to places throughout the United States."[167] The remaining seventy counts charge one or more of the sixteen with specific acts of encouraging and aiding refugees in entering the U.S.A., shielding and harboring them, and transporting them, basically in the Mexico-Arizona part of the sanctuary network.

In addition, fifty refugees are named as "illegal alien unindicted co-conspirators," many of whom have been arrested on material witness warrants and held by the INS pending the posting of bond. Seventy-five other "unindicted co-conspirators" are also named. The reason for having "unindicted co-conspirators" is (1) to put pressure on them to testify against those indicted; (2) to make actions in concert with the unindicted co-conspirators part of the conspiracy and thus illegal; and (3) possibly to later indict them, although this is rather unlikely.

The indictment alleges that the conspiracy started "about late 1981 or early 1982" but the specific acts charged are from the period April 30, 1984, to January 7, 1985. This was when the Justice Department and the INS placed two informant infiltrators and two agents, all wired for sound, into the Arizona sanctuary network, and it is their tapes and testimony upon which the government is primarily relying. In addition, several of the residences of sanctuary workers were broken into and their records and files were seized, which records the government will also seek to use as evidence at trial.

Not content with their attempts to criminalize the activities of sanctuary workers under statutes that carry penalties of up to five years in prison for each violation (and some of the defendants have as many as sixteen charges against them), the government further seeks to prevent them at trial from explaining or defending their work. In a motion *in limine* filed with the indictment, the U.S. attorney asks the court to rule that those charged should not be permitted to even raise at trial any of the following: the legality of their acts under international and domestic law; that their acts were justified

---

*Jeffrey Haas is a lawyer with the People's Law Office, Chicago.

206

based on their religious beliefs; that their humanitarian motives negated any criminal intent; or that their acts were compelled by the necessity to prevent greater death and destruction in Central America. Further, the government motion also asks the court to rule in advance of trial that no witness be permitted even to make reference to "refugees or asylees"; "any past or present policy of the U.S. . . . regarding its foreign policy to any Central American countries"; "any alleged episodes of civil war or terrorism that may have occurred or are occurring in Central American countries"; "the number of refugees who have applied for, and have been granted or denied asylum"; and "amnesty or extended voluntary departure regarding El Salvadoreans and/or illegal alien unindicted co-conspirators in the indictment."

The government has further indicated that it will seek through immunity and other "appropriate procedures" to obtain (coerce) the testimony of unindicted refugees against the sixteen.

The serious charges against so many sanctuary workers, including church leaders; the wholesale arrest and holding of refugees as potential witnesses; the methods of infiltration and bugging of church and religious meetings used to obtain this evidence; and the current effort to gag the defendants and their attorneys at trial—all this shows that the government has seriously escalated its attack against the sanctuary movement and against all those, including sanctuary refugees and workers, who would bear witness against its policies.

This must be seen as part of the overall plan to escalate U.S. intervention in Central America and to prevent the building of resistance inside the U.S.A. on religious, humanitarian, and political grounds. The government gave approval to the Civilian Military Assistance Group in Alabama for training, arming and fighting alongside the contras to terrorize the Nicaraguan civilian population—all in violation of the U.S. Neutrality Act and international law. At the same time it indicts the sanctuary movement because it assists and provides a forum for the victims of this policy, thus exposing the genocidal effect of this policy on the peoples of Central America. Direct and indirect aid to the Somocistas who murder and maim Nicaraguan civilians is sanctioned because President Reagan has declared these killers our "brothers" (he should speak for himself), whereas it has become a crime to provide food and shelter to the refugees who flee the U.S.-provided helicopter gunships in El Salvador, and the reign of terror by the U.S.-imposed Guatemalan government.

The U.S. government is well aware that the sanctuary movement provides Central American refugees a safe and public forum for exposing the drastic human costs of the war "made in the U.S.A.," from which they fled. By April 1984, the Reagan administration had concluded that this support system and flow of information were adversely affecting public support for its plans to increase intervention. Therefore they had to be stopped. INS agents and informants working with the U.S. attorney then infiltrated the sanctuary movement, taped religious meetings, and gathered information that resulted in the indictment. The seriousness of the charges and the government motions to prohibit any reference to the illegality of U.S. intervention, as well as to bar religious and political defense material, reveal the U.S. government belief that the sanctuary movement is effective and must be silenced if the government is to increase control over Central America.

Four things are clear from this. First, *the government is serious in its attack on the sanctuary movement, domestic dissent, and resistance to U.S. foreign policy.* If the community of faith continues in its commitment to religious, humanitarian, and political principles, some persons will be sent to prison for providing sanctuary to fleeing refugees. Although sanctuary members may assert that their actions are legal—both because they do not violate the letter or spirit of U.S. and international law, and because they stem from well-founded and long-held religious beliefs—it is unlikely that such arguments will prevail against the pointed attack by the government. Judge Carroll, who presides over the Phoenix case, is known for supporting the most reactionary government policies. They are left vulnerable if they believe that the government, or a court sympathetic to its most repressive actions, will honor these defense arguments or even hear them. They know very well that the government wants to silence and stop the sanctuary movement with prison and threats of prison. Nor can they blind themselves to the willingness of the judiciary to effect such efforts by assisting convictions and other potential means, such as grand juries.

Secondly, *security must be a factor in the way the sanctuary movement functions.* Its supporters now know that they are targets of a government plot to stop them. They need not become closed or secret in their work, but they also need not publicize information that might jeopardize the movement. Further, they cannot ignore activity they recognize to be suspicious, particularly when it occurs at the heart of the movement, as they did when they knew that some "helpers" (who turned out to be undercover INS agents) were asking refugees in Phoenix for the names and addresses of persons with whom they had stayed. Their awareness of the government plan to close them down, and their knowledge of its history of using whatever means to accomplish such an objective (informants, bugging devices, the offer of immunity, etc.), together with their common sense and good judgment, make them better able to protect themselves.

Thirdly, *the best defense is a good offense.* The trials provide an opportunity to expose the instigation, maintenance, and escalation of U.S.-sponsored genocide in Central America and the extent to which the government will use repression to conceal it. There have been other court cases where government motivation for indictments (i.e., to make easier the escalation of intervention in Central America) was not articulated. Defendants can build public support for sanctuary and public denouncement of U.S. intervention by putting the government on trial for its war crimes at every opportunity and by showing that the present indictment is an effort to persecute those who bear witness to those crimes.

Building public support by denouncing and exposing the indictment for what it is becomes the *real* defense for sanctuary defendants. Resultant public opposition to U.S. sponsored warfare in Central America may make the government decide that sanctuary prosecutions, rather than furthering its foreign policy objectives, actually make them more difficult, and may require some alteration of those objectives. Although one or more defendants may avoid conviction because of a legal technicality, or (though it is unlikely) have their penalties reduced by refusing to identify themselves with refugees and their cause, the fact remains that putting government policy in Central America on trial is the only way to promote nationwide acceptance of the ultimate justification of sanctuary, and build support for defendants who will be named in future indictments.

This does not mean that every defense measure, legal and religious, should not be raised. Certainly they should, and acquittals are certainly part of defense objectives. But the whole defense case should be put in the context of the stance that the indictment itself is an illegal and immoral adjunct to a foreign policy that anticipates creating greater and greater destruction in Central America, and greater and greater repression at home against those who would expose it.

The sanctuary movement is faced with political prosecution motivated by the most heinous and illegal foreign policy objectives. Those who promote these objectives think nothing of blocking the exercise of religious and other constitutional rights and freedoms within the U.S.A. Religious communities in El Salvador and Guatemala practicing their beliefs and exercising their rights to set up cooperatives and oppose human rights violations have systematically "disappeared" or have been slaughtered.

Sanctuary supporters understand that the pretext behind U.S. intervention in Central America—to spread democracy abroad—is just that, a pretext. Religious and political rights are in fact not protected in those countries where U.S. arms back up reactionary regimes. The Reagan administration has now brought the repression home in futherance of its perceived need to silence or imprison those who expose its machinations or the death and destruction in Central America. Though the level of repression against sanctuary workers does not approach the level of terrorism against those who oppose the U.S.-supported regimes in Guatemala, El Salvador, and Honduras, the indictment helps everyone recognize that the pretext of democracy is being seen through, at home and abroad.

Fourthly, *repression of the sanctuary movement must be seen and understood in historical perspective.* Although attacks on the sanctuary movement have certainly reached a new level, repression against those who give shelter to victims of oppression is not new. Abolitionists who intervened to protect runaway slaves were jailed. Protesters were jailed when they opposed the 1898 invasion of the Philippines and the subsequent killing of hundreds of thousands of Filipinos. Similarly many of those who protested U.S. intervention in Indochina in the 1960's, particularly draftees who refused induction into the U.S. military, received jail sentences. Repression in this country is also not new to blacks, Puerto Ricans, Mexican-Americans, and native Americans. Supporters of Puerto Rican independence have been systematically jailed for noncollaboration with federal grand juries that subpoenaed them to testify against the independence movement.

The Reagan administration has lobbied for laws that would permit incarceration of anyone who supports movements for national liberation. A proposed "anti-terrorist" bill, if passed, would probably be used against all those who oppose U.S. policies in Central America, because such opposition assists "terrorists." Under this bill the secretary of state would have unbridled discretion to label "terrorist" any government or movement of which the U.S. disapproves. Secretary of State Shultz has said before Congress that the Sandinista government is "bad news." All those who opposed the Vietnam war could have been guilty of violating such a law. Moreover, even without criminal prosecutions, the FBI and other federal law enforcement agencies are continually harassing and trampling on the constitutional rights of persons who legally oppose U.S. intervention abroad. Boston offices of Central American support and solidarity groups have been broken into, and records have been taken. The government has admitted placing informants in peace groups that oppose U.S. military intervention abroad. Large corporations that participate in war efforts are setting up their own private security apparatus aimed at spying on those who protest their role. The effect is to create a climate of fear for those who would dare to denounce the government and its collaborators in war crimes.

The attack on the sanctuary movement is clearly part of the escalation of repression inside the U.S.A. directed at silencing those who oppose the escalation of U.S. military intervention abroad and particularly in Central America. It will not cease until the sanctuary movement is silent . . . or until it proves itself strong enough to turn the government attacks into strengthening both itself and opposition to the war effort.

NOTES

1. *Catholic Herald,* Milwaukee, Wisc., Nov. 1982.

2. Gary MacEoin and Nivita Riley, *No Promised Land: American Refugee Policy and the Rule of Law,* Boston, Oxfam America, 1982, p. 41.

3. Philip Hallie, *Lest Innocent Blood Be Shed: The Story of the Village of Le Chambon and How Goodness Happened There,* New York, Harper & Row, 1979.

4. Phillip Berryman, *Religious Roots of Rebellion,* Maryknoll, N.Y., Orbis, 1984, pp. 278-79.

5. William J. O'Malley, *The Voice of Blood,* Maryknoll, N.Y., Orbis, 1980, pp. 43-46.

6. Berryman, *Religious Roots,* p. 124.

7. "El Salvador 1984," *NACLA Newsletter,* March/April 1984, p.36.

8. Ibid., pp. 36-37; MacEoin and Riley, *No Promised Land,* p. 9.

9. Jenny Pearce, *Under the Eagle,* Boston, South End Press, 1981, p. 206.

10. *¡Basta!,* newsletter of the Chicago Religious Task Force on Central America, July 1984.

11. Authors' interview with Jim Harney.

12. Ibid.

13. Howard Zinn, *A People's History of the United States,* New York, Harper & Row, 1980, p. 468.

14. Allen Nairn, "Endgame," *NACLA Newsletter,* May/June 1984, pp. 37-38.

15. *Press Herald,* Portland, Maine, Aug. 19, 1984, p. 3.

16. Authors' interview with Jim Harney.

17. Steve Vanderstacy, "University Church Receives First Refugees," *The Daily,* Seattle, Wash., vol. 90, no. 48.

18. Jonathan L. Fried et al., eds., *Guatemala in Rebellion,* New York, Grove, 1983, p. 55.

19. Ibid., pp. 57-59.

20. Stephen Kinzer and Stephen Schlesinger, *Bitter Fruit,* Garden City, N.Y., Doubleday, 1982, p. 184.

21. Walter LaFebre, *Inevitable Revolutions,* New York, Norton, 1983, p. 257.

22. Nairn, "Endgame," p. 31.

23. Fried, *Guatemala,* pp. 330, 332.

24. Ibid., pp. 242-47.

25. *Chabil 'J Tinamit,* newsletter of Otto René Castillo, spring 1984, quoting *Uno Mas Uno.*

26. *Amnesty International Newsletter,* vol. 14, no. 8, Aug. 1984.

27. Suzanne Jonas et al., eds., *Guatemala: Tyranny on Trial,* San Francisco, Synthesis Publ., 1984, p. 266.

28. Penny Lernoux, *Cry of the People,* London, Penguin, 1980, frontispiece.

29. *Honduras: A Look at the Reality,* Quixote Center, Washington, D.C., 1984, p. 6.

30. Ibid.

31. Ibid.

32. Authors' interview with Center for Defense Information researcher.

33. "Technology in the Desert," *Covert Action Information Bulletin,* Washington, D.C., no. 20, winter 1984, pp. 33–34.

34. *NACLA Newsletter,* May/June 1984, pp. 44–46, 52.

35. Nairn, "Endgame," p. 53.

36. "Sanctuary Advocates Are Wrong," *USA Today,* April 20, 1984.

37. UNHCR statement, May 29, 1981.

38. MacEoin and Riley, *No Promised Land,* p. 37.

39. Ibid.

40. Laurie Beckland, "U.S. Quietly Acts to Deny Asylum to Salvadorans," *Los Angeles Times,* July 15, 1981.

41. MacEoin and Riley, *No Promised Land,* p. 41.

42. *The Fate of Salvadorans Expelled from the United States,* ACLU, Political Asylum Project, Sept. 5, 1984.

43. MacEoin and Riley, *No Promised Land,* p. 41.

44. See David Quammen, "Knowing the Heart of a Stranger," *New Age,* Aug. 1984.

45. Jessica Savitch, "Sancturay" (television documentary of WGBH), *Frontline,* July 12, 1983.

46. MacEoin and Riley, *No Promised Land,* p. 57.

47. Ibid.

48. See Quammen, "Knowing."

49. MacEoin and Riley, *No Promised Land,* p. 60.

50. *Catholic Agitator,* Aug. 1984.

51. Beverly Medlin, "Underground Railroad Still Runs in the Open," *Arizona Daily Star,* Dec. 25, 1982.

52. *Village Voice,* July 19, 1984.

53. Alice Felt Tyler, *Freedom's Ferment: Phases of American Social History from the Colonial Period to the Outbreak of the Civil War,* New York, Harper & Row, 1944, pp. 532–33.

54. See Vincent Harding, *There Is a River: The Black Struggle for Freedom in America,* New York, Vintage, 1983.

55. Charles Blackson, "The Underground Railroad," *National Geographic,* vol. 166, no. 1, July 1984.

56. Harding, *River,* p. 123.

57. Letter to Congressman George Miller, Nov. 20, 1984.

58. Press statement, Dec. 5, 1984.

59. Press statement, Dec. 5, 1984.

60. Statistics taken from the presentation by Marc VanderHout at the National Sanctuary Convocation, Jan. 1985.

61. See *CARECEN News Bulletin,* vol. 1, no. 3, Nov. 1984.

62. Ibid.

63. "Free Fire: A Report on Human Rights in El Salvador," a study done by Americas Watch and the Lawyers' Committee for International Human Rights, 1984.

64. "Misled on El Salvador Congressmen Charge," *Chicago Tribune,* Feb. 11, 1985.

65. See Heather Foote, "The Fate of Tenancingo," *Crucible of Hope,* Washington, Sojourners, fall 1984, p. 20.

66. See Joy Hachel, "Pentagon May Fly Private Aid to Nicaraguan Rebels," *National Catholic Reporter,* Jan. 18, 1985.

67. "Visit to Honduran Air Bases," memorandum written by Rev. M. Ted Steege, May 9, 1984.

68. See Mary Jo McConahay, "Relief Workers Wary of U.S. Vietnam-Style Pacification Plans for Displaced Salvadorans," *National Catholic Reporter,* Jan. 18, 1985.

69. Ibid.

70. See note 61, above.

71. Committee of Santa Fe, "A New Inter-American Policy for the Eighties," Washington, D.C., Council for Inter-American Security, 1980.

72. David MacMichaels, "Calling the Bluff," *Crucible of Hope* (note 65, above), p. 43.

73. Santa Fe Committee (note 71, above).

74. From the transcript of a telephone conversation between Rev. Dick Lundy and the Chicago Religious Task Force on Central America.

75. See Penny Lernoux, *Fear and Hope,* Field Foundation, 1984 (quoting the *Wall Street Journal,* Dec. 8, 1983), p. 44.

76. See O'Malley, *Voice of Blood* (note 5, above), p. 46.

77. MacMichaels, "Calling the Bluff," p. 46.

78. "All Things Considered," National Public Radio, April 19, 1984.

79. Ibid.

80. Richard Gillete, "Jailing Grand Jury Resisters: Implications for Church Activists," *Christian Century,* Sept. 26, 1984.

81. Ibid.

82. See Mary Lou Suhor, "Hispanics Wait Jail Sentences," *The Witness,* April 1983.

83. See *National Catholic Reporter,* Dec. 30, 1983, pp. 1, 22.

84. James Harrar, "Reagan Orders Concentration Camps," *The Spotlight,* vol. 10, no. 17, April 23, 1984.

85. Kate Skelton-Caban, "Public Statement Following Indictments," Albany, N.Y., First Unitarian Society, Jan. 22, 1985.

86. *Akwesasne Notes,* late winter 1983.

87. Ibid.

88. Amnesty International, *Special Briefing,* July 1982.

89. See Luisa Frank and Philip Wheaton, *Indian Guatemala: Path to Liberation,* Washington, EPICA Task Force, p. 88.

90. See Victor Perera, "Pawns in the Political Game," *The Nation,* Nov. 12, 1983.

91. Bill Lasswell, *Register Guard,* Eugene, Oregon; *Guatemala Newsletter,* no. 13, Sept. 7, 1984.

92. Ibid.

93. Authors' interview with Rev. Alice Hageman.

94. *Wall Street Journal,* June 24, 1984, pp. 1, 18.

95. Ibid., p. 18.

96. Phillip Berryman, *Religious Roots* (note 3, above), p. 323.

97. See Sergio Torres and John Eagleson, eds., *The Challenge of Basic Christian Communities,* Maryknoll, N.Y., Orbis, 1981, p. 168.

98. René Hurtado, "Inside a Death Squad," *Harpers,* July 1984, pp. 14–15.

99. See Allan Nairn, "Endgame" (note 14, above), p. 47.

100. Allan Nairn, "Behind the Death Squads," *The Progressive,* May 1984, pp. 1, 20.

101. Nairn, "Endgame," p. 35.

102. For an in-depth look at press coverage of Salvadoran and Nicaraguan elections, see "CIA, the Press, and Central America," *Covert Information Bulletin,* n. 21, spring 1984.

103. See *Press Herald,* Portland, Maine, Aug. 25, 1984, the Jack Anderson column.

104. *Between Honesty and Hope,* Maryknoll, N.Y., Maryknoll Publ., 1970, p. 82.

105. See Fried, *Guatemala* (note 18, above), pp. 3–4.

106. Ibid., p. 25.

107. Statistical background can be found in Penny Lernoux, *Fear and Hope* (note 75, above), and Phillip Berryman, *What's Wrong in Central America,* Philadelphia, American Friends Service Committee, 1983.

108. Berryman, *Religious Roots,* p. 43.

109. See *We Continue Forever,* Women's International Resource Exchange, Nov. 1983, p. 35.

110. Fried, *Guatemala,* pp. 194–95.

111. See Berryman, *Religious Roots,* pp. 283–84.

112. Ibid., p. 44.

113. Pearce, *Under the Eagle* (note 8, above), p. 211.

114. In Berryman, *Religious Roots,* p. 147.

115. Unpublished research by the Campaign for Global Justice.

116. Ibid.

117. Ibid.

118. See Jim Hightower, *Eat Your Heart Out,* New York, Crown Publ., 1975, pp. 214–16.

119. Ibid., p. 216.

120. See Francis Moore Lappé and Joseph Collins, *Food First,* New York, Houghton-Mifflin, 1977, pp. 194, 256, 262.

121. Ibid., pp. 181–82.

122. Tom Barry, Beth Woods, and Deb Preusch, *Dollars and Dictators,* New York, Grove, 1983, pp. 38, 40.

123. Zinn, *People's History* (note 13, above), p. 153.

124. Ibid., pp. 152–53.

125. See *Changing Course: Blueprint for Peace in Central America and the Caribbean,* rev. ed., Washington, D.C., Institute for Policy Studies, 1984, p. 42.

126. Joe Holland, *The American Journey,* New York, IDOC North America, 1976, p. 31.

127. Zinn, *People's History,* p. 292.

128. Harvey Wasserman, *Harvey Wasserman's History of the United States,* New York, Harper-Colophon Books, 1972, pp. 55–56.

129. Pearce, *Under the Eagle,* p. 11.

130. Zinn, *People's History,* p. 293.

131. Ibid., p. 290.

132. *Changing Course,* p. 18.

133. Pearce, *Under the Eagle,* p. 17.

134. Ibid., pp. 17–19.

135. Ibid., pp. 20–23.

136. Zinn, *People's History,* p. 291.

137. Pearce, *Under the Eagle,* p. 20.

138. Gustavo Gutiérrez, *The Power of the Poor in History,* Maryknoll, N.Y., Orbis, 1983, p. 48.

139. Jon Sobrino and Juan Hernández Pico, *Theology of Christian Solidarity,* Maryknoll, N.Y., Orbis, 1985, p. 61.

140. Gustavo Gutiérrez, *We Drink from Our Own Wells,* Maryknoll, N.Y., Orbis, 1984, p. 97.

141. In Tyler, *Freedom's Ferment* (note 54, above), p. 500.

142. Ibid., p. 485.

143. Howard Zinn, *The Politics of History,* Boston, Beacon, 1970, p. 171.

144. Tyler, *Freedom's Ferment,* p. 511.

145. Harding, *River* (see note 54, above), p. 167.

146. In Tyler, *Freedom's Ferment,* p. 542.

147. Harding, *River,* p. 125.

148. Ibid., pp. 126–27.

149. Ibid., p. 127.

150. Zinn, *Politics,* pp. 139, 145–46.

151. In Tyler, *Freedom's Ferment,* p. 520.

152. New York, International Publ., 1976, p. 161.

153. Albert Weinberg, *Manifest Destiny,* Gloucester, Mass., Peter Smith, 1958 (reprint).

154. Robert McAfee Brown, *Religion and Violence,* Philadelphia, Westminster, 1973, pp. 95, 96, 99.

155. Ibid., p. 101.

156. Gil Dawes, *¡Basta!,* Newsletter of the Chicago Religious Task Force on Central America, Jan. 1985.

157. In Sergio Torres and John Eagleson, eds., *Theology in the Americas,* Maryknoll, N.Y., Orbis, 1976, p. 302.

158. In Torres and Eagleson, *Challenge* (note 97, above), p. 64.

159. For a thorough treatment of the Hebrew concept of knowledge, see James Muhlenberg, *The Way of Israel: Biblical Faith and Ethics,* London: Routledge and Kegan Paul, 1962.

160. Ernesto Cardenal, *The Gospel in Solentiname,* vol. 3, Maryknoll, N.Y., Orbis, 1979.

161. "Breaking the Veil of Darkness," *Crucible of Hope* (note 65, above), p. 95.

162. Gutiérrez, *We Drink,* p. 117.

163. Memoriam card for Carlos Ishee, quoting one of Ishee's letters to his wife, 1984.

164. *Envío,* Instituto Histórico Centro América, Nicaragua, 1984.

165. Miguel D'Escoto, "An Unfinished Canvas," *Crucible of Hope,* pp. 84–85.

166. Julia Esquivel, "Christian Women and the Struggle for Justice in Central America," unpublished paper.

167. Those indicted were: María del Socorro Pardo de Aguilar; Antonio Clark; Phillip M. Conger; James A. Corbett; Cecilia del Carmen Juarez de Emery; Mary Kay Espinosa; John M. Fife; Katherine M. Flaherty; Peggy Hutchison; Wendy LeWin; Nena MacDonald; Bertha Martel-Benavidez; Darlene Nicgorski; Ana Priester; Ramón Dagoberto Quiñones; Mary Waddell. Charges against Ana Priester and Mary Waddell were later dismissed. Bertha Martel-Benavidez and Carmen Juarez de Emery pleaded guilty to reduced misdemeanor charges. María del Socorro Pardo de Aguilar and Ramón Dagoberto Quiñones, Mexican nationals, have not appeared in court.